The Jewish Question

The Jewish *Question*

A Marxist Interpretation

ABRAM LEON

PATHFINDER

New York London Montreal Sydney

ISBN 0-87348-134-8 paper; ISBN 0-87348-133-X cloth
Library of Congress Catalog Card Number 76-108721
Manufactured in the United States of America

First edition, 1950
Second edition, 1970
Sixth printing, 1993

Cover design by Eric Simpson

Pathfinder
410 West Street, New York, NY 10014, U.S.A.
Fax: (212) 727-0150

Pathfinder distributors around the world
Australia (and Asia and the Pacific):
Pathfinder, 19 Terry St., Surry Hills, Sydney, N.S.W. 2010
Britain (and Europe, Africa except South Africa, and Middle East):
Pathfinder, 47 The Cut, London, SE1 8LL
Canada:
Pathfinder, 6566, boul. St.-Laurent, Montreal, Quebec H2S 3C6
Iceland:
Pathfinder, Klapparstíg 26, 2d floor, 101 Reykjavík
Postal address: P. Box 233, 121 Reykjavík
New Zealand:
Pathfinder, La Gonda Arcade, 203 Karangahape Road, Auckland
Postal address: P.O. Box 8730, Auckland
Sweden:
Pathfinder, Vikingagatan 10, S-113 42, Stockholm
United States (and Caribbean, Latin America, and South Africa):
Pathfinder, 410 West Street, New York, NY 10014

CONTENTS

Abram Leon

1918-1944

PUBLISHER'S FOREWORD

This is the first U. S. edition of *The Jewish Question.* The English text is that of a limited edition published in Mexico City in 1950. Leon's book and the biographical sketch of Leon by Ernest Germain were translated from the original French edition of 1946.

This pioneering Marxist study went all but unnoticed until a few years ago, when it began to receive much attention in scholarly circles. A new edition was published in France in 1968, setting off anew the controversy which Marxist work on this question has aroused.

The new French edition included an introduction by Professor Maxime Rodinson, author of *Israel and the Arabs* and an acknowledged authority in the field. Professor Rodinson's critique of Leon's fundamental thesis, the theory of the people-class, reviewed Leon's work in the light of new scholarship. This first U. S. edition contains an introduction by Nathan Weinstock which answers the critique made by Professor Rodinson.

Weinstock has contributed articles on the Palestinian problem and on Jewish affairs to several European socialist journals, including *Partisans, Revue Internationale du Socialisme,* and *Quatrieme Internationale.* Currently on the editorial board of the Belgian revolutionary Marxist weekly *La Gauche,* he is also the author of *Le sionisme contre Israël,* a book that was pronounced by the London *Times Literary Supplement* to be "the most consequential and up-to-date Marxist analysis of the Israel-Arab problem yet published."

In 1968 he wrote the foreword to the Italian edition of *The Jewish Question*. The present article takes into account recent research and debates on key issues of Jewish history as well as the latest developments in Israel, Poland, Cuba, and the advanced capitalist countries.

TRANSLATOR'S FOREWORD

Writing in the shadow of Nazi occupation, the possibility of conforming his work on the Jewish question to certain formal standards of scholarship simply did not exist for the author. In making the English translation of his work, considerable time and effort were devoted to locating and identifying Leon's source material and quotations, so as to eliminate, insofar as possible, this purely technical shortcoming. We were not always successful in this research project, and it has considerably delayed the appearance of the work in English, but it is hoped that even this limited success will prove helpful to serious students of Jewish history and the Jewish question.

One further word as regards quoted material: English sources have in all cases been used as they appear in English editions — they are not retranslations from the French text. In all other cases, we have utilized standard English translations of foreign works, where they exist; and where the sources remain untranslated we have checked Leon's text against the original French, German, or Yiddish editions.

Mexico City, 1950

A BIOGRAPHICAL SKETCH OF ABRAM LEON

By ERNEST GERMAIN

The period of relative peace and prosperity experienced by Western Europe in the era between 1876 and 1914 was hardly propitious for the making of genuine revolutionists. In order for the mind to free itself completely from the influence of ruling-class ideology and in order for the will to be concentrated on a single goal —the conquest of power by the proletariat— it is not enough just to assimilate correctly the Marxist method and heritage. Life itself must propel men outside the routine of "respectable" existence and drive them into direct contact with all the violence, the cruelty, the degradation and barbarism inherent in the capitalist system. It was in the crucible of illegality, imprisonment, emigration and merciless struggle against autocracy that the great revolutionary generation of Bolsheviks was forged in Russia. In order for a new revolutionary generation to be created in the countries of the West, mankind had to enter into the very fire of the crises of wars and revolutions.

It was war and revolution which cradled Abram Leon, and which later closed his eyes. On the day of his birth the footsteps of the revolution rang through the streets of his native city, Warsaw. Two rival Soviets were contending for power. On the horizon, the Soviet Republic was already taking shape. Defeated armies brought their tatters, their bitterness and their thirst for justice into the popular assemblies. Human beings from the obscurest depths of mankind flowed in wave upon wave across the political arena: men and women, young and old, all the poor and oppressed, all the disinherited who had lived with their mouths shut and their backs bent and who now suddenly discovered their voices.

But while their hands bore the red flag deeper and deeper into the tortured city, there already fluttered over the fortress the red and white flag with the Polish eagle, hoisted by legionaires under the command of a "socialist," Pilsudski. These two symbols, these two currents of ideas, international socialism and petty-bourgeois social-patriotism, were struggling passionately for supremacy over the masses. The short but fruitful life of Leon was to pass entirely under the sign of this struggle.

Partitioned at every historical turning-point, Poland could not avoid saddling its labor movement with the heavy heritage of a miserable past: militant nationalism. The Jews of Poland, victims of every political and social crisis, who had witnessed pogroms under the Czars, under the revolution, under the Whites, under the Russians, under the Poles, under the Ukrainians and under the Lithuanians, sought a desperate solution through the formulation of a nationalist myth of their own: Zionism. An expression of the complete blind alley in which Jewish petty-bourgeois thought had arrived, this reactionary utopia was nevertheless, among the youth and above all the proletarian youth, an expression also of the will to realize the socialist ideal, to participate actively in the world proletarian struggle.

The contradiction between the petty-bourgeois character of Zionism and the rigorously internationalist conclusions of Marxism drove the Zionist working-class leaders to formulate a new theory which, by combining their socialism —which they wanted to be scientific— with their Zionist aspirations, would invest the latter with some semblance of Marxist justification. This is how the strange theory called "Borochovism" —from the name of its author, Ber Borochov— was born, a theory which was destined to become the official theory of Jewish revolutionists throughout the world for several decades.

The family in Leon's household adhered to "official" petty-bourgeois Zionism. On his first contact with reality, the child felt the attraction of the Zionist myth like a religious intoxication. The myth was to be realized in life: the family left for Palestine when the boy was old enough to enter grammar school. The wonderful procession of scenes on this trip became engraved in his memory like a fairy tale. He remembered how the sun blazed on the roofs of Constantinople, the sound of the sea among the enchanted islands of the Archipelago, and how the rugged coast of the Promised Land looked to him the first time. But the fairy tale did not last long; a year later they started back for their native country.

Amid these changing conditions of his life, the boy observes, strives to understand, and assimilates the idea of the constant movement of men and things. His mind goes traveling and doesn't as yet come to rest. We must wait until 1926, when the family decides to emigrate to Belgium, before Abram begins to get intensely interested in companions of his own age and makes contact with the Zionist socialist youth movement, "Hashomer Hatzair," "The Youth Guard." Other forces begin to act upon him. At school he feels the barriers set up before the Jew, before the foreigner, separating him from his classmates. How can he fail to understand that he is "different" from the others or that he has special problems, when he constantly notes that he is being treated differently, that he is not allowed to participate in games like any other little boy, but remains the butt of some comment or ironical jest? Upon his way homeward along the swarming streets of populous old sections of Brussels, he is sharply reminded of all the contradictions in modern society. He is greatly moved by the picture of the world's division into the rich and the poor. How could he help naturally taking sides with the downtrodden, feeling himself, as he does, the victim of a double injustice?

This is how young Leon becomes an ardent militant in the Jewish Socialist Zionist youth. His mind begins to explain the indignation and revolt that his heart feels. Gradually, through a systematic Marxist education, Leon grows to understand society and the solution toward which the struggle of the workers is directed. Within the framework of this youth movement — which is, despite its confused political ideas, a model organization, and one of the best schools of morals and proletarian thought — everything begins to dissolve — family ties, traditions, heritage of age-long petty-bourgeois calculation, heritage of submissive fear of authorities. He grows as free in his character as in his mind; he learns to govern himself, he lets himself be governed by reason, he learns to subordinate himself to the pursuit of the goal. His will becomes tempered in the ideal. His personality is formed in concentrating upon the struggle for socialism; he finds the highest satisfaction in thought and action which are placed in the service of the world proletariat.

It is not long before the young Leon outstrips his comrades in the movement. As the most intelligent, the firmest and the most comprehensive, he at the same time possesses a calmness and a reasoned confidence that completely and naturally draw the respect of all those around him. Born to lead, he has no need to raise his voice, or to charm with beautiful phrases or to attract by extraordinary deeds in order to have everybody accept his authority. He moves up rapidly along the various rungs of the elected apparatus of the "Hashomer" and soon finds himself in the leadership of the Brussels section and also on the national leadership.

The living conditions of his family compel him to give up

his studies for a time. Because he has to be constantly on the move all over Belgium in order to make a livelihood, he is able to renew his contact with the working masses who are once again going into the streets to demonstrate their strength and to demand their rights. During the sunlit days in the summer of 1936 the fever spreads from the coal pits of Charleroi to the somber villages of the Borinage miners. While the police patrol the crossroads, the workers gather to hear a new leader. It has been years since they heard a genuine revolutionary voice.

The workers come by the thousands to Flénu, to Jemappes, to Quaregnon, to Frameries and to the great stadium of Bouverie in order to listen to the fiery speeches of Walter Dauge, the young founder of the Revolutionary Socialist Party. Leon attends the meetings of Dauge. He learns to distinguish Trotskyism from Stalinism. He studies and it does not take him long to side with those ideas which appear to him to be the product of genuine Marxism, and which are inspired by the genuine interests of the world proletariat and not by the miserable falsifications concocted by the master of the Kremlin. Concurrently the series of the monstrous Moscow Trials leads him to take a definite position. From this year on, as against the entire world organization of "Hashomer" which leans somewhat toward Stalinism, he becomes a resolute "Trotskyist" and defends his ideas vigorously and not unsuccessfully at national and international congresses and gatherings.

But even while rapidly advancing in his knowledge of Marxism and while pursuing deeply his study of political economy, he remains profoundly attached to Zionism. While serving for one year as chairman of the Belgian Zionist Federation, he devotes all his energy, all his revolutionary zeal in the service of this cause. When a group of young militants departs for Palestine, an enthusiastic call is launched for the establishment of a "com-

*munist" colony there. But Leon begins to doubt. Side by side with him are the representatives of petty-bourgeois and bourgeois Zionist organizations. Isn't he united with them for the present, even though he expects to fight against them mercilessly after "nationality" and the "possibility of waging an effective struggle" * have been conquered in Palestine? Isn't this "social-patriotism," even if in a rather unusual form? Leon has his Lenin at his finger tips. The lengthy and lucid arguments in* Against the Stream *ring in his ears. How can he reconcile his consistent Leninism with Zionism? Where can one find a common ground for the Jewish national struggle and the struggle of internationalist socialism?*

In this way, twenty years after Borochov, Leon in his turn, took up the trail of the Hashomer "theoretician" in order to discover a Marxist justification of Zionism. He questioned everything; he methodically re-explored the connections between the ideas, accepting none of the axioms of the Zionist ideology, cutting his way through the tangled prejudices of Jews and non-Jews on the subject of the history of the Jews, a history which seems so astonishing and extraordinary and which his rigorously scientific mind seeks to explain by the Marxist method. In the course of his researches, he forwarded several articles to the Belgian Trotskyist weekly, La Lutte Ouvrière (The Workers' Struggle). *The editors of this periodical established contact with him. He was astonished to find treasures of historical, economic, and political knowledge among these simple workers. He sensed that this was the vanguard. He turned for the last time to his past, resolving to break with it harmoniously, with complete consciousness, after clarifying to himself and to his comrades the*

---

* "Hashomer Hatzair" defends the position that Jewish workers and revolutionary socialists are able to struggle "effectively" for the proletarian revolution only in Palestine.

profound reasons for his break, after demonstrating to his friends the truth which he had himself just discovered. His "Theories on the Jewish Question" took form; his book The Jewish Question, A Marxist Interpretation *would constitute the amplified elaboration of these theses.*

Meanwhile, a wave of uneasiness had seized the Jewish masses all over the Old Continent. They sensed the approach of war; premonitions of the terrible catastrophe that would befall them threw them into a crisis of nervousness and fear. The world congress of "Hashomer" convened. The menacing shadow of Hitler was already hovering over Brussels. In heated debate the delegates came out either for a "conditional" support of British imperialism, or for "neutrality," or for an "independent defense" of Palestine should it be threatened by a fascist army. Despite angry shouts of the assembly against this "renegade from Israel," Leon, even before breaking definitely with Zionism, defended courageously the position of complete "revolutionary defeatism." "Woe to those who with their own social-patriotism instill chauvinism in the workers in enemy countries. This weapon will boomerang against those who wield it. Woe to those who sow false hopes that the miserable lot of Jews in Central Europe will improve as a result of the war of British imperialism against its German rival! They will themselves prove to be its most sorely stricken victims." It was in this sense that Leon must have spoken. And what stupefaction must his words have aroused among those wavering centrists who seek at every turn for cheap solutions and for compromises, who are incapable of reacting to the rigors of history with an equally rigorous mind.

As the waves of imperialist war broke closer and closer to Belgium before engulfing it in May 1940, Leon completed his "Theses on the Jewish Question" and submitted them for discussion to his organization. In his attempt to grasp the meaning of

Jewish history Leon found himself in collision with Borochov's "metaphysical materialist" theory, and his first attempt was to eliminate this obstacle. Borochov maintained that the Jewish question was rooted in the fact that the Jews, and above all the Jewish workers, played no important role in the vital sectors of economy (heavy industry, metallurgy, coal, and so on) but instead occupied important positions solely in the peripheral spheres of economic life. The social composition of other peoples resembled a pyramid having as its base hundreds of thousands of miners, metal workers, railroad workers, etc., and then passing through large layers of handicraftsmen, topped off by ever thinner strata of businessmen, industrialists and bankers. But the social composition of the Jewish people resembled an "inverted pyramid" in which large handicraft strata rested on narrow layers of workers —who were moreover engaged in non-vital sectors of industry— and had to bear the full weight of an enormous mass of businessmen.

Borochov cut his analysis short at this point; he accepted this as a historical fact, without making any attempt at an explanation, and used it as the starting point for his "solution" of the question: It was first of all necessary to "reverse the inverted pyramid," i. e., to create a "normal" Jewish society like those of other peoples; until this was done the Jewish proletariat could not seriously undertake revolutionary struggle; and such a society could be created only in Palestine.

Leon quickly grasped everything that was "non-dialectical" in this theory: The existing social condition of the Jews could not be approached as a "fact," but as the product of historical development. How did this different historical evolution of the Jews come about? Linking up Borochov's thread of reasoning with several casual statements of Marx, who with his habitual genius had laid bare the entire "mystery" of Jewish history, Leon commenced to reconstruct the entire past of the Jews.

The explanation for the religion of the Jews and for their preservation must be sought in the social role they played. Gathering together the mass of existing documentation he elaborated the theory of the "people-class," astonishing in its simplicity, and providing the indispensable key for understanding the past and present role of the Jews and for finding a solution to their misery.

Borochovism erred, however, not alone in its point of departure but even more so in its conclusions. It approached the "solution" of the Jewish problem not only outside the past historical process but also outside the existing social reality. In the epoch of imperialism and of capitalism in its death agony, the "will" of a few million Jewish workers to "create a society like the rest" appeared as a pathetically weak force amid the imperialist giants fighting over every unoccupied nook and cranny on the globe, amid the violent collisions of classes on the world arena. Borochov had no comprehension whatever of the law of uneven and combined development in the imperialist era, whose operation prevents every nation without exception from solving any of its problems under the capitalist regime in its death throes. The tragic peculiarities of Jewish society could not be eliminated by seeking to isolate it from decaying society as a whole. The "inverted pyramid" of the Jews could not possibly be "reversed" while the "normal" pyramid of other peoples was itself in the process of disintegration. The world proletarian revolution is alone capable of normalizing Jewish history. Within the framework of decaying capitalism no solution is possible.

This was the manner in which Leon completely settled all the accounts with his own past. He not only exposed the petty-bourgeois utopian character of the Zionist ideal, but also showed how this ideal, like the rest of the petty bourgeoisie's "own" ideology, is bound to become in the imperialist epoch an instrument in the hands of world capitalism. He denounced Zionism as a brake upon the revolutionary activity of the Jewish workers throughout the world, as a brake upon the liberation of Palestine from the yoke of English imperialism, as an obstacle to the complete unity of Jewish and Arab workers in Palestine. Candidly, without any reservations or evasions, he condemned his own entire past activity. He understood what had completely conditioned it and how it had served as a necessary stage in his own development. His mind, steeped in the dialectic, delighted in presenting each clear piece of knowledge, each phase of consciousness, as the product of the struggle to surmount the counter-truth and error. "In order to understand one must begin by failing to understand," he would frequently say. "No conviction is so deeply held as the one gained in the course of a prolonged and sincere internal ideological struggle." The few years he lived thereafter demonstrated to him how exact these observations were in his own case. Having surmounted the nationalist stage of his own development, Leon rooted out from his thought every vestige of Zionism and his internationalism was of a purity that is rarely met.

No longer constrained to pursue two contradictory paths and to consume itself in internal controversy, his energy was henceforward able to strike out with all its power on a single road, that of the Fourth International. Leaving the "Hashomer" with about a score of comrades, Leon organized a study circle with the aim of leading his followers to Trotskyism. Most significant of all was the date of this "conversion." When Leon came to international communism, the workers' movement seemed dead in Belgium. Henri De Man —who began his evolution as an ardent antimilitarist only to become in rapid succession a social-patriot, a theo-

retician of insipid "revision" of Marxism, His Majesty's Minister and a charlatan patcher-up of capitalism— had just completed the circle of his "socialist" life by dissolving his party, whose president he was, and by calling upon his comrades to collaborate with Hitler in building a new order in Europe. Isolated from the masses who had been stunned by the May-June 1940 events, the Communist Party, following instructions from Moscow, prudently retired and even went so far as to publish a Flemish weekly which meekly reprinted Goebbels' interminable anti-British tirades side by side with ritualistic paeans to the "land where life was so joyous and so happy." The former Trotskyist leader Walter Dauge, whose intellectual baggage proved too light for this long ordeal, became profoundly demoralized and abandoned his party to its fate. The few Trotskyist cadres, dispersed all over the country, had hardly re-established contact. The situation seemed to justify only resignation and watchful waiting. Any other attitude appeared like a manifestation of desperate and impotent revolt.

What was lacking was not so much courage to act as courage to think, and to think correctly. Marxist analysis enabled one to penetrate through the totalitarian lid pressing on Europe and to discover there gestating forces which would in the end throw it off. Correctly establishing the reasons which we had for hope, Leon noted that the workers' movement in Europe had already reached the lowest point of its ebb. It was now necessary to count upon a new rise. It was necessary not to await it passively but to prepare for it, preparing for it the cadres and insofar as possible the masses. Even in darkest moments of history, a party that is later capable of leading the masses in struggle can be forged only in constant contact with the day-to-day life, difficulties and aspirations of the people. Behind every reason for despair, one must discover a reason for hope.

This motivating thought of Leon is not only a symbol but

the beginning of action. When on August 20, 1940 we were overwhelmed by the tragic news of the assassination of L. D. Trotsky, Leon immediately wrote the first illegal pamphlet of the Belgian Trotskyist movement. He established contact with several former regional leaders of the party in Brussels. The first leadership began to take form. The illegal Trotskyist organization was born on the day following the death of its spiritual father. The vitality of the ideas of the Fourth International, which are nothing else but the conscious expression of historical reality, seeks only the occasion and the men in order to become reaffirmed at every turn. It had just discovered both.

There ensued a period of incessant, stubborn and unyielding work in the face of difficulties which kept constantly arising and which seemed each time insurmountable. From this moment on, the story of Leon was linked with the history of the Trotskyist movement in Belgium. The principal inspirer of the party, he served as political secretary from the time the first executive committee was set up. As a journalist, with an incisive, lively and clear style, he made his readers feel that he understood thoroughly every problem with which he dealt. The editorial board of the illegal Voie de Lénine (Lenin's Road) *worked under his direction and its first issues contained a masterly study from his pen of the structure and future of the various imperialist powers. In this study he traced the main line of future events in the war exactly in the way in which they later unfolded. An exemplary organizer and educator, he guided the branches, tried to build the party under conditions of illegality, and concentrated with infinite patience on winning the confidence of workers' districts and on forming a recognized and responsible national leadership on the basis of this confidence.*

I met him personally for the first time on the first central committee of the party which was reconstituted by his efforts in July 1941.

Although he was absorbed to the exclusion of everything else in the enormous daily tasks, organizational as well as political, Leon did not for a moment suspend his ideological work which constitutes the most precious heritage he left us. On the one hand he systematically completed his book on the Jewish question, constantly working over the details, reflecting for weeks on a particular aspect of this or that question, devouring all the existing documentation, but prepared, once his mind was made up, to defend his views to the end. That is how this book came to be written. It is not only a model of the application of the Marxist method to a specific historical problem; it not only "liquidates" the Jewish question as a problem from the historical materialist point of view, but it contains in addition a wealth of observations and formulations on many problems in political economy, history, and contemporary politics.

On the other hand, he devoted himself to elaborating an exact Leninist conception of the problem which was at the time agitating all revolutionists in the occupied countries, namely: the national question and its relation to the strategy of the Fourth International. Let those who so readily incline to criticize the Trotskyist policy in Europe in relation to the national question read and study the documents which Leon elaborated during this period. Let them find out how preoccupied he was, as was the entire leadership of our party, with safeguarding, on the one hand, the Leninist program from the virus of chauvinism while defending Leninist tactics, on the other hand, against the myopia of sectarians, and they will see how foolish are their accusations to the effect that we "underestimated" the national question.

Whatever he had clarified in theory he sought to execute in practice. The smallness of our cadres did not permit us to start consistent work among the resisters. But each time a genuine movement became apparent, whether on the occasion when the University of Brussels was closed, or during the first great strikes at Liège, or during the deportations or actions against the Jews, our party invariably applied its political line of "supporting and promoting mass movements aimed against the occupying imperialism with a view to directing them toward the revolutionary proletarian movement." It was with justifiable pride that Leon pointed out at the illegal party congress in July 1943 that there was not a single event in Belgium since 1941 in which our party had remained on the sidelines.

*As soon as the party was reconstituted, Leon began to worry about international relations. An internationalist to his marrow, he found it intolerable that the Belgian section should live in isolation from its brother movements in Europe and throughout the world. The need for contact with the other sections of the Fourth International did not arise solely from his desire to compare the political line of the Belgian party with that of its brother parties; it also corresponded to a very clear realization that the great military and revolutionary shocks would in the future inevitably assume a continental character and that no political leadership could any longer function effectively on a national scale. An attempt to establish contact with Holland failed. We had more success in France. Thanks to this connection the last documents of L. D. Trotsky reached us via Marseilles from where we received the Manifesto of the Emergency Conference which was issued as a pamphlet by our party. Later, in August 1942, in a small village in Ardennes, the first meeting of representatives of the Belgian and French leaderships took place, Leon and Marcel Hic**

---

* Marcel Hic, Secretary of French Trotskyist Party and leading member of European Executive Committee of Fourth International. Editor of *La Vérité*, first illegal newspaper in occupied France. Responsible editor of *Arbeiter und Soldat*, revolutionary paper circulated

were the principal inspirers of this meeting. They laid the groundwork for the future Provisional European Secretariat which was in its turn to reconstitute an international leadership under conditions of complete illegality.

This period of illegal activity under the most dangerous conditions, when one's heart involuntarily jumped each time the doorbell rang or an automobile pulled up close to the house, was a time of extreme nervous tension, of continuous waiting for an explosion that would finally make a breach in the walls and bring closer the day on which would explode all the gates of the enormous prison into which Europe had been transformed. We awaited this explosion from the very depths of this prison. Our thoughts were centered on the reserves of revolutionary energy stored up during the long years of suffering by the proletariat on the Old Continent. When Leon personally assumed the direction of party work among the proletarian soldiers of the Wehrmacht or when he attended meetings of the underground factory committees set up in the Liège metallurgical plants, he invariably invested these various tasks with a meaning which transcended the present; he wished to sow that the party would be able to reap when the decisive moment came. Many times he would pose the question of whether we would be capable of gathering the harvest in view of the numerical weakness of our cadres. He could not foresee that he himself would be lost to the party during the decisive days of the "liberation" and that the absence of an effective leadership would prevent the party from profiting as it might have from the extraordinary conditions of that hour.

Then came the downfall of Mussolini. We finally felt the rising wind of the revolution; our activities multiplied. Each of

---

among German occupation troops. Betrayed by agent-provocateur and arrested by Gestapo in December 1943. Tortured at Buchenwald and later at Dora concentration camp where he died. *Tr.*

us expended himself unsparingly; the culmination was approaching. There took place a number of secret trips to France where Leon participated actively in the work of the European Conference of the Fourth International in February 1944. We halted our work of self-preparation; it was now a question of intervening actively in the workers' struggles which were erupting everywhere. In the Charleroi region, the Trotskyist organization took the initiative in organizing an illegal movement of miners' delegates. This movement spread rapidly to about fifteen pits: in complete illegality the party's ideas began to take root among the masses. Understanding the full importance of this movement, Leon wished to follow it step by step. He decided to locate himself in Charleroi in order to collaborate daily with the revolutionary workers of the region. News of Allied landing in Europe and fears lest connections between the various regions be broken, hastened the preparation for the shift. After living for two years in complete illegality, he went to settle at Charleroi with his wife. On the very evening of his arrival the house into which he had moved was searched by the police. He was arrested and sent to prison.

Then followed long days of moral and physical torture. The Gestapo used every means to make him talk. He was torn with worry about the party which had lost five of its first rank leaders within the period of two years. He succeeded in gaining the confidence of one of the soldiers of the guard. A contact was established with the party. The letters which he sent are the most convincing testimonial that in the most difficult hours of his life all his thoughts were centered on the organization, its immediate projects, its future. He wanted so much to continue his work shoulder to shoulder with his comrades. Destiny willed it otherwise. The rapidity with which he was deported frustrated the preparations to effect his escape undertaken by the party and he was flung into the hellish place where five million human beings were to perish—Auschwitz.

Leon was the type least able to withstand the regime of Nazi concentration camps. He possessed a sense of human dignity which found intolerable contact with the degradation and cruelty which became the common denominator of human conduct inside the concentration camps. The nobility of his character was shattered against the implacable bestiality of desperate egoism, just as his body became broken by physical exertions to which it was not accustomed and by malignant disease. After several weeks of labor in a road-building gang, he was sent to a quarantine camp. There one had to devise tricks, grovel before the masters, engage in petty trading and steal in order to survive. He could not rise above his companions in misery along these lines. Chained to his miserable cot, he passed his last days in reading and meditation. He was certain that the end was near. There came the final "medical inspection." The sick destined for the gas chambers were selected. He was among them.

It is difficult if not impossible to give an estimation of a revolutionary leader who reached only his 26th year. Despite all his incessant labors he has left us few works. He did not write a great deal; before confiding his ideas to paper he preferred to think them out to the end. Nevertheless that which he did leave us, his book and a thin volume of articles, suffices to discern in him, alongside of Marcel Hic, an individual of very exceptional talent and of the most serious promise possessed by the Fourth International on the Continent. By his strength of character as much as by the maturity of his political judgment, by his natural authority as much as by his qualities as leader, Leon was destined to lead our movement and to guide it through incessant struggles to victory. The void he leaves behind will not be quickly filled by a figure of similar stature.

Those who knew him will retain the memory of A. Leon as an example to emulate and a constant source of inspiration. Those *who read his book will admire the clarity and vigor of his reasoning and will be astounded by the maturity of a mind at the age of 24 years. Among those who learn the story of his life there may be some who will perhaps ask why a man of such remarkable qualities tied his destiny to a small revolutionary organization; they will praise his sincerity, his complete ideological honesty that caused him to live in complete harmony with his ideas. They will ask themselves: Why did the Marcel Hics, the Martin Widelins*, the A. Leons, who were among the most gifted European intellectuals, choose a movement which could promise them neither success nor glory nor honors nor even a minimum of material comfort, but which on the contrary demanded of them every sacrifice, including their lives, and which required long ungrateful work, frequently in isolation from the proletariat to whom they wanted to give everything? And if they are able to recognize in these young revolutionists, along with their intellectual gifts, exceptional moral qualities, they will then say to themselves that a movement capable of attracting such men solely by the power of its ideas and the purity of its ideal and capable of leading these rationalist dialecticians to such heights of self-denial and devotion—is a movement that cannot die because in it lives everything that is noble in man.*

---

* Martin Widelin. Leader of "Hashomer Hatzair" in Berlin and close friend of A. Leon. Worked as Trotskyist in French and Belgian Sections. Organizer of underground work among German soldiers and an editor of *Arbeiter und Soldat*, Trotskyist propaganda paper directed at Wehrmacht. Trapped by French Fascist "Brigade Spéciale" in Bois de Vincennes, shot and left for dead. Hospitalized, denounced to Gestapo, and immediately shot. *Tr.*

INTRODUCTION

By NATHAN WEINSTOCK

Few problems, if any, have cropped up as persistently during the last twenty-five years as the Jewish question. As a matter of fact, the history of the socialist movement since the 1930s shows that many of the decisive issues the working class has had to face have involved the Jewish question.

Thus, the rise of fascism in Western Europe was accompanied by the mass extermination of European Jewry which stands to this day as the most atrocious case of calculated genocide ever perpetrated. After the fall of fascism, public opinion discovered the plight of the "displaced persons," the uprooted survivors of the genocide. The birth and the consolidation of the state of Israel in 1948 ushered in a new era in the national and social struggle of the Arab masses. The reappearance of anti-Semitism in the Soviet Union, abetted by the ruling bureaucracy and publicized by the nauseating "Doctors' Plot" and the Prague frame-up trials in the early 1950s, exposed the cynicism of the Stalinist leadership. In 1956, the Suez affair illustrated the consequences of the Zionist alliance with imperialism in the Middle East. Meanwhile, after the Twentieth Congress of the Communist Party of the USSR, the cold-blooded murder of the leading Yiddish writers and artists—a glaring instance of bureaucratic degeneration—was revealed by the Warsaw *Folksstimme.* The Arab-Israeli war of 1967 and the deliberate exploitation and fostering of anti-Semitic prejudices which followed in Poland have once again brought the Jewish question to the fore.

So, time and again, the various aspects of the Jewish problem have been highlighted by the rise and fall of fascism, the postwar revolutionary upsurge in the Middle East, and the acute crisis of Stalinism in the Soviet Union and Eastern Europe. Thus, whether one considers the advanced capitalist countries, the workers' states, or the "Third World" (at least its Arabic-speaking component), the issues raised by the course of history appear to have put the Jewish question in dramatic relief. And since the major Jewish communities are presently situated in the USA, the Soviet Union, Israel, Western Europe, and Latin America, the future of the Jews is clearly a worldwide issue intimately related to the future history of mankind.

True, the events mentioned above were of such tremendous import that they dwarf the specifically Jewish aspects of the problems involved—although obviously not to the Jews themselves, who quite rightly refuse to consider their own future a side issue. Undoubtedly, the traditional view that the treatment of minorities—and especially of the Jews—serves as a thermometer of civilization has received a most sinister confirmation.

In our epoch humanity is faced with the alternative of socialism or barbarism. The tragedy of the Jewish people in the twentieth century is certainly one of the most ghastly illustrations of the barbaric depths to which man can sink. Such is the terrible price mankind must pay for delay in carrying out the socialist revolution or for failure to arrest its degeneration. And this again corroborates the remark made above: if the Jewish problem is linked up with the destiny of mankind, clearly the future of the Jews will be determined by the rhythm of the worldwide struggle for socialism. Obviously, a problem of planetary dimensions cannot conceivably be solved by artificially abstracting the issue from its global context.

Even though the Jewish problem remains a live issue, periodically highlighted by new trends in world politics, there has been an astounding lack of analysis of the question from a Marxist angle. One good reason for this strange silence immediately suggests itself: for many years, Marxist research appeared to be quasi-monopolized by the Communist Party. And the sharp twists and turns of the Stalinist leadership precluded a serious investigation, as this would have exposed the leadership's opportunism. Besides, one can hardly discuss the Jewish problem in the USSR—which has the largest community in the world after the United States—without a thorough study of Soviet society and politics, an undertaking no Marxist subservient to Moscow yet dares. Finally, one should not forget the sterilizing influence of Stalinist practices on creative Marxist theory and research. It is this incredible impoverishment of Marxism, transformed by Stalinist zealots from a radically critical method of analysis and action into a self-justifying ritual, which explains why so many independent socialists and radicals rejected Marxism as a whole, especially in countries where the Communist Party has no mass following and its ideology consequently does not even appear to be relevant to reality.

In this context, Abram Leon's brilliant essay stands out as a unique achievement, and the present edition should be hailed as a major step enabling the new generation of radicals to clarify an agonizing problem. Of course, many Marxist scholars, starting with Marx himself, devoted essays to the Jewish problem before Leon did (and it is worth noting, as we shall see, that they all were generally in agreement on the main points of their analysis). However, Leon's book is the first Marxist approach to be based on a thorough study of Jewish history and sociology; the first to follow the development of the Jewish communities from the days of the Romans until the present era of decaying capitalism; the first, too, to relate the major phases of Jewish history to the social history of capitalism. The author had a secure grasp of Marxist thought, and a quarter of a century after he finished his essay it remains a classical model of Marxist methodology. Leon also provides insight into numerous fields besides Jewish history.

Incidentally, although *The Jewish Question: A Marxist Interpretation* is absolutely free from sectarian bias, it is clearly no coincidence that the author, a leader of the Belgian Trotskyist movement, belonged to a non-Stalinist Marxist organization. As mentioned above, in its heyday Stalinism all but succeeded in killing creative Marxist thought. If only in the field of theory, the Trotskyist struggle to maintain the Leninist heritage found ample justification in that it succeeded in preserving the original standard of Marxist thought while the main body was decaying and rotting. Of this historical task of assuring the continuity of the socialist heritage on a theoretical and organizational level, Trotsky himself was painfully aware — as he showed in his spirited defense of the great figure of Rosa Luxemburg, who had been the subject of scurrilous attacks by Stalinist hacks.[1]*

As mentioned above, the first Marxist to study the subject was none other than Marx himself (*On the Jewish Question*, 1844).[2] This early essay remains a high point in the development of Marx's thought and contains a few glimpses and insights of genius on the Jewish question. It cannot be regarded as a definitive analysis of the problem, however, nor even as a thorough study. In spite of its somewhat misleading title, the essay is primarily concerned with the Jewish question *as an illustration of the need to overthrow the prevailing world order*. This explains the abstract character of the study, which contrasts sharply with the later writings of Marx, more characteristically painstaking in marshaling factual evidence.

On the Jewish Question was written to refute two major essays on the subject by Bruno Bauer, who argued that the Jews were not entitled to civil or political rights until they renounced Judaism or until the state renounced Christianity. Marx retorted that Jewish emancipation was fundamentally social, and not religious, in character. The political emancipation of the Jews was thus a necessary but by no means sufficient condition for their human emancipation. For human emancipation would require nothing less than the overthrow of the prevailing world order, in short, the emancipation of humanity from capitalism.[3]

So, in spite of its shortcomings (and, obviously, the hasty

* Notes to this article begin on page 60.

identification of the Jews with the capitalist spirit is one of the outstanding weak spots), this early essay of Marx does view the Jewish problem in its correct perspective, in stressing that the social function of the Jews kept them alive, and in viewing the Jewish question as part of the worldwide struggle for human emancipation. Furthermore, several of Marx's observations remain invaluable for any study of the Jewish question from the standpoint of historical materialism, such as his famous remark that "Jewry has survived, not in spite of, but because of history." Marx himself, however, never took up the subject again, though several incidental references to the Jews can be found in later works such as *Capital*.[4]

After Marx, many socialist scholars were induced to reopen the discussion, especially from the last quarter of the nineteenth century onwards, when anti-Semitism took on the form of a mass current in many countries of continental Europe, chiefly in Germany. It was under these circumstances that August Bebel uttered his scathing statement that anti-Semitism was the "socialism of fools." One of the first documented rebuttals of the prevalent racial theories to propound a Marxist approach to the Jewish question appeared in *Die Neue Zeit*, the leading theoretical journal of the socialist movement at the time.[5] The author of the anonymous essay (who was none other than Karl Kautsky) has obviously undertaken a careful study of the question. He dwells on the pioneering role the Jewish traders played in economic history and remarks that other people, too, such as the Scots in seventeenth- and eighteenth-century England, had been the agents of monetary economy. (These points are abundantly dealt with by Marx in his manuscript *Grundrisse der Kritik der Politischen Oekonomie* that was not unearthed and published until 1958.) Kautsky points out the unique history of the Jews in Europe since the second century A. D. as a purely urban population and stresses the fact that medieval towns usually harbored important communities of foreigners.

But it is especially interesting that the author is fully aware of the social and economic role of the Jewish population and rightly views it as a key to the survival of Jewish identity:

"In the Middle Ages, to be a Jew meant not only to be a member of a particular nation, but also of a particular profession."[6] Up to this point, Kautsky merely reiterates in detail Marx's analysis. However, the evolution in the social structure of the Jewish population, which was not clearly apparent when Marx took up the subject, could no longer be ignored half a century later. So Kautsky comments on the penetration of the Jews in new urban professions, whereby they cease to constitute a sort of corporation. A new diaspora is emerging, he observes: the migration of the Jews into the various professional occupations. This evolution tends to undermine the former unity of the Jews bound by a common interest, as the increasing class differentiation ultimately divides the Jewish population into a Jewish working class on the one hand (not necessarily an industrial proletariat) and a Jewish bourgeoisie on the other. So the evolution of capitalism implies the dissolution of Jewish particularism. And the author finally reaches the original Marxian prognosis: the emancipation of the Jewish proletariat cannot be isolated from the general issue of the emancipation of the working class.[7]

Further contributions to Marxist literature on the Jewish question were added by Karl Kautsky in later works[8] and Otto Bauer.[9] The latter devoted a long chapter of his book on the national question to what had by then become a burning issue in the Austro-Hungarian Empire. His discussion of the subject is analogous to the essay in *Die Neue Zeit.* He pointed out that the Jews had been the pioneers of money economy in the Middle Ages and that as a particular social group they were endowed at that time with indisputably national characteristics. However, capitalism had undermined these traditional foundations of Jewish national existence since the specific function of the Jews had come to an end. Bauer was also much concerned with the growth of anti-Semitism and he quoted approvingly the saying that national hatred is in fact nothing else but a perverted form of class hatred.

Lenin was also much concerned about the Jewish question since he feared that the increasingly nationalistic and separatist tendencies of the *Bund* (Jewish Labor Party) would jeopardize the unity of the Social Democratic Party in Russia. However, he did not undertake any personal research on the subject, relying heavily on Kautsky and Otto Bauer. He counterposed the situation in the advanced capitalist states, where Jewish particularism was disintegrating as a result of the disappearance of Jewish specific economic functions and the abolition of religious discrimination, to that in the Czarist empire with its barbaric oppression of the Jewish people. Here the Jews — "the most oppressed nation" — were "maintained by violence in the situation of a caste."[10] Clearly Lenin had grasped the social roots of the Jewish problem. As for the causes of anti-Semitism, who could possibly have ignored the deliberate exploitation of national antagonism by the Czarist regime in a desperate effort to divert the masses from the class struggle?

These classical theses of the Marxist analysis of the Jewish question were finally synthesized in Otto Heller's *Decline of Jewry* (1931),[11] a notable work unfortunately marred by the author's unconditional allegiance to Stalinism.

Finally, reference should also be made to Trotsky[12] for, although he disclaimed "any special authority" in this subject, his views are unquestionably of importance as he witnessed the mounting wave of anti-Semitism and fascism, the development of the Zionist enterprise in Palestine, and the unfortunate Birobidjan experiment in Soviet Russia. In an interview granted to the representatives of the Jewish press in Mexico in 1937 he admitted that he now no longer believed in his former prognosis that the Jewish problem would disappear in a quasi-automatic fashion in the different countries by means of assimilation. "The historical development of the last quarter of a century has not confirmed this perspective," he noted. "Decaying capitalism has everywhere swung over to an exacerbated nationalism, one part of which is anti-Semitism." This trend, combined with the growth of Jewish culture, meant that "one must therefore reckon with the fact that the Jewish nation will maintain itself for an epoch to come."[13] But Trotsky's conclusion did not differ from that of his predecessors. Foreseeing the mass extermination of Jewry—"the next development of world reaction signifies with certainty the physical extermination of the Jews," he wrote in 1938[14] —he warned that "the fate of the Jewish people—not only their political but also their physical fate—is indissolubly linked with the emancipating struggle of the international proletariat."

In view of the importance of this book, which presents a fundamentally new approach to Jewish history and a stimulating interpretation of its development, it is quite surprising how little response it evoked from the specialists. Although *The Jewish Question: A Marxist Interpretation* conforms to the traditional academic standards, the political persuasion of the author apparently accounts for the book having remained virtually ignored in learned circles until Professor Maxime Rodinson of the Sorbonne raised it to scientific respectability in 1968 by providing a thought-provoking preface to the second French edition.[15] One of the very rare exceptions to this deathlike silence comes from Professor Werner J. Cahnman, and his tribute to Leon is all the more remarkable as he disagrees with Leon's interpretation of Jewish history. Mention should also be made of Professor Oscar Handlin's stimulating review of Leon's work in *Commentary*.[16]

The present book can be considered in a certain sense as the spiritual testament of Abram Leon, who assumed the heavy duty of leading the Trotskyist organization in Belgium during the Nazi occupation. It provides a striking illustration of his exceptional capacities. All the more so since the reader should bear in mind that the author was compelled to gather his material and write his manuscript under extremely difficult circumstances and in the midst of exceedingly demanding activities devoted to the cause of the revolution. These formidable obstacles notwithstanding, the book he left us may certainly be ranked among the masterpieces of Marxist historiography.

Proceeding from Marx's comments on the fact that the secret of Jewish survival resides in Jewish history, Leon developed his concept of the people-class as the key to Jewish history. It is the historical role fulfilled by the Jews during their history which provides the explanation of their survival as a distinct community. Analyzing the successive economic functions assumed by the Jews in the precapitalist era, under manufacturing and industrial capitalism, and finally under imperialism, the author succeeds in unraveling the various Jewish modes of existence corresponding to those stages in social history. The discovery of this periodization enables Leon to rebut in a most convincing manner the idealistic premises that are commonly resorted to in order to interpret Jewish history. He leads us through the intricate maze of the Jewish saga, describing the growth of modern anti-Semitism generated by the incapacity of crisis-ridden capitalism to integrate the Jewish masses from Eastern Europe who had been evicted from their traditional occupations by the disintegration of the feudal economy. Leon also provides us with an explanation that sheds light on the psychological mechanisms that support the fascist ideology and its exploitation of the persisting medieval stereotype of the Jewish usurer in order to pervert the spontaneous elementary anticapitalism of the masses into anti-Semitism. Finally, having sketched the decline of East European Jewry from the nineteenth century onwards, he explains the development of the Zionist utopia as an ideological reflection of the problems of the declassed Jewish petty bourgeoisie, supplanted in the economy by the rising indigenous middle class and deprived of all prospects in the framework of decadent capitalism.

The conclusion of Leon's analysis is that no lasting solution to the Jewish question is conceivable under capitalism. The position of the Jews in society remains precarious so long as the menace of a major economic crisis looms in the future, with the attendant peril that the ruling class will once again resort to racist slogans. Insofar as the Jewish problem is intimately linked up with the social structure, clearly only a socialist revolution can offer a definitive answer to the problem, just as none of the vital problems of society can be solved under the present class structure.

This masterly work remains the only attempt to provide a *general* Marxist interpretation of Jewish history. Obviously it bears the stamp of its epoch: more than a quarter of a century has elapsed since Leon was deported by the Nazis — an unspeakable loss for his next-of-kin and his comrades. Since then the Jewish question has acquired new and terrifying dimensions. The present-day reader will regret that Leon's untimely death prevented him from analyzing the consequences of the genocide perpetrated on European Jewry, the effects of the Stalinist degeneration on the Jewish communities in the workers' states, or the significance of the establishment of the state of Israel. However, armed with the results of his research, other militants will resume the task where he was compelled to leave off. And, truly, compared to the considerable achievement of this pioneering work, the remainder will prove a much less arduous undertaking.

Yet the case of the Jews is not absolutely unique in history, although the Jews are doubtless the most perfect illustration of a process which many other peoples have experienced. It would certainly be a rewarding task to apply Leon's theory of the people-class to a large number of other allogeneous communities which, in the midst of host populations, have survived with their particular religious, linguistic, and cultural traits by virtue of their specific social and economic functions. Examples of these are the Gypsies, the Armenians living in exile, the Chinese merchants of Southeast Asia, the Copts, the Indian usurers in Burma, the German communities in Slavonic regions, etc. Such cases simply generalize the original pattern of an initially foreign group surviving in precapitalist society as an agent of monetary economy. American readers might be tempted to carry this line of reasoning a step further: in a sense the Afro-Americans in the United States who were shipped to the continent as slaves and who represent today an essentially proletarian community, in fact the lowest stratum of the American working class, can also be held to illustrate Leon's theory. Possibly a study of their history in this perspective could enrich our understanding of their present situation and future outlook.

Most historians tend to take an idealist view of Jewish history and explain the survival of the Jewish people by the intensity of their religious feelings or of their national consciousness, an interpretation that at best begs the question of why the religious or national consciousness arose in the first place.

Some sociologists, however, have anticipated the main lines of Leon's thesis or have independently expounded a similar interpretation, being naturally inclined to seek the answer to social problems in social processes. The most striking example is that of Max Weber who coined the term "pariah capitalism"[17] to describe the capitalism of socially ostracized marginal traders, originally strangers among host nations, who fulfill economically necessary but morally impugned functions. The Belgian sociologist Eugene Dupreel[18] observed in one of his essays that during the Middle Ages the Jews had practiced professions based on exchange value in rudimentary civilizations, fulfilling the role of specialists. A somewhat similar view is taken by Howard Becker in his reference to the Jews as a marginal trading people.[19]

Substantiations of Leon's concept of people-class can be found in the work of an Israeli historian, Michael Avi-Yonah,[20] who has described the gradual process of assimilation of Palestine Jewry in the second century A. D., except for the small minority engaging in trade and allied occupations, a point that we will elaborate below. Much the same can be said of Professor Goitein's study of the metamorphosis of the Jews in Islamic civilizations who entered *en masse* into commerce,[21] and this point too will be discussed below. Nor should we forget the fate of the Jewish congregations which were converted wholesale to Christianity (the Chuetas of the Balearic Isles) or to Islam (the Dunmeh of Turkish Salonika) and which retained their common identity in spite of conversion because the socioeconomic feature that differentiated them from the surrounding population had not been modified. These instances offer a negative proof of Leon's theory.

In accepting the assignment to write the preface to the second French edition of *The Jewish Question: A Marxist Interpretation,* Professor Maxime Rodinson enhanced Leon's book with his considerable scientific and personal prestige. And credit is due to him for consenting to lend his authority to Leon's work. The major part of his long introduction — forty-two pages — is devoted, however, to a sharp criticism of the author's thesis. Although in Rodinson's opinion Leon proved himself "above all capable of sketching in a substantially correct manner the main outline of the 'Jewish question,'" and notwithstanding the fact that he is praised for having "been right on what is essential, the fundamental point," the reservations that Rodinson makes are so important that they practically call into question the validity of the concept of the people-class as an explanatory principle of Jewish history.

The purpose of this discussion should not be misunderstood. Nothing could be further from my thoughts than an absurd faithfulness to the letter of the text. It would be unworthy of a Marxist to deny scientific evidence and to cling morbidly to outworn conceptions for the sake of some sort of misguided "fidelity" to the writer, an attitude that would amount in fact to betraying Leon's spirit. Nonetheless it is important to examine whether Rodinson's observations really blast Leon's conclusions. In my opinion this is not the case at all. In order to be brought into line with present-day knowledge, the concept of people-class calls for a reinterpretation rather than a revision.

We will start by summarizing Rodinson's criticisms. On the strength of the writings of various specialists, he comes to the conclusion that the theory of the people-class "within certain limits has a certain value regarding Western Christianity, especially from the Crusades onwards. . . ." But it would seem that this factor played no part at all for a period of "[at least] a thousand years."[22] In these regions, as well as in the West before the eleventh century, it would appear that no functional specializations of the Jews have been recorded: all Jews were not merchants nor were all merchants Jews. The explanation of the enduring existence of the Jewish people, then, should be sought in the characteristic pluralism of the precapitalist states of Islam and of Western Christianity prior to the Crusades. It is this "open" character of these multinational societies which would appear to account for the triumph of the "normal tendency of communities to persist in their existence and defend their interests and the aspirations of their members on a communal level."[23] It is only in Western Europe from the late Middle Ages onwards, that the orientation of many Jews towards trade in general and moneylending in particular seems to have crystallized, finally resulting in the effective transformation of the Jews into a people-class. This is the gist of Rodinson's refutation.

Before attempting to assess the value of these objections, it is necessary to provide an accurate definition of the meaning of the concept people-class, which is quite often interpreted by Rodinson in so schematic and narrow a sense that it borders on caricature.

When he stated that the Jews were a people-class, Leon did not at all mean to imply that all Jews *without any exception whatever* had been distinguished in the past by a history of functional specialization from which *all* the non-Jews of the country *without any exception whatever* were excluded. We are obviously dealing with a *tendential law*, admitting of numerous exceptions. In fact, the essence of the theory does not lie in the statement that Jews were traders but in the finding that Jewish professional occupations appeared as a *visible materialization of monetary economy in a society that rested essentially on use-values.* The point will be made further on that, paradoxically, the very structure of the people-class presupposes the existence of other, noncommercial Jewish strata. Besides, Leon never denied the existence of these atypical Jewish social strata. In fact, his thesis is precisely that the categories of Jews independent of commercial and usurers' capital *tend to melt away in the mass while those that specialized in these branches retained their group identity thanks to their specific function.*[24]

It is also erroneous to ascribe to Leon the view that the specific function of Jews in precapitalist society implies that they were all traders (or usurers). On the contrary, he insisted on the fact that in the Roman Empire "the majority was certainly made up of small people, some of them making their living directly or indirectly from trade: peddlers, stevedores, petty artisans, etc."[25] This information is of prime importance as, in the East, Jewry happens to have maintained to a large extent a professional structure akin to that of the Jewish communities of Roman Antiquity.

Leon described how the Jews were transformed into a people-class—the key to their conservation by history—as a *process of permanent selection* extending over several centuries and which has been continuously starting anew and going on since the initial functional specialization.[26]

Now that these preliminary points have been settled, we can systematically grapple with Rodinson's objections. We will successively examine his obervations pertaining to the belated appearance of functional specialization, the existence during the Middle Ages of Jewish professions in Western Christianity that appear to be incompatible with the status of a people-class, the atypical social structure of the Jews in the East, and the explanation of the survival of the Jewish people by the multinational character of precapitalist states.

1. *The belated appearance of functional specialization.*

The long description Goitein devotes to the process of transformation of the Jews, a population until then mainly plying manual trades, into a group whose chief occupation was trade and commerce[27]—a mutation that was accelerated by the economic evolution of the Muslim Empire after its decomposition—does not at all represent a refutation of Leon's theory;

far from it. On the contrary, it offers a remarkable illustration of his perception of the formation of the people-class. The same applies to Baron's analysis of the metamorphosis of the Jews into a predominantly mercantile population, with a strong emphasis on the money trade, a process which had been going on for centuries until it finally reached its climactic stage in the thirteenth century.[28] These basic trends which took place most distinctly under Western Christendom precisely *illuminate* the process portrayed by Leon. And to these accounts of the formation of the people-class should be added a third corroboration which is supplied, as mentioned above, by Michael Avi-Yonah,[29] who has studied the progressive assimilation of Palestinian Jewry, especially the Galilean agriculturists, by the surrounding population. Only the small fraction of the community that stood out through its commercial pursuits survived as such, that is, in the very measure in which it exhibited the socioeconomic peculiarities characterizing the Jewish communities of the diaspora.[30] Surely it is rather paradoxical to strive to rebut Leon's theory by referring to the selection process that happens to highlight the formation of the people-class.

Moreover, while the authors quoted above insist on the belated *completion* of the selection process, they explicitly add that the transformation itself had started several centuries before. Now Leon never claimed that the changeover in Jewish professions had been an abrupt or rectilinear process: like all tendential laws, the constitution of a people-class should be viewed through the actual dialectics of history which do not preclude *a priori* the possibility of intermittent fluctuations.

2. The professions at variance with the hypothesis of a people-class which were practiced by the Jews during the early Middle Ages in Western Europe.

Relying heavily on Bernhard Blumenkranz's[31] research, Rodinson emphatically challenges that the Jews had undergone a functional specialization during this period of history. Incidentally, attention should be called to a recent study by a Dutch historian, based on firsthand research, which upholds in all its main points the peculiar social structure of the Western Jews during the reign of the Merovingians and the Carolingians.[32]

But, as a matter of fact, the result of Blumenkranz's investigations are far from being as decisive as Rodinson would have us believe. According to this author's enumeration of the professions practiced by the Jews during this period, they were mainly connected with trade (traders, merchants, proprietors of handicraft workshops, moneylenders, shipowners, slave traders, goldsmiths, and silversmiths).[33] Nevertheless, on the list of occupations he has drawn up one does come across some professions which appear at first sight to invalidate the theory of the people-class. Such is the case, for instance, of the poor Jews of Sicily who were often small peasants (although Blumenkranz points out,[34] and this remark is obviously of prime importance, that they soon became converted to Christianity: so Leon's thesis on the assimilation of the strata which lose their specific function is proved to be *correct* after all) and that of the Jewish vinegrowers and landowners.

As far as landed property is concerned, Leon directed attention to the fact that the land belonging to Jews essentially represented the fruits of speculative operations of a usurious or commercial nature,[35] whereas the real Jewish landowners soon became assimilated after they had lost their specific features. As for the Jewish agriculturists and the vinegrowers in particular, we shall deal with them a little further on.

3. The atypical social structure of the Jews living in the Muslim world.

The diversified professional structure of the Oriental Jewish communities unquestionably constitutes Rodinson's main challenge to the validity of the people-class concept. Most research work on Oriental Sephardic Jewry was published after the Second World War so that Leon was not able to get acquainted with it. These studies underscore the fact that the Jewish population in the East differs from Western Jewry mainly by the exceptional importance of the artisan class, a characteristic that is common to Mediterranean Jewry in general.[36]

Therefore we must examine the role and significance of this stratum that most historians have disregarded. If one takes the trouble to try and define the structure of this Jewish artisan class, it will be found to consist of three distinct groups of professions.

The first comprises the corporations whose members catered directly for the internal needs of the Jewish community (bakers, millers, butchers, barbers, etc.) and who appear to be absolutely necessary for the very maintenance and conduct of the community.[37] Clearly, Rodinson was wrong in supposing that the concept of people-class excluded the coexistence in the midst of the Jewish people of noncommercial occupations side by side with commercial activities. Perhaps we should include the vinegrowers in this category (ritualistic importance of wine), although their profession is linked up with international trade, as well as the communal bureaucracy (scribes, rabbis, etc.).[38]

The second group of occupations *derives directly from the specific trading activity of the people-class* and constitutes its natural extension. Artisans belonging to this group generally enjoy a privileged status: silversmiths, goldsmiths, jewellers, silk workers, and people producing luxury articles.[39] So this labor force derived its livelihood directly from the main trading activity.

Here one is fully justified in resorting to Rodinson's description of a community *centered* around its members who are engaged in trade, without considering this state of affairs to be, as he suggests, an exception to the theory of the people-class.[40]

The last series of occupations is that of the *depressed crafts*, the marginal artisan sector that developed out of the degradation of the former Jewish merchant status, as in the Yemen.[41]

This downfall is strangely reminiscent of the status of the declassed Jews in Western Europe at the close of the Middle Ages: ragmen, peddlers, dyers.[42] Here we can observe a particular case of the *interstitial nature* of Jewish economic activity — the tangible expression of capitalism in a predominantly agrarian society — which undoubtedly flows from the intermediary functions fulfilled by the people-class.[43] One is reminded of Marx's striking description of the Polish Jews living in the pores of society.

On the whole, the Jewish artisan class naturally belonged to the Jewish middle layers situated between the aristocracy and the laboring classes.[44] It can be said to have been directly or indirectly dependent on trade, in accordance with Leon's description of the Jews in the Roman Empire. Moreover, the majority of the Jewish artisans were small entrepreneurs selling their wares to the customer in their own booths on credit. Thus, to a certain extent, their condition was similar to that of the moneylenders.[45] Finally, Cahnman[46] emphasizes the fact that all of these craftsmen without exception were employed exclusively by Jewish employers, and this clearly points to their position in a specific economic circuit as well as to the marginal character of their activity. So the diversity of the Jewish professions does not contradict the *specific character of their social function.* Oriental Jewry simply represented a *differentiated* people-class. It is true, however, that here we are manifestly dealing with a borderline case.

The existence during certain periods of history of a class of Jewish agriculturists does not invalidate the theory, provided one does not confuse them with Jewish *farmers* (who did not till the soil themselves) — and this was the most frequent case[47] — whose way of life is proof of Jewish landed property being a result of commercial transactions. Indeed, Jewish cultivators were not ordinary peasants. They specialized in viticulture, the cultivation of orchards, or dairy or truck farming, all of which, as Baron[48] is careful to point out, were *forms of agriculture intimately linked up with the urban economy, requiring heavy capital investments, and producing for exchange.* It is precisely because this intensive agriculture was integrated into the monetary economy that it was practiced in the immediate vicinity or sometimes even within the confines of the medieval towns.

Obviously this is a far cry from classical feudal agriculture based mainly on use-values!

As regards the traditional Jewish agriculture that dates from the times preceding the process of selection which converted the Jews into a people-class, it declined steadily from the end of Antiquity onwards and finally disappeared with the rise of Islam.[49]

4. The explanation of the preservation of the people-class by the multinational character of the precapitalist states.

Finally, one cannot help feeling disappointed on reading Rodinson's unconvincing interpretation of Jewish survival in precapitalist society. No doubt the atmosphere of tolerance peculiar to the pluralistic "Barbarian" states elucidates up to a certain point the comparative absence of religious coercion (though this line of reasoning awkwardly reminds one of Moliere's pun on the dormitive virtue of opium as an explanation for its action as a soporific). But it does not provide us with a key to understanding the survival of the Jewish community in history — in contradistinction to other peoples of the Ancient East — and still less with the reason for that community's remarkable class structure. In fact, it is rather astonishing that such a distinguished Orientalist as Rodinson was not struck by the obvious parallelism between the preservation of the Jewish minority and the survival of other religious communities, such as the Copts or the Nestorian Christians in the Near East. This comparison suggests that the correct interpretation of the phenomenon consists in a *generalization* of the theory of the people-class in order to extend its scope to the whole spectrum of socioreligious or allogeneous minorities fulfilling intermediary economic functions within precapitalist society. In this connection, it is worth remembering the point Lenin made in his *Agrarian Program of the Russian Social Democracy* (1902),[50] namely that in precapitalist society, class differentiation is accentuated by the division of society into *castes*, each caste having a specific legal status.

The crystallization of people-classes becomes especially significant within this context.

One of the most striking illustrations of the case for extending the concept worked out by Leon to other ethnic communities, is that of the Chinese in Southeast Asia.[51] Like the Jewish merchants of the Middle Ages, they were the traders in luxury articles; like the Jews also, they formed in the Southeast Asian cities a community of merchants and usurers. And when an indigenous bourgeois class developed, the Chinese were forced to face oppressive governmental measures (in Indonesia, the Philippines, Burma, etc.) and even, occasionally, actual pogroms (Indonesia).[52]

It is significant that the agriculture of the Overseas Chinese in Malaysia, for instance, is specifically oriented towards highly profitable crops produced for the urban market economy. Finally, the growing mass of Chinese proletarians overseas is an indication of the gradual breakdown of the people-class into antagonistic social classes — a process quite similar to the evolution of the Jewish communities in Eastern Europe since the end of the eighteenth century.

These remarks do not purport to exhaust the subject. Their only purpose was to try and show that the facts that have been marshaled in order to criticize the theory of the specific function of the Jews as representatives of capital in a society based on natural economy, can be easily dealt with within the framework of the people-class concept.

Professor Rodinson's brilliant and controversial introduction to Leon's book reopens a debate which will undoubtedly enrich Marxist thought.

The rise of capitalism ushered in the liberal era which resulted in the emancipation of the Jews and the demolition of the walls of the ghettos. Leon describes how the loss of their specific function, coupled with the disappearance of discrimination, hastened the process of integration of the Jews of Western Europe and was followed by the rapid assimilation of the Jewish communities in that part of the world. This process was particularly evident in Germany.[53] In Eastern Europe, however, where the feudal structure of the countryside hampered the development of capitalism, this perspective never really materialized. The Jewish masses lost their traditional role, but the feeble growth of capitalist economy prevented their absorption in industry. The same structural weakness of capitalist society in Eastern Europe explains why the ruling class, faced with a permanent social and economic crisis, was compelled to resort to Jew-baiting and persecution in order to divert the masses from revolutionary struggle. This situation forms the backdrop to the Jewish tragedy of the nineteenth and twentieth centuries in Eastern Europe.

As a result of the massive emigration of the Jews from Central and Eastern Europe between the last quarter of the nineteenth century and the First World War, the Jewish problem was "exported" to Western Europe and North America. But, in its decaying phase, capitalist society racked by periodic economic crises was no longer able to absorb the immigrants permanently into the social structure. Moreover, as Leon has shown, imperialism is reflected in the ideological sphere by the emergence of a jingoistic and racist ideology and chauvinism. Now racism and anti-Semitism soon proved to be invaluable instruments for the nationalist capitalist oligarchies who sought to channel the budding anticapitalist consciousness of the petty bourgeoisie and the class consciousness of the workers into politically harmless directions. Like fascism itself, fascist racism represented a desperate attempt to consolidate the crisis-ridden capitalist regime imperiled by the rising militancy of the working class.

It is significant that the Jews were not, as commonly believed, the only minority to suffer mass extermination under fascism. An identical fate awaited another people-class in Nazi Europe: the Gypsies.

If this interpretation of anti-Semitism is correct, then clearly there is nothing to warrant that a similar catastrophe will not occur in the future. The systematic use of weapons specifically designed to annihilate civilian populations, as demonstrated by American imperialism in Vietnam, is sufficient proof that there are no inherent limits to the barbarism of decaying capitalism. And there is no safeguard to guarantee that imperialism would refrain from resorting to the time-honored weapon of anti-Semitism if faced once again with a major economic and political crisis. As a matter of fact, the experience of the last few years in the country which presently harbors the largest Jewish community in the world, the U. S., is that the ruling class is getting ready to use the most sophisticated armament (nerve gas, for instance) against the Afro-American people and their class allies. And, incidentally, the treatment meted out to the Afro-Americans should serve as a useful reminder of the ripe experience accumulated by the American power elite in manipulating race hatred. So there is no reason to vouch for the fact that it "couldn't happen here." This was the sober warning addressed to the Western Jewish communities by Isaac Deutscher. And as George Novack[54] has pointed out: "Such a prediction may seem farfetched and unduly alarmist to those privileged and shortsighted Anglo-American Jews who have been sunning in the prolonged prosperity and social stability of the postwar decades. Yet it is based upon a keen insight into the ultimate direction of the main motive forces of capitalist development in our time."

The only safeguard consists in uprooting the system that generates the evil: capitalism cannot be reformed.

Any attempt to convince the Jewish masses of the accuracy of Leon's analysis will unfailingly raise the following retort: "Well, assuming you are right about this, how do you account for what happened in the Soviet Union or in Poland?" And this indeed calls for some explaining.

The reasons why the Soviet Union did not succeed in solving the Jewish problem have been dealt with most competently by Isaac Deutscher in his essay on the Russian Revolution and the Jewish problem.[55] He describes how the Lenin era brought forth an unparalleled Jewish (especially Yiddish) cultural flowering in the Soviet Union, in accordance with the Bolshevik program for the national minorities. No pains were spared in attempting, with considerable success, to resettle the impoverished Jewish petty bourgeoisie. Many found employment in the agricultural sector; the majority, however, were absorbed in industry after the first Five Year Plan was launched.

But the Jews could not remain unaffected by the retrogression of the Russian Revolution which became manifest in every field after Lenin's death and the defeat of the left-wing opposition. Trotsky was the first, in *Thermidor and Anti-Semitism* (1937),[56] to warn that the growth of chauvinism under the Thermidorian reaction implied the rebirth of the anti-Semitic tendencies the Revolution had eradicated. He pointed out the anti-Semitic innuendos implicit in the Moscow trials of 1936. And it is now a well-established fact that the anti-Jewish drive initiated in the late 1920s was intensified just before the Second World War, reversed altogether during the struggle against Nazi Germany, and pursued again with renewed energy from 1948 onwards, culminating in the closing down of all Jewish cultural institutions (press, theater, schools), the wanton murder of the foremost Yiddish writers, and the sinister anti-Semitic "Doctors' Plot" in 1953, a frame-up trial halted in the nick of time by Stalin's death.

The connection between the persecution of Jewish culture and the discriminatory measures against Soviet Jewry, on the one hand, and the bureaucratic degeneration of the regime, on the other hand, is obvious. And it is highly significant that Yevgeny Yevtushenko, the author of *Stalin's Heirs*, a bitter indictment of the Soviet bureaucracy, is also the author of *Babi Yar*, a poem that ends with the defiant assertion that "The International shall ring when the last anti-Semite will have disappeared." Yevtushenko has apparently made his peace now with the Soviet leadership; but the new vanguard of Russian intellectuals and workers are carrying on the struggle against the perversions of Stalinism, and fortunately they are made of sterner stuff.

So it is hardly astonishing that the criminal record of Stalinism has disgusted a whole generation of Jewish militants with the Soviet regime. Unfortunately, the shock of Nazi genocide and the subsequent disillusion with Stalinism often resulted in people despairing of socialism altogether as a solution for the Jewish problem. Nor is it surprising that the Communist movement has been unable to offer a Marxist analysis of the Jewish problem in the USSR, a task that would imply, as stated above, a clear-cut denunciation of the Soviet bureaucracy. [57]

But the fate of Soviet Jewry is not an isolated case. Chauvinistic Great Russian tendencies are equally manifest in the national oppression of the Ukrainian people, the Baltic nationalities, and especially in the wholesale deportation of the Kalmuks, the Crimean Tartars, the Volga Germans, and a host of other communities — all that was officially admitted by Khrushchev in his famous "secret" speech at the Twentieth Congress of the Soviet Communist Party. So the Jewish problem in the USSR is but an aspect of national oppression in the Soviet Union. The problem is to regenerate socialism altogether, a task that implies overthrowing the whole parasitical bureaucratic structure that defaces the land of October.

The case of Poland is quite similar. Although Stalinist Poland initially took great pride in its effort to help the remnants of the Jewish community, it should not be forgotten that the new regime started by driving out the German minority in 1945-46, using German workers as slave labor on Russian state farms in and outside of Poland, and deporting them *en masse* (including the women) to Russia in an attempt at calculated revenge. [58] All this on the basis of the Stalinistic assumption that the German proletariat was "guilty" of the crimes of the Nazi rulers who had oppressed them — as if the German workers had not been the very first victims of Nazism! Members of the German minority left in Poland were not even recognized as Polish citizens until 1950, and German schoolchildren were deprived of German schools until 1951. [59] Much the same could be said of other "People's Democracies" as regards their treatment of national minorities (the Germans and the Hungarians in Czechoslovakia, the Hungarians in Rumania, etc.).

So, as we can see, Polish Stalinism was linked with racism and chauvinism from the very beginning of its regime. Nor is this the whole story: the bureaucratic nature of the regime and the subservience of its leaders to Moscow made it especially unpopular. In order to gain the allegiance of the population, the government embarked on a program of extreme chauvinism, pandering to the prejudices of the Nationalists, often former fascists. A well-known instance of this unholy alliance is the privileged position of Mr. Boleslaw Piasecki, leader of the "Pax" movement and enterprises (press, publishers, dealers in religious articles), who gained wide notoriety in prewar Poland as a pogromist and fascist. Apparently, the idea was that in patronizing this unsavory figure the Stalinist leadership would somehow earn the gratitude of the Catholic working class. On top of all this, the direct executors of the policy were often of Jewish origin, a fact that naturally fed the traditional popular anti-Semitic prejudices; nor were some bureaucrats averse to encouraging these racist feelings, since they provided a "harmless" outlet for political opposition.

The Polish October of 1956 brought the hope of a new turn in Polish politics with the appearance of workers' councils and the awakening of the masses. But the "liberal" bureaucrats like Gomulka, propelled to power by the workers and students, were able with consummate art to liquidate the emerging workers' democracy within a few months.[60] A new opposition enlightened by this bitter experience started to take shape around 1965, centered around the Warsaw students and a number of revolutionary intellectuals. The student demonstrations of March 1968, supported by Polish Communist intellectuals such as Kolakowski and by the vanguard of the industrial proletariat, indicated the extent of popular support for the program of the left opposition (2330 people were arrested). At this juncture, Jozef Kepa, first secretary of the Polish CP, denounced the sinister designs of the "Zionists"[61] and laid stress on the alleged Jewish origin of the leaders of the student movement.

True, officially sponsored anti-Jewish tendencies were already perceptible since the end of the June war in 1967 — although the alleged rejoicing over Israel's victory was certainly not restricted to the Polish Jews who, incidentally, were mostly stalwart opponents of Zionism with a lifelong record of fidelity to the Communist movement. But now the so-called "anti-Zionist" drive—directed against nonexistent Zionists—became the major theme of an official campaign meant to rally the masses around the authorities and against the students. The so-called "spontaneous anti-Zionist" meetings were supported by a sickening press campaign which included statements in the Polish parliament on the "excessive concentration and representation in key areas" of Jews. Clearly, once again the Jewish problem sidelights the shameful degeneration of the bureaucratic caste.

This is how the promise that the October Revolution held out for the Jews and other oppressed minorities has been turned into bitter mockery: a reflection of the worldwide effect of the Stalinist distortion of socialism.

Yet, only ninety miles from the American shore, one can catch a glimpse of what socialism really could mean for the Jews. Although the present-day Cuban Jewish community has been reduced by emigration to a thousand souls, its situation illustrates the deeply humanitarian approach to all problems socialism implies. To quote an American conservative rabbi's report[62]: "Speaking with many Jews of varying outlooks—some sympathetic to the revolution, some neutral, some hostile—I found unanimous agreement on one point: the revolutionary government of Cuba has been beyond criticism in its respect for and consideration of Jewish religious needs."[63] Not only do the synagogues function in Havana, but in spite of the severe food rationing in Cuba, the government also provides special rations for the Jewish community to ensure that a weekly kosher meal is available to the entire community as well as appropriate dinners for the Holy Days. Any Jewish child who wishes to may attend the Albert Einstein school, now nationalized (as are all schools) but still giving classes in Jewish studies, and bus transportation is provided to and from the school for all those who live at any distance. The Jewish cemetery is state-supported so that free ritual funerals are available to all. Jewish cultural activities are regularly engaged in at the community center.

And the results of this absolutely correct approach to the Jewish problem by the Cuban leadership are rewarding indeed: deeply religious Jews who were formerly unconcerned with politics have been won over to the Revolution! Rabbi Gendler quotes the queries of practicing Jews "who related the biblical tradition to the Cuban experiment." And it is certainly appropriate to quote his conclusion:[64]

"Numerically, the Cuban Jewish community is much diminished, and it will likely be reduced yet further by continuing emigration. Institutionally, despite basic governmental respect and consideration, it faces powerful challenges from the whole spirit of Cuban life today, and like other religious communities both there and elsewhere it must develop new relevance for society if it is to survive as a vital part of life. Yet, personally, for a small number of deeply dedicated and intensely aware Jews, Cuba represents, at this period of its history, a vivid re-enactment of the desert period of our own people, a period of radical change, severe trial, and the formation of a new generation of human beings. Strange as such notions may be to our established ways of thinking, and despite some misgivings which I may have about the Cuban experiment, it seems to me, on reflection, that this seemingly perverse judgment of this tiny minority of Jews may yet prove more correct than the prevailing negative assessments of the Cuban experiment.

"Why do I say this? Because nowhere in the Western Hemisphere have I seen a society in which there is such morale, such social dedication, such feelings of fellowship, such concern for children and young people. Nowhere have I seen in practice such a radical interpretation of human brotherhood expressed in the attempt at economic equality and sharing (not yet fully achieved) which converts from theory to fact the notion of our human interdependence. Nowhere outside Israel have I seen such social concentration on education or such respect for teachers and learning, and nowhere else have I seen such attention and resources focused on the previously poorest and least esteemed."

Socialism, then, not only means rooting out racial discrimination — as the Cuban record shows in regard to the Negro population — it also holds out the challenge to all who are seriously committed to their religious faith, of acting out their principles in a fraternal society.

Last but not least, the results of the Zionist enterprise in Palestine offer further proof of the impossibility of finding a lasting solution to the Jewish problem within the framework of capitalism. Zionism is based on the assumption that the concentration of the Jewish masses in a national homeland would insulate them from anti-Semitism. For the Zionist considers anti-Semitism to be an inevitable phenomenon in non-Jewish society — or, as Pinsker put it, a psychosis peculiar to the gentiles — and not an outgrowth of the social structure. But it is an illusory solution. Aside from the fact that at most it could only provide a *partial* answer to the Jewish problem (since more than four-fifths of world Jewry live outside Israel) it ignores the fact that the fundamental roots of anti-Semitism lie in the *worldwide crisis of capitalist society.* If a new wave of fascism were to arise, there is no reason why its racist policies should mysteriously stop short at Israel's frontiers. After all, if Hitler had conquered Palestine would he have exempted Palestine Jewry from the gas chambers?

Still, it is true of course that *within* the almost purely Jewish society of Israel (at any rate before the 1967 conquests), anti-Semitism is out of the question. But it is a dubious achievement: ironically, the Israelis appear to be today the *only* Jewish community in fear for their physical existence. Nor does Israel extend help to world Jewry. On the contrary, its emissaries tour the world begging for support in every Jewish community. Israel has not proved to be an independent Jewish state standing on its own. Quite the reverse: Israel is absolutely dependent (economically, politically, diplomatically) on the assistance of imperialism. And surely, in a world in which the power of imperialism is steadily declining, especially in the underdeveloped countries, this should be a source of preoccupation to all those who are sincerely concerned with the future of the Israelis.

Now that the Israelis are engulfed by a wave of mounting hostility to Zionism, how prophetic Trotsky's warning sounds that Palestine might prove to be a bloody trap! And how true Leon's premonition that a Jewish state in Palestine would inevitably become a pawn of Anglo-American imperialism!

But let us recall how the present situation arose. The Zionist enterprise could not but reflect European colonial expansion of the nineteenth century. (In his *Judenstaat,* Theodor Herzl patterned the "Society of the Jews" he wished to set up as the backbone of Jewish colonization on the model of the British chartered companies in Africa.) And its aim — the establishment of a Jewish state in an Arab land — obviously had to clash, sooner or later, with the interests of the native population. Now it is a fact that the Zionist pioneers, imbued with socialistic ideals — and there is no reason to question their dedication or their idealism — hoped to evade the consequences of colonialism. They were bitterly opposed to the exploitation of the cheap Arab labor they were competing with, and they set out to build their own segregated economy, based on Jewish investments, exclusively Jewish labor, and inasmuch as feasible, exclusively Jewish produce. This policy of deliberate separatism had a lasting effect on the outline of Zionist colonization. If Israel appears to be a full-fledged nation today, a society consisting of a Jewish bourgeoisie exploiting a Jewish proletariat (and not as a mere layer of *colons* thriving on Arab labor), this is unquestionably the result of their ideology. And it was in this spirit that the exclusively Jewish trade union, the *Histadrut,* the collective and cooperative rural settlements (*kibbutzim* and *moshavim*) were founded.

But for the Arab peasants, the *fellaheen,* the policy of exclusively Jewish labor had dramatic results. It meant not only that they were evicted from the land they tilled after the Arab landowner had sold it to the Zionist concerns, but also that they were prevented on principle from finding employment on the Jewish farms or in industry. Likewise the policy of Jewish produce (i.e., the boycotting of Arab produce) impeded the development of an Arab bourgeoisie and proletariat in Palestine. Thus Arab resentment[65] to Zionist colonization could be channeled into neither bourgeois nationalism nor proletarian socialism, since the social classes that normally convey these policies remained embryonic owing to the Zionist segregationism which blocked their emergence. Therefore, the embittered Arab masses of Palestine fell prey to the rapacious, obscurantist, feudal leadership (the very same people who were selling their land to the Zionist settlers at a handsome profit, thus preparing the eviction of the *fellaheen*). And, as the feudal leadership was reactionary and leaned heavily on British support, they diverted the Arab Palestinian masses from their real interest—the struggle against imperialism and Zionist colonization—and initiated a chauvinistic anti-Jewish policy.

The implementation of the Zionist program also served to alienate the Jewish immigrants from their long-term interests. The Zionist enterprise could only be put in force against the wishes of the local population and with the help of foreign rulers (first the Turks, then the British). So the growing Jewish community became the mainstay of the hated foreign rule. This fitted in wonderfully with imperialism's traditional exploitation of religious and national prejudices in the Middle East in order to divide its opponents. In the past this policy had been used to pit Christians against Muslims, Turks against Arabs, Sunni Muslims against Shia Muslims, Copts against Muslims, Druse against Maronites, etc. The new antagonisms between Jews and Arabs followed the same pattern and served the same ends. Furthermore, the policy of class collaboration of the Zionist leadership (motivated by the so-called common interests of the Jewish bourgeoisie and working class in Palestine) widened the rift between the Jewish and Arab masses, for the common benefit of the Arab feudalists, the Zionist bourgeoisie, and the British administration.

The Palestine war of 1948 highlighted this distortion of the social and national currents in the Jewish and Arab society. The Jews (who had by now become Israelis, a new Hebrew-speaking nation with its own economy and society distinct from other Jewish communities) fought under a bourgeois leadership, assisted by American imperialism and the Soviet bureaucracy. Their aim was to set up a purely Jewish state in Palestine, as large as possible. They succeeded in forcing this program on British imperialism and in conquering close to 80 percent of the Palestinian territory. But the result of their victory was the expulsion of some 750,000 Palestinian Arab refugees. And the new state of Israel, surrounded by a hostile sea of Arabism, was compelled to seek the helping hand of Uncle Sam. Israel has become increasingly dependent on U. S. imperialism ever since, while embarking on a policy of institutionalized oppression of the Arab minority. On the Arab side, the war—though basically progressive since it was part of the worldwide anticolonial struggle—was fought under the guidance of British imperialism and the corrupt feudal leaderships which led their armies and peoples to disaster. The wars of 1956 and 1967 merely repeated the 1948 pattern: Israel was proving itself to be more and more dependent on imperialism and hostile to the forces of Arab liberation. And the Arab leadership was meanwhile unable to set the issue in its true perspective: a struggle of the popular masses of the Middle East (Arab and non-Arab) under a revolutionary socialist leadership against the forces of imperialism, Zionism, and Arab reaction.

Since 1967 Israel has occupied vast expanses of Arab territory, expelling many inhabitants (many of them refugees of 1948). It would seem that this new situation will eventually lead to the implementation of an officially segregationist policy, since the Zionist leadership does not wish to relinquish its new conquests but insists on maintaining a purely Jewish power structure. On the Arab side, hostility to the presence of the Zionist enclave has increased, and since 1965 the new militancy of the Palestinian refugees has been expressing itself in guerrilla warfare, to which should now be added the passive and active resistance of the population in the occupied territories.

It is obvious that the continuation of the present Zionist policy (and there is no other way of maintaining an exclusively Jewish power structure) of oppression of the Arab masses and cooperation with imperialism can only pave the way of the Israeli masses to catastrophe. The Israeli position is becoming untenable: the authorities admit their failure to crush the Palestinian partisans, who are eating away at the foundations of the surrounding Arab bourgeoisies, Israel's secret allies. And the Israeli authorities have no outlook to offer the Jewish population except further warfare. On the other hand, the growing left wing of the Palestinian freedom fighters is increasingly aware that the Israeli population is a victim of exploitation and manipulation and that it must be won over. They also realize that the outcome of their struggle depends in the first place on the elimination of the enemy waiting to shoot them in the back: the Arab reaction.

The Middle Eastern scene is in a state of flux. The Palestinian guerrilla is radicalizing the coming generation of Arabs and forcing the Arab bourgeoisie to admit that they prefer peaceful coexistence with Zionism and imperialism to the perils of revolution. The Arab petty bourgeoisie, which is mirrored in Nasserism, now appears to be thoroughly discredited in the eyes of the vanguard after having demonstrated its utter corruption during the war of June 1967 (a *political* defeat as well as a military defeat). The essential task now is to combine the struggles of the revolutionary elements of the Arab world, spearheaded by the Palestinians, into one common front including the Israelis who raise their banner against the Zionist power structure, the revolutionary Kurds, the South Sudanese, etc. The future of the Israeli population rests in its integration, with due respect of its right to national self-determination, in a united socialist Middle East. As Deutscher pointed out, the Zionist policy has turned the Israelis into political scapegoats. The only way out of this trap is an alliance with the forces of the socialist revolution.[66]

So, whether one considers the advanced capitalist countries, the workers' states, or Israel, the lesson of history is the same:

the solution of the Jewish problem is indissolubly bound up with the victory of socialism. Therefore, assuming that one could spell out a "Jewish" stand in the political struggle, it could only be the admission of the fact that the Jewish people have a vested interest in the emancipation of humanity and that socialism has a particular relevance to their fate. Socialism is the only road to Jewish survival.

Autumn 1969

NOTES

1. Leon Trotsky, "Bas les pattes devant Rosa Luxemburg!" in *Ecrits (1928-1940)*, tome I, Paris, 1955.
2. Karl Marx, *Early Writings*, T. B. Bottomore (ed.), New York, 1964.
3. In accord with the prevailing opinion among left Hegelians in Germany at that time, Marx identified Jewry *(Judentum)* with the bourgeois or commercial spirit. This was, he wrote, the secular basis of Judaism.
4. The famous description of the "Jews [living] in the pores of Polish society" appears in *Capital*, vol. III, Moscow, 1959, p. 325. Countless references to foreign merchant communities living in agrarian society are also given by Marx in his famous *Grundrisse* (pp. 38, 108, 146, 163, 200, and 449 of the French edition, *Fondements de la critique de l'economie politique*, tome I, Paris, 1967).
5. S., "Das Judentum," *Die Neue Zeit*, 1890, pp. 22-30.
6. Ibid., p. 28.
7. The increasing class differentiation among the Jewish population, resulting in the appearance of compact masses of Jewish workers in Eastern Europe and, as a result of large-scale immigration, in London and New York, also struck Engels, who commented on the combativity of the Jewish proletariat and emphasized the outstanding contribution of Jewish revolutionists to socialism. Letter of April 19, 1890, to an unknown correspondent, in Karl Marx and Frederick Engels, *Selected Correspondence*, London, 1943, p. 471.
8. Karl Kautsky, *Are the Jews a Race?*, New York, 1926; and *Foundations of Christianity*, New York, 1925.
9. Otto Bauer, *Die Nationalitaetenfrage und die Sozialdemokraten*, Vienna, 1907.
10. V. I. Lenin, *Notes critiques sur la question nationale* (1913), Moscow, 1951, pp. 12-13.
11. Otto Heller, *Der Untergang des Judentums*, Vienna, 1931. Among the lesser essays devoted to the subject by authors of the Stalinist school one should mention I. Rennap, *Anti-Semitism and the Jewish Question*, London, 1943.
12. Leon Trotsky, "Interview with Jewish Correspondents in Mexico (January 18, 1937)," *On the Jewish Question*, New York, 1970, pp. 20-22.
13. Ibid., p. 20.
14. Ibid., "Appeal to American Jews Menaced by Fascism and Anti-

Semitism (December 22, 1938)," p. 29.

15. Abram Leon, *La conception materialiste de la question juive,* Paris, 1968.

16. Werner J. Cahnman, "Socio-Economic Causes of Antisemitism," *Social Problems,* vol. 5, no. 1, July 1957, p. 22. Oscar Handlin, "Does Economics Explain Racism?" *Commentary,* vol. 6, no. 1, July 1948, pp. 79-85. Handlin holds that racial prejudice arises out of a total situation in which both the prejudiced and the object of his prejudice are victims. But as capitalism permeates every aspect of social life, this thesis does not invalidate Leon's economic determinism, though he is right in warning against schematic excesses.

17. Cf. C. Wright Mills and Hans Gerth, *Character and Social Structure,* London, 1965, p. 216. Max Weber, *Gesammelte Aufsaetze zur Religions-Soziologie,* Bd. II, Zweite Auflage, Tuebingen, 1923, p. 39.

18. Eugene Dupreel, "Le probleme de l'antisemitisme," *Revue de l'Institut de Sociologie,* no. 1, Brussels, 1948, p. 8.

19. Cited by Werner J. Cahnman, in "Role and Significance of the Jewish Artisan Class," *Jewish Journal of Sociology,* vol. VII, no. 2, December 1965, p. 207.

20. Michael Avi-Yonah, *Geschichte der Juden im Zeitalter des Talmud,* Berlin, 1962.

21. S. D. Goitein, *Jews and Arabs,* New York, 1955.

22. Leon, *La conception. . . ,* p. xiv.

23. Ibid, p. xxxi.

24. See pp. 42-43 and 83-84.

25. See p. 77.

26. See pp. 83-84.

27. Goitein, op. cit., pp. 115-124.

28. Salo W. Baron, *A Social and Religious History of the Jews,* 2d ed., vol. IV, New York, 1957, p. 150.

29. Avi-Yonah, op. cit., especially pp. 85*ff.* and 133*ff.*

30. Ibid., p. 272.

31. Bernhard Blumenkranz, *Juifs et Chretiens dans le monde occidental 430-1096,* Paris-La Haye, 1960.

32. Lea Dasberg, *Untersuchungen ueber die Entwertung der Judenstatus im 11. Jahrhunderts,* Paris-La Haye, 1965, pp. 93*ff.*

33. Cf. Blumenkranz, op. cit., pp. 30-32 and 336, as well as, by the same author, *Les auteurs chretiens latins du Moyen Age sur les Juifs et le Judaisme,* Paris-La Haye, 1963, especially p. 74, note 6.

34. Blumenkranz, *Juifs. . . ,* p. 32. Also Cahnman, "Role. . . ," pp. 209 and 211.

35. This is corroborated by Baron, op. cit., p. 13.

36. Cahnman, "Role. . . ," especially p. 209.

37. Ibid., p. 213. Cf. Baron, op. cit., pp. 157-158 and 164.

38. Baron, op. cit., p. 215.

39. Ibid., p. 211; and Cahnman, "Role . . .," pp. 213-215. Also S. D. Goitein, "Jewish Society and Institutions under Islam," *Cahiers d'Histoire Mondiale*, vol. XI, no. 1-2, 1969, p. 179.

40. Leon, *La conception . . .*, p. xxxviii.

41. Cahnman, "Role . . .," p. 211. Cf. Sidney Mendelssohn, *The Jews of Asia, Especially in the Sixteenth and Seventeenth Centuries*, London-New York, 1920, pp. 176*ff.*

It should be noted, however, that things are not as simple as they appear on first sight. In a recent study Goitein has shown that the despised work imposed on the Yemenite Jews (cleaning latrines, etc.) most certainly represented the deliberate humiliation of a non-Muslim community, but that paradoxically it did not in the least affect the social status of the members of the Jewish community. Jewish artisans were addressed respectfully as "Master" by their fellow citizens, a token of deference indeed. (Goitein,"Jewish Society . . .," pp. 175-176.)

42. See p. 115.

43. Cahnman, "Role . . .," pp. 215*ff.*

44. Ibid., p. 219.

45. Ibid., p. 216.

46. Ibid.

47. Baron, op. cit., p. 155, and Goitein, "Jewish Society . . .," p. 175.

48. These features of Jewish agriculture are specifically stressed by Baron, op. cit., p. 29 and especially p. 162.

49. Ibid., pp. 151 and 164.

50. V. I. Lenin, in *Collected Works*, vol. 6, Moscow, 1964, p. 115.

51. Cf. Lois Mitchison, *The Overseas Chinese*, London, 1961.

52. The title of one of the first anti-Chinese pamphlets that was published in Siam in 1914 and which is written in a frankly "anti-Semitic" style is revealing: *The Jews of the East.*

53. For a typical description of the scale of the conversion movement among German Jews, cf. A. Menes, "The Conversion Movement in Prussia During the First Half of the 19th Century," *YIVO Annual of Jewish Social Science*, vol. VI, New York, 1951, pp. 187-205.

54. George Novack, *How Can the Jews Survive? A Socialist Answer to Zionism*, New York, 1969.

55. Isaac Deutscher, "The Russian Revolution and the Jewish Problem," in *The Non-Jewish Jew and Other Essays*, London, 1968.

56. Cf. Trotsky, *On the Jewish Question*, New York, 1970.

57. A typical instance of this helplessness is the introduction the well-known Italian Communist Senator Umberto Terracini has provided for a collection of highly critical essays on the Jews in the Soviet Union. The remarkable fact is that while Terracini has had the courage to edit the book, none of the contributors, least of

all Terracini himself, offers a *Marxist* interpretation of this flagrant case of degeneration. (*Gli Ebrei nell'URSS*, Milan, 1966.)

58. Elisabeth Wiskemann, *Germany's Eastern Neighbours*, London, 1956, pp. 89-95 and 113*ff.*

59. Ibid., p. 271.

60. Jacek Kuron, Karol Modzelewski, et al., *Revolutionary Marxist Students in Poland Speak Out*, New York, 1968.

61. *Tribuna Ludu*, March 12, 1968.

62. Rabbi Everett Gendler, "Holy Days in Habana," *Conservative Judaism*, vol. XXIII, no. 2, Winter 1969, p. 19.

63. Marxists certainly believe that socialism will ultimately ring the knell of religion—*not* as a result of the suppression or the curtailment of religious activities or feelings—but as a logical consequence of the disappearance of the social roots of alienation of which religious alienation is a particular aspect. To persecute religion would not merely be contrary to socialist ethics, it would also be self-contradictory for those who hold, as Marx wrote, that social being determines consciousness. (Karl Marx and Frederick Engels, *Preface to a Contribution to the Critique of Political Economy*, in *Selected Works*, vol. I, Moscow, 1950, p. 329; Frederick Engels, *Anti-Duehring*, Moscow, 1954, pp. 338-340; V. I. Lenin, "The Attitude of the Workers' Party Towards Religion" (1909), in *Marx-Engels-Marxism*, 4th English ed., Moscow, 1951, pp. 272-286; Otto Bauer, *Sociaaldemocratie, Godsdienst en Kerk*, Amsterdam-Brussels, 1928, pp. 79-94.)

64. Gendler, op. cit., pp. 23-24.

65. Arab opposition to Zionism had nothing to do with anti-Semitism. They would probably have reacted in the same way if the Zionists had been Hottentots or Mongolians. It is worth recalling in this connection that the Afro-American settlers had to fight some bloody battles against the native African population in Liberia when they landed and colonized the country.

66. For a full discussion on the Zionist issue, see my *Le sionisme contre Israel*, Paris, 1969.

CHAPTER I

THE PREMISES FOR A SCIENTIFIC STUDY OF JEWISH HISTORY

The scientific study of Jewish history is yet to transcend the stage of idealist improvisation. Serious historians have boldly attacked the field of history as a whole in the spirit of Marx, and have in large measure conquered it for the materialist outlook. Jewish history, however, still remains the chosen land of the "god-seekers" of every variety. It is one of the few fields of history where idealist prejudices have succeeded in intrenching and maintaining themselves to so great an extent.

How many oceans of ink have been spilled to celebrate the famous "miracle of the Jew!" "What a strange spectacle are these men who have, in order to preserve the sacred trust of their faith, braved persecutions and martyrdom," exclaims Bédarride.[1]

The preservation of the Jews is explained by all historians as the product of their devotion through the centuries to their religion or their nationality. Differences among these historians begin to appear only when it comes to defining the "goal" for which the Jews preserved themselves, the reason for their resistance to assimilation. Some, taking the religious point of view, speak of the "sacred trust of their faith"; others, like Dubnow, defend the theory of "attachment to the national idea." "We must seek the causes for the historical phenomenon of the preservation of the Jewish people in their national spiritual strength,

---

[1] I. Bédarride, *Les Juifs en France, en Italie et en Espagne*, París, 1867, p. i.

in their ethical basis and in the monotheistic principle," says the *General Encyclopedia* which contrives in this way to reconcile the various viewpoints among the idealist historians.[2]

But while it is possible to reconcile these idealist theories with one another, it is hopeless to try to find some ground for reconciling these same theories with the elementary rules of historical science. The latter must categorically reject the fundamental error of all idealist schools which consists of putting under the hallmark of free will the cardinal question of Jewish history, namely: the preservation of Judaism. Only a study of the economic role played by the Jews can contribute to elucidating the causes for the "miracle of the Jew."

To study the evolution of this question is not exclusively of academic interest. Without a thorough study of Jewish history, it is difficult to understand the Jewish question in modern times. The plight of the Jews in the Twentieth Century is intimately bound up with their historical past. Every social formation represents a stage in the social process. *Being* is only a moment in the process of *becoming.* In order to undertake an analysis of the Jewish question in its present phase of development, it is indispensable to know its historical roots.

In the sphere of Jewish history, as in the sphere of universal history, Karl Marx's brilliant thought points the road to follow. "We will not look for the secret of the Jew in his religion, but we will look for the secret of the religion in the real Jew."[3] Marx thus puts the Jewish question back on its feet. We must not start with religion in order to explain Jewish history; on the contrary, the preservation of the Jewish religion or nationality can be explained only by the "real Jew," that is to say, by the Jew in his

---

[2] *General Encyclopedia* (Yiddish), Paris, 1936, vol. III, pp. 454-455. Article of Ben-Adir on anti-Semitism.

[3] "On the Jewish Question," *Selected Essays by Karl Marx*, New York, 1926, p. 88.

economic and social role. The preservation of the Jews contains nothing of the miraculous. "Judaism has survived not in spite of history, but by virtue of history."[4]

It is precisely by studying the historical function of Judaism that one is able to discover the "secret" of its survival in history. The struggles between Judaism and Christian society, under their respective religious guises, were in reality social struggles. "We transmute the contradictions of the state with a specific religion, like Judaism, into the contradiction of the state with specific secular elements."[5]

The general pattern of Jewish history is presented (with various slight nuances) somewhat as follows according to the reigning idealist school: Up to the destruction of Jerusalem, as late as the rebellion of Bar Kochba, the Jewish nation was in no wise different from other normally constituted nations, such as the Roman or the Greek. The wars between the Romans and the Jews resulted in dispersing the Jewish nation to the four corners of the world. In the dispersion, the Jews fiercely resisted national and religious assimilation. Christianity found no more rabid adversaries in its path and despite all its efforts did not succeed in converting them. The fall of the Roman Empire increased the isolation of Judaism which constituted the sole heterodox element after the complete triumph of Christianity in the West.

The Jews of the Diaspora, in the epoch of the barbarian invasions, did not at all constitute a homogeneous social group. On the contrary, agriculture, industry, commerce were widely prevalent among them. It was the continuous religious persecutions which forced them to intrench themselves increasingly in commerce and usury. The Crusades, by reason of the religious fanaticism they engendered, violently accelerated this evolution which

---

[4] *Ibid.*, p. 92.
[5] *Ibid.*, p. 52.

transformed the Jews into usurers and ended in their confinement in ghettos. Of course the hatred against the Jews was also fanned by the latter's economic role. But the historians attribute only a secondary importance to this factor. This condition of Judaism continued up to the French Revolution, which destroyed the barriers that religious oppression had raised against the Jews.

Several important facts challenge the truth of this pattern:

1. The dispersal of the Jews does not at all date from the fall of Jerusalem. Several centuries before this event, the great majority of Jews were already spread over the four corners of the world. It is certain that well before the fall of Jerusalem, more than three-fourths of the Jews no longer lived in Palestine.[6]

For the great masses of Jews dispersed in the Greek Empire, later in the Roman Empire, the Jewish kingdom of Palestine was of completely secondary importance. The tie with the "mother country" was manifested solely in religious pilgrimages to Jerusalem, which played a role similar to that of Mecca for the Moslems. Shortly before the fall of Jerusalem, King Agrippa said to the Jews: "There is no people upon the habitable earth which have not some portion of you among them."[7]

The Diaspora was consequently not at all an accidental thing, a product of acts of violence.[8] The fundamental reason for Jewish emigration must be sought in the geographic conditions of Palestine. "The Jews in Palestine were the possessors of a mountainous country which at a certain time no longer sufficed for assuring its inhabitants as tolerable an existence as that among

---

[6] See Arthur Ruppin, *The Jews in the Modern World,* London, 1934, p. 22.

[7] Flavius Josephus, *Works*, London, 1844, p. 693.

[8] "In the first place we know of no hostile power which might have forced our people before the final destruction of Jerusalem to spread out through all of Asia Minor, the Mediterranean islands, Macedonia and Greece." Dr. L. Herzfeld, *Handelsgeschichte der Juden des Alterthums,* Braunschweig, 1879, pp. 202-203.

their neighbors. Such a people is driven to choose between brigandage and emigration. The Scots, for example, alternately engaged in each of these pursuits. The Jews, after numerous struggles with their neighbors, also took the second road... Peoples living under such conditions do not go to foreign countries as agriculturalists. They go there rather in the role of mercenaries, like the Arcadians of Antiquity, the Swiss in the Middle Ages, the Albanians in our day; or in the role of *merchants,* like the Jews, the Scots and the Armenians. We see here that a similar environment tends to produce similar characteristics among peoples of different races."[9]

2. The overwhelming majority of Jews of the Diaspora unquestionably engaged in trade. Palestine itself since very remote times constituted a passageway for merchandise, a bridge between the valleys of the Euphrates and the Nile. "Syria was the inevitable highway of the conquerors... Trade and ideas followed the same route. It is easy to see that from a very early date these regions were thickly populated, and possessed great cities whose very situation lent itself to commerce."[10]

The geographic conditions of Palestine therefore explain both the Jewish emigration and its commercial character. On the other hand, among all nations, at the beginning of their development, the traders are foreigners. "The characteristic of a natural economy is that each sphere produces everything consumed by it and consumes everything it produces. There is consequently no pressure to buy goods or services from others... Because what is produced is consumed in this economy, we find among all these peoples that the first traders are foreigners."[11]

---

[9] Karl Kautsky in *Neue Zeit.*

[10] Adolphe Lods, *Israel from Its Beginnings to the Middle of the Eighth Century,* London, 1932, p. 18.

[11] Lujo Brentano, *Die Anfange des Modernen Kapitalismus,* Munich, 1916, pp. 10, 15.

Philo enumerates many cities where the Jews were established as traders. He states that they "inhabited countless cities in Europe, in Asia, in Libya, on the mainland and in the islands, along the coasts and in the interior." The Jews who inhabited the Hellenic islands, as well as the mainland and further to the west, had installed themselves there with commercial objectives.[12] "As well as the Syrians, the Jews were to be found in all the cities, living in small communities; they were sailors, brokers, bankers, whose influence was as essential in the economic life of the time as was the Oriental influence which made itself felt at the same time in the art and the religious thought of the period."[13]

It is to their social position that the Jews are beholden for the wide autonomy granted them by the Roman emperors. The Jews, "and they only were allowed to form, so to speak, a community within the community, and —while the other non-burgesses were ruled by the authorities of the burgess-body— [they were permitted] up to a certain degree to govern themselves."[14] Caesar advanced the interests of the Jews in Alexandria and in Rome by special favors and privileges, and protected in particular their peculiar worship against the Roman as well as against the Greek local priests."[15]

---

[12] Herzfeld, *op. cit.*, p. 203.

[13] Henri Pirenne, *Mohammed and Charlemagne*, New York, [1939], pp. 18-19.

[14] Theodor Mommsen, *The Provinces of the Roman Empire*, New York, 1887, vol. II, p. 179.

[15] Theodor Mommsen, *The History of Rome*, London, 1911, vol. IV, p. 509.

Sombart, in his work of such uneven value, *The Jews and Modern Capitalism*, (London, 1913), wherein the worst of absurdities are mixed with highly interesting researches, states: "I think that the Jewish religion has the same leading ideas as capitalism." (p. 205). This affirmation is correct provided we understand by "capitalism," — precapitalist trade and usury. (As we shall see later (Chapter IV), it is false to attribute a preponderant role to the Jews in the building of modern capitalism.) In support of his thesis, Sombart

3. Hatred for the Jews does not date solely from the birth of Christianity. Seneca treated the Jews as a criminal race. Juvenal believed that the Jews existed only to cause evil for other peoples. Quintilian said that the Jews were a curse for other people.

The cause of ancient anti-Semitism is the same as for medieval anti-Semitism: the antagonism toward the merchant in every society based principally on the production of use values. "Medieval hostility toward merchants is not solely of Christian or pseudo-Christian inspiration. It also has a 'real' pagan source. The latter was strongly rooted in a class ideology, in the disdain which the leading classes of Roman society —the senatorial gentes as well as the provincial curia— felt, out of a deep peasant tradition, toward all forms of economic activity other than those deriving from agriculture."[16]

---

cites many passages from the Talmud and other Jewish religious books which reflect this close connection between the Jewish religion and the commercial spirit. Here are, for example, several of these quotations: "He that loveth pleasure shall be a poor man, he that loveth wine and oil shall not be rich." *Proverbs*, 21.17. "Thou shalt lend unto many nations, but thou shalt not borrow." *Deuteronomy*, 15.6. "The righteous therefore is prosperous here, and the wicked here suffers punishment." "Rabbi Eleazar said: 'The righteous love their money more than their bodies." *Sota* xiia. "And Rabbi Isaac also taught that a man always have his money in circulation." *Baba Mezia*, 42a

It is naturally difficult to get a complete picture from a confused welter of texts, written and supplied with commentaries at different epochs and in different countries. The imprint of the commercial spirit is nevertheless clearly discernible in most of these writings. The work of Sombart is in this sense only an illustration of the Marxist thesis that religion is an ideological reflection of a social class. But by maintaining that it is religion which must have been the primary factor, Sombart, like other bourgeois scholars, strives to invert the causal relation.

[16] Henri Laurent, "Religion et Affaires," *Cahiers du Libre Examen*.
Aristotle says in his *Politics* (Jowett translation, Oxford, 1885, vol. I, p. 19): The most hated sort [of money-making], and with the greatest reason, is usury, which makes a gain out of money itself,

However, while anti-Semitism was already strongly developed in Roman society, the condition of the Jews, as we have seen, was quite enviable there. The hostility of classes that live from the land toward trade does not eliminate their dependence upon the latter. The landowner hates and despises the merchant but he cannot get along without him.[17]

The triumph of Christianity did not bring any notable changes in this regard. Christianity, at first the religion of the slaves and the downtrodden, was rapidly transformed into an ideology of the ruling class of landed proprietors. It was Constantine the Great who laid the foundation for medieval serfdom. The triumphal march of Christianity across Europe was acompanied by an extension of feudal economy. The religious orders played an extremely important role in the progress of civilization, which consisted in that epoch of developing agriculture on the basis of serfdom. There is little astonishing in the fact that "born in Judaism, formed at first exclusively of Jews, Christianity nevertheless nowhere during the first four centuries found more difficulty than among them in acquiring partisans for its doctrine."[18] As a matter

---

and not from the natural use of it. For money was intended to be used in exchange, but not to increase at interest. And this term, usury, which means the birth of money from money, is applied to the breeding of money, because the offspring resembles the parent. Wherefore of all modes of making money this is the most unnatural." Further (p. 221), "citizens... must not lead the life of mechanics or tradesmen, for such a life is ignoble and inimical to virtue."

[17] Contrary to the opinion of some historians, ancient economy was, despite a fairly important development of commercial transactions, based essentially on the production of use values. "This system [of home or family economy] prevails not only in primitive societies but even in those of Antiquity.... Under this system... each group suffices unto itself, consuming hardly anything but what it has itself produced, and producing almost nothing beyond what it will consume." Charles Gide, *Principles of Political Economy*, Boston, 1905, p. 132.

[18] Jean Juster, *Les Juifs dans l'Empire Romain*, Paris, 1914, vol. I, p. 102.

of fact, Christian mentality during the first ten centuries of our era viewed everything connected with economic life from the basic standpoint "that a merchant can with difficulty do work pleasing to God" and that "all trade implies a greater or lesser amount of cheating."[19] The life of the Jews appeared completely incomprehensible to St. Ambrose who lived in the Fourth Century. He despised the wealth of the Jews profoundly and firmly believed that they would be punished for it by eternal damnation.

The fierce hostility of the Jews toward Catholicism and their determination to preserve a religion which admirably expressed their social interests are therefore quite natural. It is not the loyalty of the Jews to their faith which explains their preservation as a distinct social group; on the contrary, it is their preservation as a distinct social group which explains their attachment to their faith.

Nevertheless, like the hostility in Antiquity toward the Jews, Christian anti-Semitism, in the first ten centuries of the Christian era, never went to the extreme of demanding the annihilation of Judaism. Whereas official Christianity mercilessly persecuted paganism and heresies, it tolerated the Jewish religion. The condition of the Jews continued to improve during the decline of the Roman Empire, after the complete triumph of Christianity and up to the Twelfth Century. The more economic decay deepened, all the more did the commercial role of the Jews grow in importance. In the Tenth Century, they constituted the sole economic link between Europe and Asia.

4. It is only from the Twelfth Century on, parallel with the economic development of Western Europe, with the growth of cities and the formation of a native commercial and industrial class, that the condition of the Jews begins to worsen seriously,

---

[19] Laurent, *op. cit.*

leading to their almost complete elimination from most of the Western countries. Persecutions of the Jews take on increasingly violent forms. As against this, in the backward countries of Eastern Europe, their condition continues to remain flourishing up to a fairly recent period.

From these few preliminary considerations, we can see how false is the general conception prevailing in the sphere of Jewish history. *Above all the Jews constitute historically a social group with a specific economic function. They are a class, or more precisely, a people-class.*[20]

The concept of class does not at all contradict the concept of people. It is because the Jews have preserved themselves as a social class that they have likewise retained certain of their religious, ethnic and linguistic traits.[21]

This identification of a class with a people (or race) is far from being exceptional in precapitalist societies. Social classes were then frequently distinguished by a more or less national or

---

[20] "The peasant and the lord during the Middle Ages are not producers of merchandise.... It is true that they exchange their surpluses on occasion, but exchange is for them something fundamentally alien, an exception. Thus, neither the lord nor peasant generally possesses large sums of money. The greatest part of their wealth consists of use values, of wheat, cattle, etc... Circulation of merchandise, circulation of money-capital, and money economy in general are fundamentally alien to this form of society. Capital lives, according to the clear expression of Marx, in the pores of this society. It is into these pores that the Jew penetrated." Otto Bauer, *Die Nationalitätenfrage und die Sozialdemokratie*, Vienna, 1907, p. 367.

[21] Pirenne explains the preservation of the national character by the Germans in the Slav countries as follows: "The principal explanation [of this preservation] is the fact that among the Slavs they were the initiators and for long centuries *par excellence* the representatives of the urban life. The Germans introduced the bourgeoisie into the midst of these agricultural populations, and the contrast between them was, perhaps, from the very first, that of social classes rather than national groups."
Henri Pirenne, A *History of Europe*. London, 1939, p. 328.

racial character. "The higher and lower classes... are in many countries the lineal representatives of the peoples conquering and the peoples conquered of an anterior epoch... The race of the invaders... formed a military nobility... the invaded race... not living by the sword but by the compulsory labor of their hands..."[22] Kautsky speaks in the same vein: "Different classes may assume the character of different races. On the other hand, the meeting of many races, each developing an occupation of its own, may lead to their taking up various callings or social positions within the same community: *race becomes class.*" [23] [24]

There is evidently a continuous interdependence between racial or national and class characteristics. The social position of the Jews has had a profound, determining influence on their national character.

---

[22] Augustin Thierry, *History of the Conquest of England by the Normans*, London, 1856, vol. I, pp. xix-xx.

[23] Karl Kautsky, *Are the Jews a Race?*, New York, 1926, p. 58. My emphasis. Inasmuch as the divisions between the various classes in precapitalist times are airtight, it often happens that national differences persist for a very long time. They manifest themselves particularly in language differences. The language of a conquered people used to be demoted to the role of a despised popular tongue, while the language of the conquerors became the language of "high society." In England, the Norman aristocracy continued for many centuries to use French while the people spoke Saxon. It is from the fusion of these two languages that modern English was formed. In the long run, the language differences faded away. The Burgundians, the Franks and other barbarians quickly started speaking the language of their subjects. On the other hand, the Arab conquerors imposed their own language on conquered peoples. These language differences between classes disappeared completely only with the advent of the bourgeoisie to power.

[24] "Some classes, the ruling, the peasant and the merchant classes, for instance, arose from the union of different ethnological elements... their characteristic differences are original. Such classes antedate the state and are the more easily maintained in it because their differences are both anthropological and moral." Ludwig Gumplowicz *The Outline of Sociology*, Philadelphia, 1899, p. 134.

There is no contradiction in this idea of a people-class; and it is even easier to show the correspondence between class and religion. Whenever a class attains a certain degree of maturity and consciousness, its opposition to the ruling class takes on religious forms. The heresies of the Albigenses, the Lollards, the Manichaeans, the Cathari and other innumerable sects that swarmed in medieval cities, were the initial religious manifestations of the growing opposition to the feudal order by the bourgeoisie and the people as a whole. These heresies nowhere reached the level of a dominant religion because of the relative weakness of the medieval bourgeoisie. They were savagely drowned in blood. It was only in the Seventeenth Century that the bourgeoisie, increasing in power, was able to bring about the triumph of Lutheranism and above all of Calvinism and its English equivalents.[25]

Whereas Catholicism expresses the interests of the landed nobility and of the feudal order, while Calvinism (or Puritanism) represents those of the bourgeoisie or capitalism, Judaism mirrors the interests of a precapitalist mercantile class. [26] [27]

What primarily distinguishes Jewish "capitalism" from genuine capitalism is that, by contrast with the latter, it is not the bearer of a new mode of production. "The merchant's capital is

---

[25] This scientific view has been perforce accepted for a long time by all serious historians.

[26] "...Jewish capitalism was speculative pariah-capitalism, while Puritan capitalism consisted in the organization of citizen labor." Max Weber, *General Economic History*, New York, 1927, p. 381.

[27] The correspondence between class and religion is, naturally, not absolute. All of the gentry were not Catholics, nor were all adherents of Calvinism bourgeois. But the classes do leave their imprint on religion. Thus, "revocation of the Edict of Nantes at the end of the Seventeenth Century exiled about 100,000 Protestants, almost all inhabitants of the cities and belonging to the industrial and commercial classes; for the Huguenot peasants, converted only in name, hardly left the kingdom." Henri Sée, *Economic and Social Conditions in France during the Eighteenth Century*, New York, 1927, p. 9.

pure, separated from the extremes, the spheres of production, between which it intervenes." "The trading nations of the ancients existed like the gods of Epicurus in the intermediate worlds of the universe *or rather like the Jews in the pores of Polish society.*" "Both usury and commerce exploit the various modes of production. They do not create it, but attack it from the outside."[28]

The accumulation of money in the hands of the Jews did not arise from a special mode of production, from capitalist production. Surplus value (or surplus product) came from feudal exploitation and the lords were obliged to yield part of this surplus value to the Jews. Hence the antagonism between the Jews and feudalism, but hence likewise came the indestructible bond between them.

As for the lord, so too for the Jew, feudalism was mother earth. If the lord needed the Jew, the Jew also had need of the lord. It is by reason of this social position that the Jews were nowhere able to rise to the role of a ruling class. In feudal economy, the role of a merchant class could only be a clearly subordinate one. Judaism could only remain a more or less tolerated cult.[29]

We have already seen that the Jews in Antiquity had jurisdiction over their own community. The same was true in the Middle Ages. "In the plastic society of the Middle Ages, each class of men lived according to its own customs, and under its special jurisdiction. Outside the judical organization of the state, the church had its ecclesiastical courts, the nobility its feudal

---

[28] Karl Marx, *Capital*, Kerr Edition, vol. III, p. 716.

[29] The sole known exception was a Mongol tribe, the Khazars, on the shores of the Caspian Sea, who adopted Judaism in the Eighth Century. Was there perchance a relation between the commercial function of this tribe and its conversion to Judaism?

courts, and the peasants their manorial courts. The burghers in their turn, obtained their *échevins'* courts."[30]

The specific organization of the Jews was the *Kehillah*. Each cluster of Jews was organized into a community (Kehillah) which lived its own social life and had its own juridical organization. It was in Poland that this organization attained its highest degree of perfection. According to an ordinance issued by King Sigismund II in 1551, the Jews had the right to choose judges and rabbis whose duty it was to administer all their affairs. Only in actions between Jews and non-Jews did the Voyevoda courts intervene. Each Jewish community was free to choose a community council. The activities of this council, called *Kahal,* were very extensive. It collected taxes for the state, apportioned the general and special taxes, directed the elementary schools and high schools *(Yeshibot)*. It had jurisdiction over all questions concerning trade, artisanry, charity. It took care of settling conflicts between members of the community. The power of each Kahal extended to the Jewish inhabitants of surrounding villages.

With time the various councils of Jewish communities made a practice of assembling regionally at regular intervals to discuss administrative, juridical and religious questions. These assemblies thus assumed the aspect of miniature parliaments.

On the occasion of the great fair of Lublin, a sort of general parliament assembled in which the representatives of Great Poland, Little Poland, Podolia and Volhynia participated. This parliament was called *Vaad Arba Aratzoth,* or the "Council of the Four Lands."

Traditional Jewish historians have not failed to discern a form of national autonomy in this organization. "In old Poland," says Dubnow, "the Jews constituted a nation having autonomy,

---

[30] Henri Pirenne, *Belgian Democracy*, London, 1915, p. 46.

with its own internal administration, courts and a certain juridical independence."[31]

Clearly, it is a gross anachronism to speak of national autonomy in the Sixteenth Century. This epoch knew nothing of the national question. In feudal society, only the classes had their special jurisdictions. Jewish autonomy is to be explained by the specific social and economic position of the Jews and not at all by their "nationality."

Its linguistic evolution also reflects the specific social position of Judaism.

Hebrew disappeared very early as a living language. The Jews everywhere adopted the languages of the peoples among whom they lived. But this linguistic adaptation generally occurred in the form of a new dialect in which we again find some Hebraic expressions. There existed at various times in history Judo-Arabic, Judo-Persian, Judo-Provencal, Judo-Portuguese, Judo-Spanish and other dialects, including, of course, Judo-German which has become present-day Yiddish. The dialect thus expresses the two contradictory tendencies which have characterized Jewish life; the tendency to integration in the surrounding society and the tendency to isolation, deriving from the socio-economic situation of Judaism. [32] [33]

It is only where the Jews cease constituting a special social

---

[31] Lecture by Dubnow at a meeting of the Ethnographic Historical Society of St. Petersburg. (See also S. M. Dubnow, *History of the Jews in Russia and Poland,* Philadelphia, 1916, vol. I, p. 103. *Tr.*)

[32] As early as the Fifth Century before Christ, the Jews of the Diaspora spoke Aramaic. Later, they mainly used Greek. "The inscriptions [in the Jewish cemeteries in Rome] are mainly in Greek, some written in an almost unintelligible jargon; some are in Latin, none in Hebrew." Ludwig Friedländer, *Roman Life and Manners under the Early Empire,* London, 1910, vol. III, p. 178.

[33] It would be interesting to investigate why the Jews in the Slavic countries kept the German dialect (Yiddish) for so long a time.

group that they become completely assimilated in the surrounding society. "Assimilation is no new phenomenon in Jewish history," states the Zionist sociologist Ruppin.[34]

In reality, while Jewish history is the history of the preservation of Judaism, it is at the same time the history of the assimilation of large sections of Judaism. "In Northern Africa, in pre-Islamic times, great numbers of Jews were engaged in agriculture, but of these, too, the vast majority have been absorbed by the local population."[35] This assimilation is explained by the fact that the Jews by turning agriculturalists ceased to constitute a separate class. "Could they at all have taken to agriculture, they could hardly have done so without scattering through the country and its numerous villages, which, in spite of the difference in religion, would probably in a few generations have resulted in complete assimilation. Engaged in commerce and concentrated in towns, they formed agglomerations and developed a social life of their own, moving and marrying within their own community."[36]

Let us also recall the numerous conversions of Jewish landed proprietors in Germany in the Fourth Century; the complete disappearance of the Jewish warrior tribes of Arabia; the assimilation of the Jews in South America, in Surinam, etc.[37]

---

[34] Ruppin, *op. cit.*, p. 271.

[35] *Ibid.*, p. 132.

[36] *Ibid.*, p. 132.

[37] In the epoch of the development of capitalism, from the Sixteenth to the Nineteenth Century, assimilation in Western Europe generally meant penetration into the Christian capitalist class. The penetration of the Jews into the capitalist class may be compared to the "capitalization" of feudal properties. In the latter case, too, the struggle of the bourgeoisie against feudalism terminated in some cases with the total expropriation of the feudal class (as in France), and in other cases with the penetration of feudal elements into the capitalist class (as in England and Belgium). Capitalist

The law of assimilation might be formulated as follows: Wherever the Jews cease to constitute a class, they lose, more or less rapidly, their ethnical, religious and linguistic characteristics; they become assimilated.[38]

It is very hard to trace Jewish history in Europe at several important periods, because the economic, social and political conditions were so different in various countries. Whereas Poland and the Ukraine were completely feudal at the end of the Eighteenth Century, in Western Europe we witness an accelerated development of capitalism during this same period. It is easy to understand that the situation of the Jews in Poland bore far more resemblance to the situation of the French Jews in the Carolingian Era than to that of their co-religionists in Bordeaux or Paris. "The Portuguese Jew of Bordeaux and the German Jew of Metz are two absolutely different beings," wrote a French Jew to Voltaire. The rich bourgeois Jews of France or Holland had virtually nothing in common with the Polish Jews who constituted a class in feudal society.

Despite the marked differences in conditions and in the tempo of economic development of the various European coun-

---

development has had a similar effect upon the Jews. In some cases they were assimilated; in others they were eliminated.

[38] As a general rule the persecutions of the Jews were social in character. But the lag of ideology behind the social superstructure can account for certain *purely religious* persecutions. In some regions, the Jews were able to preserve their special religion for a fairly long time despite their transformation into agriculturalists. In such cases, the persecutions were designed to *hasten* their conversion. What distinguishes *religious* persecutions from *social* persecutions (under a religious guise) is their less violent character and the feeble resistance of the Jews. Thus, it appears that in Visigoth Spain the Jews were in part agriculturalists. Consequently, the Visigoth kings never thought of expelling them, as Ferdinand and Isabella did later. On the whole, purely religious persecutions must be considered as exceptional.

tries inhabited by the Jews, a careful study permits the delineation of the following main stages of their history.

I. Precapitalist Period

This was also the period of the greatest prosperity of the Jews. Commercial and usurious "capital" found great possibilities for expansion in feudal society. The Jews were protected by the kings and princes and their relations with other classes were in general good.

This situation lasted up to the Eleventh Century in Western Europe. The Carolingian epoch, the culminating point of feudal development, was also the apex of Jewish prosperity.

Feudal economy continued to dominate Eastern Europe till the end of the Eighteenth Century. And the center of Jewish life shifted more and more to that area.

II. Period of Medieval Capitalism.

From the Eleventh Century on, Western Europe entered a period of intensive economic development. The first stage of this evolution was characterized by the creation of a corporative industry and a native merchant bourgeoisie. The penetration of mercantile economy into the agricultural domain determined the second stage.

The growth of cities and of a native merchant class brought with it the complete elimination of the Jews from commerce. They became usurers whose principal clientele consisted of the nobility and the kings. But the mercantile transformation of agricultural economy resulted in undermining these positions as well.

The relative abundance of money enabled the nobility to throw off the yoke of the usurer. The Jews were driven from one country after another. Others became assimilated, being absorbed mainly by the native bourgeoisie.

In certain cities, principally in Germany and in Italy, the Jews became primarily loan-makers to the popular masses, the peasants and the artisans. In this role as petty usurers exploiting the people, they were often the victims of bloody uprisings.

In general, the period of medieval capitalism was that of the most violent Jewish persecutions. Jewish "capital" came into conflict with all classes of society.

But the unevenness of economic development in the Western European countries operated to alter the forms of anti-Semitic struggles.

In one country, it was the nobility which directed the struggle against the Jews; in others, it was the bourgeoisie, and in Germany, it was the people who unleashed the movement.

Medieval capitalism was practically unknown in Eastern Europe. There was no separation between merchants' capital and usurious capital. In contrast to Western Europe where "Jew" became synonymous with "usurer," the Jews in Eastern Europe remained mainly traders and middlemen. Whereas the Jews were progressively eliminated from the countries of the West, they constantly strengthened their position in Eastern Europe. It was only in the Nineteenth Century that the development of capitalism (it is no longer corporative capitalism this time, but modern capitalism, which appears on the scene) began to undermine the prosperous condition of the Russian and Polish Jews. "The poverty of the Jews in Russia dates only from the abolition of serfdom and of the feudal regime in rural property. So long as the former and the latter existed, the Jews found wide possibilities for subsisting as merchants and middlemen."[39]

---

[39] Werner Sombart, *L'Apogée du Capitalisme*, Paris, 1932, vol. I, p. 430.

III. Period of Manufacture and Industrial Capitalism

The capitalist period, properly speaking, began in the epoch of the Renaissance and manifested itself at first by a tremendous expansion of commerce and the growth of manufactures.

To the extent that the Jews survived in Western Europe —and only a few were left there— they took part in the development of capitalism. But the theory of Sombart, who attributes a decisive activity to them in the development of capitalism, belongs to the sphere of fantasy. Precisely because the Jews represented a primitive capitalism (mercantile and usurious), the development of modern capitalism could only prove fatal to their social position.

This fact does not at all exclude —far from it— the individual participation of the Jews in the creation of modern capitalism. But wherever the Jews were integrated into the capitalist class, there *they were likewise assimilated.* The Jew, as a great entrepreneur or shareholder of the Dutch or English India Company, was already on the threshold of baptism, a threshold, moreover, which he crossed with the greatest of ease. The progress of capitalism went hand in hand with the assimilation of the Jews in Western Europe.

If Judaism did not completely disappear in the West, it was owing to the mass influx of Jews from Eastern Europe. The Jewish question, which is now posed on a world scale, therefore results primarily from the situation of Eastern Judaism. This situation is, in turn, a product of the lag in economic development of this part of the world. The special causes of Jewish emigration are thus linked with the general causes behind the emigration movement of the Nineteenth Century.

The general emigration of the Nineteenth Century was caused in large measure by the failure of capitalist development to keep pace with the crumbling of feudal economy or manufacture economy. The ranks of the English peasants, evicted by the capitalization of rural economy, were swelled by the artisan or manufacturing workers displaced by machines. These peasant and artisan masses, eliminated by the new economic system, were driven to seek a livelihood across the ocean. But this situation was not indefinitely prolonged. Because of the rapid development of the productive forces in Western Europe, the section of the population deprived of its means of subsistence was presently able to find sufficient work in industry. That is the reason why, in Germany, for instance, emigration to America, which was very strong in the middle of the Nineteenth Century, dwindled almost completely toward the end of the century. The same applies to England and other countries of Western Europe.[40]

While the disequilibrium between the crumbling of feudalism and the development of capitalism was disappearing in Western Europe, it was growing worse in the backward Eastern European countries. The destruction of feudal economy and primitive forms of capitalism proceeded there much more rapidly than the development of modern capitalism. Increasingly greater masses of peasants and artisans had to seek their road of salvation in emigration. At the beginning of the Nineteenth Century, it was principally the English, the Irish, the Germans and the Scandinavians who formed the bulk of immigrants to America. The Slavic and Jewish element became dominant toward the end of the Nineteenth Century among the masses streaming to the New World.

At the beginning of the Nineteenth Century, the Jewish

---

[40] "The economic progress of the principal European countries in the last quarter of the Nineteenth Century arrested the flow of emigration, but there soon began a second wave, comprising for the most part emigrants from the agrarian countries of Europe." Vladimil Voitinski, *Tatsachen und Zahlen Europas*, Vienna, 1930, p. 60.

masses sought new roads of immigration. But at first it was toward the interior of Russia and Germany that they headed. The Jews succeeded in penetrating the great industrial and commercial centers where they played an important role as merchants and industrialists. Here we come upon a new and important fact: For the first time in centuries a Jewish proletariat was born. The people-class began to differentiate socially.

The Jewish proletariat, however, remained concentrated mainly in the sector of consumer goods industry. It was primarily of the artisan type. In the same measure as large-scale industry expanded its field of exploitation, the artisan branches of economy declined. The workshop was superseded by the factory. And it thus turned out that the integration of Jews into capitalist economy still remained extremely precarious. It was not alone the "precapitalist" merchant who was forced to emigrate, but also the Jewish artisan worker. Jewish masses streamed in ever larger numbers from Eastern Europe to the West and to America. The solution of the Jewish question, that is to say, the complete absorption of the Jews into economic life, thus became a world problem.

IV. The Decline of Capitalism.

By socially differentiating Judaism, by integrating the latter into economic life, and by emigration, capitalism has laid the bases for the solution of the Jewish problem. But capitalism has failed to solve it. On the contrary the fearsome crisis of the capitalist regime in the Twentieth Century has aggravated the plight of the Jews to an unparalleled degree. The Jews, driven from their economic positions under feudalism, could not be integrated into a capitalist economy in utter decay. In its convulsions, capitalism casts out even those Jewish elements which it has not yet completely assimilated.

Everywhere is rife the savage anti-Semitism of the middle classes, who are being choked to death under the weight of capitalist contradictions. Big capital exploits this elemental anti-Semitism of the petty bourgeoisie in order to mobilize the masses around the banner of racism.

The Jews are being strangled between the jaws of two systems; feudalism and capitalism, each feeding the rottenness of the other.

CHAPTER II

FROM ANTIQUITY TO THE CAROLINGIAN EPOCH: THE PERIOD OF COMMERCIAL PROSPERITY OF THE JEWS

A. BEFORE THE ROMAN CONQUEST

From a very remote time Syria and Palestine were the highways for the exchange of goods between the two oldest centers of culture of the ancient Mediterranean world: Egypt and Assyria.[1] The essentially commercial character of the Phoenecians and Canaanites[2] was a product of the geographical and historical situation of the countries which they inhabited. The Phoenecians became the first great commercial people of Antiquity because they located the first two great centers of civilization. It was Assyrian and Egyptian goods which at first constituted the main object of Phoenecian trade. The same was certainly true for

[1] "In the ordinary language of European science, ancient life is that which developed chiefly round the Mediterranean basin." J. F. Toutain, *The Economic Life of the Ancient World*, New York, 1930, p. 1.

[2] It was probably the commercial prosperity of Palestine which made it appear to the Israelites as a land of "milk and honey." It is also probable that the Israelite invasion dealt a serious blow to Palestinian commerce. But with time the Israelites in their turn renewed the profitable relations with the countries of the Nile and the Euphrates.

the Palestinian merchants.[3] According to Herodotus, Assyrian goods were the most ancient and most important articles of Phoenecian commerce. No less ancient, however, was the connection of the Phoenecians with Egypt. The legends of biblical Canaan, as well as Phoenecian myths, reveal continuous relations by land and by sea, between the inhabitants of these countries and the Egyptians. Herodotus also speaks of Egyptian goods which the Phoenecians had been bringing to Greece from very remote times.[4]

But if the geographical situation of Palestine was as favorable as that of Phoenecia for mercantile trade between Egypt and Assyria,[5] the facilities for navigation at the disposal of Syria were completely lacking in Palestine. Phoenecia was abundantly provided with everything necessary for sea travel; the cedar and cypress of Lebanon furnished it with timber; copper and iron were also plentiful in the mountains of Lebanon and in the outskirts. On the Phoenecian coast, many natural ports were available for navigation.[6] It is therefore not surprising that at a very early date Phoenecian ships, heavily laden with Egyptian and Assyrian products, should have begun to ply the navigable routes of the ancient world. "The political and mercantile relations of Phoenecia

---

[3] Thus, from the very beginning, it was a specific geographic and historic situation which determined the commercial character of the Phoenecians and the Jews. It is obvious that only the proximity to centers of civilization equipped with a relatively important industry, only the closeness to countries already producing in part for exchange, could permit the development of such specifically commercial peoples as the Phoenecians and the Jews. It was alongside the first great centers of civilization that the first great commercial peoples developed.

[4] F. K. Movers, *Die Phonizier*, Berlin, 1856, vol. II, p. 18.

[5] "Even before the advent of the Israelites in Canaan, commerce was highly developed there. In the Tell-el- Amarna letters (Fifteenth Century B. C.) reference is made to caravans crossing the country under protective escort." F. Bühl, *Die Sozialen Verhaltnisse der Israeliten*, Berlin, 1899, p. 76.

[6] Movers, *op. cit.*, vol. II, pp. 19-20.

with the great states of the Nile and the Euphrates, relations established more than two thousand years before Christ, permitted the expansion of Phoenecian trade to the coastal countries of the Indian Ocean."[7] The Phoenecians brought the most diversified peoples and civilizations of Antiquity closer together.[8]

For many centuries the Phoenecians maintained a monopoly of trade between the relatively developed countries of the East and the less civilized countries of the West. In the era of the commercial hegemony of the Phoenecians, the islands in the Western Mediterranean and the countries bordering it were economically still very backward. "This does not mean that trade was unknown to the society of the day [Homeric Society], but for the Greeks it consisted essentially of importations.... In payment for these purchases [for the raw or precious materials, the manufactured goods, which the foreign navigators came to offer them], the Greeks seem to have given chiefly cattle."[9] This situation, so highly disadvantageous for the natives, was not long maintained. Phoenecian commerce itself became one of the principal stimulants for the economic development of Greece. The rise of Greece was also favored by Hellenic colonization which expanded greatly between the Ninth and Seventh Century before Christ. The Greek colonists spread in all directions over the Mediterranean. Greek cities multiplied. Thucydides and Plato attribute the Greek emigration to the shortage of land.

The development of Greek colonization was accompanied by a tremendous rise, at least for that era, in Hellenic industry and

---

[7] *Ibid.*, vol. II, p. 18.

[8] "By their indefatigable commercial enthusiasm and their entrepreneur spirit, the Phoenecians acquired a name as a commercial people far exceeding that of any other people of Antiquity. It was only later, during the Middle Ages, that this name, with all the invidious connotations attached to it, passed to their neighbors and commercial heirs, the Jews of the Diaspora." *Ibid.*, vol II, p. 26.

[9] Toutain, *op. cit.*, pp. 19-20.

commerce. This economic development of Greece inevitably brought about the commercial decline of Phoenecia. "In the past, the Phoenecians had landed their goods at the Greek anchorages and had exchanged them against native products —usually, it seems, cattle. Henceforward, the Greek mariners[10] would themselves go to Egypt, to Syria, to Asia Minor, and among the peoples of Europe, the civilized Etruscans and the barbaric Scythians, Gauls, Ligurians and Iberians, taking with them manfactured goods and works of art, tissues, weapons, jewelry and painted vases, which had a great reputation and were eagerly bought by all the barbarians."[11] The period extending from the Sixth to the Fourth Century appears to have been the era of the economic apogee of Greece. "The characteristic of this new period was that the professions had become more numerous, organized and specialized. The division of labor had been greatly developed."[12] At the time of the Peloponnesian War, Hipponikos employed 600 slaves and Nikias 1,000 in the mines.

This important economic development of Greece has stimulated most bourgeois scholars to speak about a "Greek capitalism." They go so far as to compare Hellenic industry and trade with the vast economic movement of the modern industrial era.

In reality, agriculture continued to be the economic foundation of Greece and its colonies. "The Greek colony was not a trading colony: it was practically invariably military and agri-

---

[10] These "Greek mariners" appear to have been mainly "metics," foreigners who had established themselves in Greece. The commercial role of the Phoenecians had been tied up with the development of Egyptian and Assyrian civilizations; the rise of Hellenic civilization brought as a consequence the commercial prosperity of the metics.

[11] Toutain, *op. cit.*, p. 31.

[12] *Ibid.*, p. 53.

cultural."[13] Thus, Strabo relates apropos of Cumes, a Greek colony in Italy, that it was not until three hundred years after settling there that the inhabitants noticed that their city was located near the sea. The essentially agricultural character of the economic life of the Hellenic world is incontestable. Nor can there be any question of an industry comparable to modern industry. "The methods of production and of organization remained on the artisan level."[14] Only the mines seem to have presented, at least insofar as labor power is concerned, a picture similar to that which we see at the present time.

The fact that despite their great expansion, industry and commerce remained for the most part in the hands of metics, of foreigners, proves best their relatively subordinate role in Greek economy. "In the immense trade of which Athens is the center, as well as in its industry, the metics play a preponderant role."[15] At Delos, the great commercial center, the inscriptions show that almost all the traders were foreigners.[16]

The Greek citizen despised trade and industry; he was primarily the landed propietor. Aristotle, like Plato, was opposed to granting citizenship to merchants.[17]

---

[13] Johannes Hasebroek, *Staat und Handel im Alten Griechenland*, Tübingen, 1928, p. 112.

[14] Hasebroek, *op. cit.*, p. 78. The production of use values remains the foundation of the economy. All that can be conceded is that production for exchange took on in Greece the maximum dimensions possible for the ancient mode of production.

[15] Pierre Roussel, *La Grèce et l'Orient*, Paris, 1928, p. 301. See also Michel Clerc. *Les Métèques Athéniens*, Paris, 1893, p. 397: "Maritime commerce was in effect largely in the hands of metics;" and Henri Francotte, *L'Industrie dans la Grèce Ancienne*, Brussels, 1900-1901, vol. I, p. 192: "This commerce [at Athens] appears to have been mainly in the hands of foreigners."

[16] Hasebroek, *op. cit.*, p. 27. In the period of its prosperity, Athens contained 400,000 slaves, 20,000 citizens and 30,000 metics.

[17] "It is no more permissible to speak of the commercialization of the world than of its industrialization. The agrarian character

It is therefore necessary to guard against exaggerating the importance of the industrial and commercial development of Greece. In fact, Greek expansion was primarily agricultural and military. It did, however, go hand in hand with an industrial and commercial development of considerable importance for its time.[18]

The Greeks never became a commercial people like the Phoenecians and the Jews; but we do find a very important commercial and industrial development in the Greek colonies and later in the Hellenic kingdoms. And, of course, the Greek states, while not really mercantile, supported commerce and industry with all their might as financial sources of the utmost importance.

It is not solely to the economic development of Greece and its colonies that we must attribute the decline of Phoenecian commerce; there was still another important cause: the growing antagonism between Persia and Greece. Paralleling the extension of Hellenic civilization was the victorious march of the Persians across Asia. The Persian Empire reached its apogee in the Fifth Century B. C. It extended over a part of Asia and over Egypt.

The parallel development of Greek and Persian civilization necessarily dealt a mortal blow to Phoenecian commerce. Trade between Asia and Europe was certainly rendered very difficult by the division of the Mediterranean world between two mutually hostile societies. The Persian and Greek worlds each created its own commercial trade.

---

of economy is predominant even in the Fourth Century B. C." Hasebroek, *op. cit.*, p. 101.

[18] "Any analogy between the ports of ancient Greece and modern Genoa or Marseilles will provoke only scepticism or a smile. Nevertheless, the spectacle afforded by all this exchange, shipping, and coming and going of goods was then a new thing in the Mediterranean. It was quite different in intensity and in nature from that previously afforded by Phoenecian trade, which had been mere sea-peddling rather than real business." Toutain, *op. cit.*, p. 65.

With the decline of Phoenecia and the development of Asiatic trade after the period of the Persian conquests, we can assume that Palestine, previously completely supplanted by Phoenecia again began to play an important commercial role. The passageway between Egypt and Babylonia recovered all its value. Whereas Phoenecian trade lost more and more of its ancient importance up to the point where, in the time of Lucian, salted products were the main cargo, the Jews played a leading role in the Persian Empire.[19]

Certain historians attribute an important role to the Babylonian exile in the transformation of the Jews into a commercial people. In Babylonia, "the Jews became transformed into a commercial people, such as we know them in the economic history of the world. They found highly developed economic relations among the Babylonians. Recently uncovered cuneiform texts show that the exiled Jews participated actively in commercial life. They were involved in credit business, highly developed among the Babylonians; they were also big traders."[20]

But the dispersion of the Jews is certainly prior to the Babylonian exile. "There are serious reasons for conceding the existence of a pre-exile Diaspora."[21] The scope of the Jewish exile under Nebuchadnezzar is very greatly exaggerated. Only a part of the ruling classes was hit by the measures of the Babylonian king. The majority of the Jews established in Palestine continued to live there. Consequently, if during the Persian epoch the Jews were to be found spread over all parts of that enormous Empire (and the Book of Esther is very eloquent on this subject), it would be childish to view this fact as a consequence of the Babylonian

---

[19] C. Autran, *Les Phéniciens*, Paris, 1920, p. 51.

[20] Lujo Brentano, *Das Wirtschaftsleben der Antiken Welt*, Jena, 1929, p. 80.

[21] Antonin Causse, *Les Dispersés d'Isräel*, Paris, 1929, p. 7.

exile, an exile which lasted altogether some 50 years. It is equally puerile to believe that the Jewish people returned to Palestine in the period of Ezra and Nehemiah. Their work was primarily of a religious character. It was a matter of rebuilding the temple and of reconstructing a religious metropolis for dispersed Judaism. "Most historians have considerably exaggerated the role of Palestinian Judaism in the Persian epoch. They reason as if Jerusalem, once restored, all the history of Israel became concentrated around the holy mountain; as if all the people had really returned from exile and had lived on a land measuring some few hundred square kilometers in Tekoa, Mitspa and Jericho. In reality, in this epoch, the Jews of Judea represented only a part, and the smallest, of Judaism. And undoubtedly it was the least vital part."[22]

The Edict of Cyrus is addressed to the Jews of the Diaspora in the following words: "And whosoever is left, in any place where he sojourneth, let the men of his place help [those who are going to Palestine] with silver, and with gold, and with goods, and with beasts, besides the freewill-offering for the house of God which is in Jerusalem" (Book of Ezra I. 4). "And all they that were round about them," continues the Book of Ezra (I. 6), "strengthened their hands [the 42,000 Jews who were returning to Palestine] with vessels of silver, with gold, with goods, and with beasts." It is obvious that we are not dealing here with a mass return of the Jews to Palestine but primarily with the reconstruction of the temple.

During the Persian epoch the principal colonies of the Diaspora were situated in Mesopotamia, in Chaldea and in Egypt. The documents which have been found at Elephantine in Egypt, dating from the Fifth Century before Christ, throw an interesting

---

[22] *Ibid.*, pp. 54-55.

light on the condition of the Jewish colonies of the Diaspora in this epoch.

According to the archives belonging to a Jewish family, it appears that the "Jews engaged in trade, bought and sold houses and land, loaned money, acted as depositaries, and were well versed in matters of law." It is very interesting to note that even the songs and chronicles are in Aramaic, which shows that as early as the Fifth Century B. C. Hebrew was no longer a customary language for the Jews.[23] Aramaic was the great Asiatic language of the period, the commercial language.

The religion of the Jews of Elephantine was not as developed as the official religion codified during the Ezra-Nehemiah era. In a petition to the Persian governor, they asked for authorization to rebuild their temple. But the reform of Ezra-Nehemiah was aimed precisely at concentrating all the Jews of the Diaspora around the single temple of Jerusalem. And it was in fact to Jerusalem that the gifts of the Jews dispersed throughout the world continued to flow up to the year 70.

It was this wealth of the temple of Jerusalem that was probably the principal reason for the offensive of Antiochus against the Jews. "Simon advised him that the public treasury at Jerusalem was full of large sums and that there were enormous public riches." (Second Book of the Maccabees, III, 6). Later, on the little island of Cos, Mithridates confiscated 800 talents that were destined for the temple of Jerusalem. In the Roman era, Cicero complained in his speeches of the immense sums which were flowing into Jerusalem.

The Hellenistic period constitutes the epoch of the economic apogee of Antiquity. The conquests of Alexander destroyed the barriers between the Hellenic world and Asia and Egypt.

---

[23] *Jüdisches Lexicon*, Berlin, 1927-1930, vol. II. Article on Elephantine, pp. 345-346.

Cities sprang up like mushrooms in all parts of the Hellenic Empire. The "greatest founders of cities, not alone of this epoch but even in all history, were Seleucos I and his son Antiochus I."[24] The Hellenistic kings created new urban centers destined to supplant the old Phoenecian and Persian cities. "On the coast of Syria, the port of Antioch causes the old cities of Tyre and Sidon to be forgotten."[25] Seleucos creates Seleucia on the banks of the Tigris in order to rob Babylonia of its central role in world commerce.[26] This goal was completely attained.

Whereas Babylonia fell into decline, Hellenic Seleucia probably became the greatest city of this epoch. According to Pliny, it had 600,000 inhabitants. Alongside of Seleucia, Alexandria and Antioch became the centers of the Hellenistic world. All of these cities experienced an unchallenged prosperity during the Hellenistic period.

The situation of the Jews appears to have been further strengthened after the conquests of Alexander. "It appears that they were able to secure special privileges equally well, both from the Seleucidae and from the Lagidae. At Alexandria, to which they had been attracted by Ptolemy I and where they abounded, they formed a separate community which governed itself and was not subject to the jurisdiction of the Greek courts."[27] "The Jews enjoyed a certain autonomy and a privileged position in Antioch, the capital of Syria. This was also true at Cyrene."[28] The privileged position and the specific economic roles of the Jews had already become the source of serious conflicts with the

---

[24] Eduard Meyer, *Blüte und Niedergang des Hellenismus in Asien*, Berlin, 1925, p. 20.
[25] Roussel, *op. cit.*, p. 486.
[26] Meyer, *op. cit.*, p. 22.
[27] Roussel, *op. cit.*, pp. 480-481.
[28] Brentano, *Das Wirtschaftsleben der Antiken. Welt, op. cit.*, p. 78.

population of the cities which they inhabited. Struggles broke out continuously in Alexandria, Seleucia, Cyrene and Cyprus, as well as in the Palestinian cities.[29] These conflicts had nothing in common with present-day national antagonisms. On the contrary, the Hellenistic empires witnessed a tremendous assimilation of their component peoples. The name Greek ceased after a while to be applied to the members of a particular nation but was assigned to the ruling and cultured sections of the population. Alexander ordered everybody, an ancient writer tells us, to consider the world as his fatherland, the well-to-do as his kin and evil-doers as foreigners.

The increased importance of Judaism in the commercial life of the Hellenistic world must also be attributed to the displacement of economic life toward the East. The prosperity of Alexandria, Antioch and Seleucia offers a striking contrast to the poverty and decay into which Greece has fallen in the same period. Polybius repeatedly stresses the decline of Greek cities. Somewhat later, in the Second Century, "visitors could hardly believe that this city, where water was scarce, the streets badly laid out, the houses uncomfortable, was the famous Athens."[30] Athens was shorn of its role as center of the civilized world. What contributed to the ruin of Greece, together with her economic decline, was the ceaseless class struggles,[31] which by virtue of the backward mode of production, could bring about no important changes.

---

[29] Meyer, *op. cit.*, p. 61.

[30] André Piganiol, *La Conquête Romaine*, Paris, 1927, p. 205.

[31] These class struggles were limited strictly to the free population of the Greek cities. "Some degree of equality in the possession of property appeared necessary to the maintenance of this political democracy. Therein lies the source of the bloody wars between the rich and the poor, the end-product of Hellenic demagogy. But the slaves, serfs, and metics took no part in these struggles..." Claude Jannet, *Les Grandes Epoques de l'Histoire Economique*, Paris, 1896, p. 8.

The victory of the plebeian was ephemeral, the redistribution of wealth could only wind up in new social inequalities, breeding centers of new social conflicts. Thus the triumph of Greece, after the conquests of Alexander, proved illusory. The displacement of the economic center of the world toward the East, which followed the conquests, brought about the rapid decline of Greece.[32] The propertied and aristocratic classes, powerless before the plebeian revolts, had to seek support from Rome[33] but the latter could only answer by dealing the final blow to Greece as well as to Hellenism. The Romans threw themselves on the Hellenistic world as on a convenient prey to be pillaged and conquered. "Between 211 and 208, according to the assuredly very incomplete information which has come down to us, five 'old cities of the Hellenes'... were sacked."[34] Corinth, the rich commercial city, was destroyed. "I was there," recounts Polybius. "I saw pictures trampled under foot, and soldiers sitting on them while throwing dice." Rome also dealt very harsh blows to Hellenism in Asia. [35] Under the combined blows of the Romans and the Parthians, the magnificent structure of Greece was destroyed.

B. ROMAN IMPERIALISM AND ITS DECLINE

In contrast to modern imperialism which is based essentially on the development of the productive forces, ancient imperialism

[32] "The Greek peninsula [in the Hellenistic period] thus increasingly lost its leading position and the economic center of the world was displaced toward the East." K. J. Beloch, *Griechische Geschichte*, Berlin, 1914-1927, vol. I, pp. 279-280.

[33] See N. D. Fustel de Coulanges, *The Ancient City*, Boston, 1874, p. 498.

[34] Maurice Holleaux, *Rome, la Grèce et les Monarchies Hellénistiques*, Paris, 1921, p. 231.

[35] Piganiol, *op. cit.*, p. 232.

was founded on the looting of conquered countries. For ancient imperialism it was not a question of opening new roads for its products and its capital; its objective was exclusively the despoiling of conquered countries. The backward state of production in Antiquity could sustain the possessing classes of the conquering countries in luxury only by means of the more or less rapid ruination of the conquered peoples. Exhaustion of the conquered countries, growing difficulties in making new conquests, the gradual softening of the conquerors, all these sooner or later brought about the decline of ancient imperialisms.

Rome provides the classic example of ancient imperialism. There have been great exaggerations concerning the commercial and industrial development of Rome. Its trade always showed a deficit.[36] Rome drew exports from the provinces without giving anything back in return.[37] The Roman ruling classes heartily despised every kind of trade. The Claudian law forbade Senators, their sons and the entire aristocracy of Rome to own ships drawing more than 300 amphoras, which corresponds to less than 225 bushels of grain or vegetables. This was equivalent to forbidding them to engage in trade. Caesar renewed this ban. Roman policy was never determined by its so-called commercial interests. The best proof of this is that Rome, after the defeat of Hannibal, still allowed the Carthaginians to bar entry into their sea.[38] "In general, it must be said that the Roman economic problems were unusually simple. The gradual conquest of Italy and the

---

[36] See Heinrich Cunow, *Allgemeine Wirtschaftsgeschichte*, vol. II, Berlin, 1926-1931, p. 61.

[37] Henri Pirenne, *A History of Europe*, *op. cit.*, p. 40. "Products flowed to the center without there being any compensating current backward." Gustave Legaret, *Histoire du Développement du Commerce*, Paris, 1927, p. 13.

[38] Tenney Frank, *An Economic History of Rome to the End of the Republic*, Baltimore, 1920, p. 116.

provinces more than occupied the surplusage of capital and population so that there was no crying need for industry and commerce," states Tenney Frank.[39] The traders at Rome were as a rule foreigners and it is that moreover which explains the continuous growth in the Jewish colony at Rome from Caesar's epoch on. Roman business men were not traders but usurers who looted the provinces.[40] The development of trade in the Roman Empire must above all be ascribed to the growing luxury requirements of the ruling classes of Rome. Strabo explains the development of the great market of Delos in this fashion: "Hence arose a proverbial saying 'Merchant come into port, discharge your freight — everything is sold.' The Romans, having acquired wealth after the destruction of Carthage and Corinth, employed great numbers of domestic slaves."[41]

The same was true of industry. Roman industry depended primarily on the luxury requirements of the aristocracy. "Tenney Frank, after observing that no appreciable progress was made in the domain of industry in the Fourth Century B. C., adds: 'In the two succeeding centuries we do not find evidence of any marked change in the nature of production at Rome. Doubtless the amount of ordinary ware produced at home increased with the growth of the city... but of goods worthy of export we do not hear. The only difference now is that work previously performed by free labor began in the Second Century to fall into the hands of slaves.' "[42]

Even those authors who consider that Italy had been a producer country in the republican epoch admit that it ceased to be

[39] *Ibid.*, p. 126.

[40] *Ibid.*, pp. 283ff.

[41] Strabo, *Geography*, London, 1854-1857, vol. III, p. 51.

[42] Toutain, *op. cit.*, pp. 234-235. Toutain does not subscribe to this opinion.

one in the imperial period. "Italy becomes less and less a producer country... Several industries which were prosperous at the end of the republican period are now in decline... Thus trade between Italy and the Orient now takes place only in one direction, and it also becomes lodged more and more in the hands of Asiatics, of Alexandrines and Syrians."[43]

Thus Italy now lived only on the exploitation of the provinces. Small property, the foundation of Roman strength, was progressively supplanted by vast domains serving the luxury needs of the Roman aristocrats and on which slave labor predominated.[44] Pliny's conclusion is known to all: "Latifundia perdidere Italiam."

The slave became more and more an item of luxury rather than a factor in production.[45] Horace, in one of his Satires, states that a minimum of ten slaves was the indispensable prerequisite of a gentleman. Thousands of slaves did in fact work in the vast *latifundia*. "In the domains of Tusculum and Tibur, on the shores of Terracina and Baiae —where the old Latin and Italian farmers had sown and reaped— there now rose in barren splendor the villas of the Roman nobles, some of which covered the space of a moderate-sized town with their appurtenances of garden-grounds and aqueducts, fresh and salt water ponds for the preservation and breeding of river and marine fishes, nurseries of snails and slugs, game-preserves for keeping hares, rabbits, stags, roes and

---

[43] Jean Hatzfeld, *Les Trafiquants Italiens dans l'Orient Hellénistique*, Paris, 1919, pp. 190-191.

[44] "The subject of the disappearance of the peasants was a common topic of discussion among the leading men of the Augustan period." M. Rostovtzev, *The Social and Economic History of the Roman Empire*, Oxford, 1926, p. 65.

[45] Karl Kautsky, *Foundations of Christianity*, New York, 1925, p. 66.

wild boars, and aviaries in which even cranes and peacocks were kept."[46]

At the same time that free labor was being eliminated by slave labor, Italy became an immense center of squandering the wealth drained from the entire empire. Crushing taxes ruined the provinces; "...the frequent and costly naval armaments and coast defenses in order to check piracy; the task of supplying works of art, wild beasts, or other demands of the insane Roman luxury in circus, theater and the chase... were just as frequent as they were oppressive and incalculable. A single instance may show how far things were carried. During the three years administration of Sicily by Gaius Verres, the number of farmers in Leontini fell from 84 to 32, in Motya from 187 to 86; in Herbita from 252 to 120; in Agyrium from 250 to 80; so that in four of the most fertile districts of Sicily, 59 per cent of the landholders preferred to let their fields lie fallow rather than to cultivate them under this *regime*... In the client states the forms of taxation were somewhat different, but the burdens themselves were if possible still worse, since in addition to the exactions of the Romans there came those of the native courts."[47]

Roman capitalism, to the extent that the term capitalism is applicable here, was essentially speculative and bore no relationship whatever to the development of the productive forces.[48]

Roman trade and banking resembled organized brigandage. "But still worse if possible and still less subject to any control, was the havoc committed by the Italian men of business among the unhappy provincials. The most lucrative portions of the landed property and the whole commercial and monetary business in the

---

[46] Mommsen, *The History of Rome, op. cit.*, vol. IV, p. 478.

[47] *Ibid.*, vol. IV, p. 501.

[48] Giuseppe Salvioli, *Der Kapitalismus im Altertum*, Stuttgart, 1922, p. 206.

provinces were concentrated in their hands... Usury flourished as it had never flourished before... 'All the communities' it is said in a treatise published in 684/70, 'are ruined'; the same truth is specially attested as regards Spain and Narbonese Gaul, the very provinces which, comparatively speaking, were still in the most tolerable economic position. In Asia Minor, even towns like Samos and Halicarnassus stood almost empty; legal slavery seemed here a haven of rest compared with the torments to which the free provincials succumbed and even the patient Asiatic had become, according to the descriptions of Roman statesmen themselves, weary of life... Even the statesmen of Rome herself publicly and frankly conceded that the Roman name was unutterably odious through all Greece and Asia."[49]

Clearly this system of parasitism and brigandage could not last indefinitely. The source of wealth from which Rome drew dried up. Long before the fall of Rome we witness a steady slowing up of trade. The arena for pillage contracted in the measure that Rome emptied the conquered countries of their substance.

The fact that the production of grain, especially wheat, diminished, while the vine and olive tree conquered vast domains in the east and west, constituted an ominous token of the state of things. Luxury products displaced products which are indispensable for production and for reproduction of the labor force. "The spread of the culture of vines and olive trees... not only meant economic ruin for Italy but might also result in a corn famine throughout the Empire."[50] Trajan vainly tried to ward off this danger by compelling Senators to buy land in Italy. His successors achieved as little. Luxury killed off production. "Soon superb buildings will leave no more land for the plough of the toiler," Horace cried out.

---

[49] Mommsen, *The History of Rome, op. cit.*, vol. IV, pp. 502-504.

[50] Rostovtzev, *op. cit.*, p. 188.

By the Third Century, the decline in trade was complete. Relations with distant countries were cut off. "Practically no Roman coins of the Third Century have been found in India," which proves a breakdown of exchange between Rome and India.[51] The decline of Egyptian agriculture became so pronounced in the Third Century that it was necessary to forego a part of the deliveries of grain from this formerly wealthy province. These Egyptian deliveries had to be replaced by grain supplies from the province of Africa (the Algeria and Tunisia of today).[52]

Commodius found it necessary to establish a flotilla for transporting the grain grown in the province of Africa. We have seen that trade in the Roman Empire was primarily based on supplying the wealthy classes of Rome. Is there any wonder then that exhaustion of the provinces was followed by a decline in trade? More and more, Roman emperors were compelled to resort to requisitions in kind, which only resulted, however, in aggravating the lot of the suffering provinces. "The system of requisitions was rampant: corn, hides, wood for spears, and draught animals had to be delivered, and payment for them was irregular and indeed problematic."[53]

A purely natural economy, producing exclusively use values, slowly displaced the exchange of products. "Whereas the Roman peace had formerly brought about a regular exchange of goods and the equalizing of living conditions between the different regions of the Empire, in the anarchy of the Third Century, each country was often condemned to live upon itself, painfully and poorly."[54]

---

[51] *Ibid.*, p. 421.

[52] Wilhelm Schubart, *Aegypten von Alexander dem Grossen bis auf Mohammed*, Berlin, 1922, p. 67.

[53] Rostovtzev, *op. cit.*, p. 374.

[54] Eugène Albertini, *L'Empire Romain*, Paris, 1929. p. 306.

An attempt has been made to explain the gradual displacement of slavery by the *coloni* system either as a result of the lack of energy on the part of landed proprietors or by a shortage of slaves caused by the termination of foreign wars. The gradual ruin of the colonies, the halt in the flow of their products, was probably the main reason. The great proprietors, more and more reduced to living on the products of their own lands, were interested in replacing slave labor, relatively low in productivity, by the *coloni* system, which resembles the system of serfdom that flourished in the Middle Ages. "The *colonus* owes his master everything that the serf will have to give his lord."[55]

The power of the landed proprietors, who often possess enormous areas of land, kept growing continuously. In Egypt, in the Fifth Century, the peasants will be completely subject to them. State administration passed entirely into their hands.[56]

It is therefore quite inaccurate to view the natural economy which flourished in the Carolingian epoch as an outgrowth of the fall of the Roman Empire and the destruction of Mediterranean economic unity.[57]

---

[55] Ernest Lavisse, *Histoire Générale du IVe Siècle à Nos Jours*, Paris, 1893, vol. I, p. 16.

[56] Schubart, *op. cit.*, p. 29. Very significant also is the gradual disappearance of the class of knights, the class of Roman "capitalists."

[57] "The demesnial organization, as it appeared from the Ninth Century on, is therefore the result of alien circumstances; nothing can be observed there in the nature of an organic transformation. This is equivalent to saying that it was an abnormal phenomenon." Henri Pirenne, *Les Villes au Moyen Age*, Brussels, 1927, p. 46. "The French Empire was destined to lay the foundations of the Europe of the Middle Ages. But the mission which it fulfilled had as an essential pre-condition the overthrow of the traditional world order; there would have been no summons to this task if historical evolution had not been turned aside from its normal course, if it had not been, so to speak, thrown off its axis by the Moslem invasion. Without Islam, the Frankish Empire undoubtedly could never have existed and Charlemagne would be inconceivable without Mohammed." *Ibid.*, *pp.*

Undoubtedly the barbarian invasions played a very important role in the decline of ancient trade and in the rise of feudal economy. But the economic decline of the Roman Empire began long before the fall of Rome and several centuries before the Moslem invasion.

Another very important indication of the evolution toward a natural economy was the monetary change which had already begun under the reign of Nero.[58] Copper increasingly replaced gold and silver. In the Second Century, there was an almost complete dearth of gold.[59]

The development of a natural economy, of an economy primarily producing use values, was consequently far from being an "abnormal phenomenon" as Pirenne claims. The Roman Empire was ruined economically before it was ruined politically. The political blow to the Roman Empire was rendered possible only by its economic decline. The political anarchy of the Third Century, like the barbarian invasion, can be explained accurately and exclusively by the economic decline of the Roman Empire.

To the extent that the provinces were ruined, an intensive exchange of goods ceased, and a return took place to a natural economy, to that same extent the very existence of the Empire became a matter of indifference to the possessing classes. Each country, each province withdrew into its shell. The Empire, with its immense administrative apparatus and its extremely costly army, became a cancer, a parasitic organism whose unbearable weight pressed down on all classes. Taxes devoured the substance of the peoples. Under Marcus Aurelius, when the soldiers after their

---

27-28. For Pirenne, feudal economy is therefore a result of the destruction of Mediterranean unity, produced primarily by the Mohammedan invasion.

[58] Rostovtzev, *op. cit.*, p. 171.

[59] Salvioli, *op. cit.*, pp. 245ff.

great victories against the Marcomanni, demanded an increase in pay, the Emperor made this significant reply: "Everything you would receive above your usual pay would first have to be drained from the blood of your relations."

The Treasury was exhausted. In order to maintain the administrative apparatus and the army, it was necessary to confiscate individual fortunes. While the lower classes were in ceaseless revolt, the possessing classes were turning away from the Empire which was ruining them. After the economic ruin of the Empire by the aristocracy, the aristocracy was in its turn ruined by the Empire. "Daily people could be seen who only yesterday were still among the wealthiest and today have to take up the beggar's staff," said Herodian. The soldiers grew more and more bestial. It was not greed alone which forced them to despoil the inhabitants; impoverishment of the provinces and the wretched state of transportation, which created difficulties in provisioning the armies, forced the soldiers to use violence in order to find their means of subsistence. Caracalla, in granting Roman citizenship to all Roman inhabitants, sought only to increase the taxable population. Irony of history: The whole world became Roman when Rome was no longer anything!

The exactions of the Roman administration and the excesses of the soldiery incited all the inhabitants of the Empire to hope for its destruction. "The quartering of soldiers was a real disaster: the population of Syria regarded an occupation by the Parthians as a relief in comparison with a prolonged stay of Roman troops."[60]

"The Roman government appeared every day... more odious and oppressive to its subjects... The severe inquisition, which confiscated their goods and tortured their persons, compelled the subjects of Valentinian to prefer the more simple tyranny of the

[60] Rostovtzev, *op. cit.*, p. 375.

Barbarians... They abjured and abhorred the name of Roman citizen, which had formerly excited the ambitions of mankind."[61] The Christian writer Salvian stated in *De Gubernatione Dei:* "Hence all the Romans in that region [Gaul and Spain] have but one desire, that they may never have to return to the Roman jurisdiction. Yet we are surprised that the Goths are not conquered by our resistance, when the Romans would rather live among them than at home... I could find occasion to wonder why all the poor and needy taxpayers do not follow their example, except for one factor that hinders them, namely, that they cannot transfer their poor possessions and homes and their households."[62]

Far from being an "abnormal" phenomenon, the barbarian invasion was the normal consequence of the economic and political decline of the Empire. Even without the invasions, the Empire would probably have been dismembered. "In Asia Minor, as well as in Syria, one of the leading features of life was the gradual reversion to the feudal system... The so-called revolt of the Isaurians in Asia Minor is another symptom of the same tendency towards the formation of almost independent states within the Empire."[63] Similarly, the attempt to create an independent Gallo-Roman Empire, the attempts at secession, prove how weak had become the bond of Empire. The barbarians only gave the *coup de grace* to the shaking edifice of the Roman state.

The fundamental cause for the decline of the Roman Empire must be sought in the contradiction between the growing luxuriousness of the possessing classes, between the incessant growth of surplus value, and the static character of the mode of production. During the entire Roman epoch, very little progress was

---

[61] Edward Gibbon. *The History of the Decline and Fall of the Roman Empire,* Heritage Press, New York, 1946, vol. II, p. 1103.

[62] Salvian, *On the Government of God,* New York, 1930, p. 146.

[63] Rostovtzev, *op. cit.*, p. 425.

registered in the sphere of production. The tools of the cultivator retained their primitive form. "Plough, spade, hoe, mattock, pick, fork, scythe, sickle and pruning knife, were, as the surviving specimens show, just as they had been handed down from generation to generation."[64] The growing luxury of the Roman aristocracy and the expenses of imperial administration were covered by a furious exploitation of the provinces, which had as its consequence economic ruin, depopulation, exhaustion of the soil.[65] Unlike the capitalist world, which must perish from the (relative) superabundance of means of production, the Roman world perished from their scarcity.

The reforms of Diocletian and of Constantine constituted an attempt to set the Roman Empire on the foundations of a natural economy. "The State had now to be based on the country and the peasants."[66] The peasant was now chained to his bit of land. Each landed proprietor became responsible for his domain and for the number of *coloni* who were established on it; the new tax was assessed on this basis. "The reform of taxation by Diocletian and the edicts of later emperors made the *colonus* a serf, bound to his domicile and to his master..."[67] The same was true of the other layers of the population; small proprietors, artisans, merchants, all were chained to their living place and to their profession. The epoch of Constantine is the epoch of the unlimited rule of the great landed proprietors, undisputed masters of vast princely domains. The aristocracy more and more abandons the cities which fall into decay and flees to sumptuous country villas where it lives surrounded by its clients and its serfs.

---

[64] Toutain, *op. cit.*, p. 282.

[65] Certain authors see depopulation and exhaustion of the soil as the essential causes for the decline of the Empire.

[66] Rostovtzev, *op. cit.*, p. 453.

[67] *Ibid.*, p. 472.

The reforms of Diocletian and Constantine constituted attempts to adapt the Empire to a natural economy. But we have seen that the Empire had, on this basis, no reason for existence. Its various parts could be held together longer only by tyranny. Thus, if from the economic and social point of view, Constantine ushers in a new historical era, symbolized by the adoption of Christianity, from the political point of view, he opens the last act in the history of the Roman Empire.

C. JUDAISM AND CHRISTIANITY

The situation which the Jews had acquired for themselves in the Hellenistic epoch appears to have undergone no fundamental transformation after the Roman conquest. The privileges conferred upon the Jews by Hellenistic laws were confirmed by the Roman emperors. "The Jews enjoyed a privileged position in the Roman Empire."[68] The fact that nearly a million Jews lived in Alexandria alone is sufficient evidence of their primarily commercial role in the Dispersion, which embraced three and a half million Jews several centuries before the seizure of Jerusalem, whereas hardly a million continued to live in Palestine. "Alexandria in Egypt, under the Roman Emperors, was what Tyre had been in the epoch of Phoenecian commercial glory... Under the reign of the Ptolemies, a direct trade between Egypt and India had been established. From Thebes, caravans went to Merowe in Upper Nubia, whose markets were also frequented by caravans from the interior of Africa... A Roman fleet went to the mouth of the Nile to receive the precious objects and distribute them in the

---

[68] Jacques Zeiller, *L'Empire Romain et l'Eglise*, Paris, 1928, p. 23.

Empire."[69] Two out of the five sections of Alexandria were inhabited by Jews.[70] The role of the Jews at Alexandria was so important that a Jew, Tiberius Julius Alexander, was appointed Roman governor of this city.

From the cultural standpoint, these Alexandrine Jews were completely assimilated and no longer spoke anything but Greek. It was on their account that the Hebrew religious books had to be translated into that language. Communities similar to that of Alexandria were located in all the commercial centers of the Empire. The Jews spread over Italy, Gaul and Spain. Jerusalem continued to be the religious center of Diaspora Judaism. "The successors of David and Solomon were of hardly more significance for the Jews of that age than Jerusalem for those of the present day; the nation found doubtless for its religious and intellectual unity a visible rallying-point in the petty kingdom of Jersualem, but the nation itself consisted not merely of the subjects of the Hasmonaeans, but of the innumerable bodies of Jews scattered through the whole Parthian and the whole Roman Empire. Within the cities of Alexandria especially and of Cyrene, the Jews formed special communities administratively and even locally distinct, not unlike the 'Jews' quarters' of our towns, but with a freer position and superintended by a 'master of the people' as superior judge and administrator... Even at this time the predominant business of the Jews was trade."[71]

In the Sibylline books of the Maccabean period, it is stated that "all the seas are overflowing with Jews." "According to Strabo it was not easy to discover a place in the entire world where Jews were not to be found and which was not ruled (financially) by them... Students of national economy have no doubt

---

[69] G. B. Depping, *Histoire du Commerce entre le Levant et l'Europe*, Paris, 1830, vol. I, pp. 3-6.

[70] Schubart, *op. cit.*, p. 8.

[71] Mommsen, *The History of Rome*, *op. cit.*, vol. IV, p. 508.

that the majority of these [Jews in Antiquity] depended on commerce and industry for their livelihood."[72]

Jerusalem was a great and wealthy city of 200,000 inhabitants. Its importance lay above all in the temple of Jerusalem. The inhabitants of the city and of its suburbs lived primarily from the mass of pilgrims who flocked to the holy city. "The Jews of Palestine regarded their God as the means by which they lived."[73] It was not alone the priests who lived from the service of Jehovah but also innumerable grocers, money-changers and artisans. Even the laborers and fishermen of Galilee certainly found markets for their products in Jerusalem. It would be erroneous to think of Palestine as entirely inhabited by Jews. In the north, there were several Greek cities; almost all the rest was "inhabited generally, as each place in particular, by mixed tribes of Egyptians, Arabians, and Phoenecians..." Strabo tells us.[74]

Jewish proselytism took on increasingly imposing proportions toward the beginning of the Christian era. "To be members of so widely ramified and prosperous a commercial organization was a prospect that must have been enticing to not a few."[75] As early as 139 B. C., the Jews were banished from Rome for recruiting proselytes. At Antioch, the larger part of the Jewish community consisted of converts.

It was solely the economic and social position of the Jews in the Diaspora which, even before the fall of Jerusalem, made possible their religious and national cohesion. But while it is ob-

---

[72] W. Roscher, "The Status of the Jew in the Middle Ages," *Historia Judaica*, April, 1944, p. 17.

[The words "and which was not ruled (financially) by them" are not found in the English work cited. The original French edition cited p. 328 of Roscher's *Die Juden im Mittelalter* for this passage. Whether they appear there, or represent an error by Leon, we cannot say, having been unable to inspect a copy of the German work. — Ed.]

[73] Kautsky, *Foundations of Christianity*, *op. cit.*, p. 272.

[74] Strabo, *op. cit.*, vol. III, p. 177.

[75] Kautsky, *Foundations of Christianity*, *op. cit.*, p. 260.

vious that the majority of Jews played a commercial role in the Roman Empire, we must not think that all the Jews were rich traders or entrepreneurs. On the contrary, the majority was certainly made up of small people, some of them making their living directly or indirectly from trade: peddlers, stevedores, petty artisans, etc. It is this mass of small people which was first hit by the decline of the Roman Empire and suffered most from Roman extortion. Concentrated in great masses in the cities, they were capable of greater resistance than peasant peoples dispersed in the country. They were also more conscious of their interests. Consequently, the Jewish mass in the great cities will prove to be a continuous hotbed of unrest and uprisings, directed simultaneously against Rome and against the rich.

It has become traditional to portray the Jewish insurrection in 70 as a great "national uprising." However, while this insurreçtion was directed against the unbearable exactions of the Roman procurators, it was just as resolutely hostile to the native wealthy classes. All the aristocrats took a stand against the revolt. King Agrippa and other members of the wealthy classes strove mightily to put it down. The Zealots first had to massacre the "men of property" before they could get at the Romans. King Agrippa and Berenice, after the failure of their efforts at "conciliation" were to be found not alongside the insurgents but side by side with the Romans. The members of the ruling classes who, like Flavius Josephus, had assumed the guise of wishing to aid the revolutionists, rushed to betray them shamefully. On the other hand, the revolt in Judea was not the only one of its kind. Several revolts broke out in the Greek cities during the reign of Vespasian. An intense social agitation was conducted by the "cynic philosophers" whom Vespasian had to drive out of the cities. The Alexandrines also showed their hostile feelings to Vespasian. "The example of Bithynia and the disturbances in Alexandria under Trajan show that the social antagonism of which we have spoken never subsided in Asia Minor or in Egypt."[76]

But social unrest was not confined to the urban masses, even though they were the most affected by the growing decay in economic life. The peasant masses also began to move. The condition of the peasants was already very bad in the First and Second Centuries. "The situation of the latter grew steadily worse. The conditions under which the masses of the Egyptian population lived were far from normal. Taxation was oppressive, the mode of collection was brutal and unfair..."[77]

Under Marcus Aurelius, the discontent spread to all the provinces. Spain refused to supply soldiers; Gaul was full of deserters. The revolts spread in Spain, in Gaul, in Africa. In a petition to Emperor Commodius, the small African farmers declared: "We shall fly to a place where we will be able to live like free men." During the reign of Septimus Severus, banditry took on unheard of proportions. Bands of homeless ravaged various parts of the Empire. In a petition, a copy of which has been found recently, the small farmers of Lydia in Asia Minor addressed Septimus Severus in these terms: "When the tax collectors of the Emperor appear in the villages, they bring nothing good; they torment the inhabitants with unbearable levies and with fines...." Other petitions speak of the brutality and arbitrariness of these same tax officials.

The poverty of the urban and rural masses offered a fertile soil for the propagation of Christianity. Rostovtzev correctly sees a link between the Jewish revolts and the popular revolts in Egypt

---

[76] Rostovtzev, *op. cit.*, p. 121. After the death of Trajan, "the Jews in Mesopotamia, Palestina, Egypt, and Cyrenaica started, dangerous and bloody revolts, the last of which almost depopulated Cyrenaica." *Ibid.*, p. 315.

[77] *Ibid.*, p. 300.

and in Cyrenaica under the reigns of Trajan and of Hadrian.[78] It was among the poor layers of the great cities of the Diaspora that Christianity spread. "The first communistic congregation of the Messiah was formed in Jerusalem... But congregations soon arose in other cities having a Jewish proletariat."[79] "The oldest... stations of Phoenecian land and sea commerce... were also the most ancient seats of Christianity..."[80] Just as the Jewish insurrections were followed by insurrections of the non-Jewish popular masses, so did the Jewish communist religion rapidly find its extension among these pagan masses.

The primitive Christian community was not born on the terrain of orthodox Judaism; it was tightly bound up with heretical sects.[81] It was under the influence of the Essenes, a Jewish communist sect "which," according to Philo, "possessed neither property, houses, slaves, lands, nor flocks." They tilled the soil and were forbidden to engage in trade.

Christianity, in its beginnings, must be considerd as a reaction of the laboring masses of the Jewish people against the domination of the wealthy commercial classes. Jesus, driving the merchants out of the Temple, expresses the hatred of the Jewish popular masses against their oppressors, their hostility to the leading role of the wealthy business people. At the start, the Christians formed only small communities of no great importance. But in the Second Century, era of great poverty in the Roman Empire, they succeded in becoming an extremely powerful party. "In the Third Century, the Christian church acquired enormous strength."[82] "In the Third

---

[78] *Ibid.*, p. 301.

[79] Kautsky, *Foundations of Christianity*, *op. cit.*, p. 382.

[80] Movers, *op. cit.*, vol. II, p. 1.

[81] See Gustav Hölscher, *Urgemeinde und Spätjudentum*, Oslo, 1928, p. 26.

[82] Rostovtzev, *op. cit.*, p. 456.

Century evidence of Christianity greatly increased in Alexandria."[83]

The popular, anti-plutocratic character of primitive Christianity is incontestable. "Blessed *are* ye poor: for yours is the kingdom of God. Blessed are ye that hunger now; for ye shall be filled.... But woe unto you that are rich!.... Woe unto you, ye that are full now! for ye shall hunger," states the Gospel according to Luke (6.20, 6.21, 6.24, 6.25). The Epistle of James is equally positive: "Come now, ye rich, weep and howl for your miseries that are coming upon you. Your riches are corrupted, and your garments are moth-eaten. Your gold and your silver are rusted; and their rust shall be for a testimony against you, and shall eat your flesh as fire... Behold, the hire of the laborers who mowed your fields, which is of you kept back by fraud, crieth out: and the cries of them that reaped have entered into the ears of the Lord of Sabaoth." (James, 5.1, 5.4).

But with the rapid development of Christianity, its leaders labored to blunt its trenchant anti-plutocratic spirit. The Gospel according to Matthew shows the change which has taken place. There it is stated: "Blessed are the poor in spirit: for theirs is the kingdom of heaven... Blessed are they that hunger and thirst after righteousness; for they shall be filled" (Matthew, 5.3, 5.6). The poor have become the poor in SPIRIT; the kingdom of God is now only the kingdom of HEAVEN; the famished now only hunger for RIGHTEOUSNESS. The revolutionary religion of the popular masses is changed into a religion of consolation for these same masses. Kautsky compares this phenomenon to social-democratic revisionism. It would be more accurate to compare this evolution to the fascist phenomenon which we are experiencing at the present time. Fascism also attempts to make use of "socialism" in order to strengthen the rule of finance capital. It

---

83 Schubart, *op. cit.*, p. 97.

unhesitatingly uses the most brazen falsehoods to deceive the masses, to represent the rule of the tycoons of heavy industry as the "rule of labor." Nevertheless the "fascist revolution" also has a certain economic and social content. It definitely closes the liberal epoch and inaugurates the epoch of the complete domination of monopoly capitalism, the antithesis of free competitive capitalism. Similarly, it is inadequate merely to say that Christianity became an instrument for deceiving the poor classes. It also became the ideology of the class of landed proprietors who seized absolute power under Constantine. Its triumph coincided with the complete triumph of a natural economy. Simultaneously with Christianity, feudal economy spread all over Europe.

It is certainly false to hold Christianity responsible for the fall of the Empire. But it furnished the ideological armament for the classes which arose on its ruins. "The most simple interest was condemned by the clergy of the East and West."[84] It thus took in hand the interests of the new possessing class whose entire wealth came solely from the land. The primary reason for the failure of "proletarian" Christianity and the triumph of "fascist" Christianity must be sought in the backward state of the mode of production of this epoch. Economic conditions were not as yet ripe for the triumph of communism. The class struggles of the Second and Third Century resulted in no gain whatever for the popular masses.[85]

This does not mean that the poor classes accepted the triumph of Catholicism without resistance. The lush growth of heresies

---

[84] Gibbon, *op. cit.*, vol. II, p. 1469.

[85] They were a manifestation of the decline of Roman economy. But the oppressed classes were not equal to the task of taking power. A new possessing class utilized their ideology for imposing its rule. A change was necessary; it took place exclusively to the profit of this new class. The same is true, *mutatis mutandis*, for the "fascist revolution."

furnishes the best proof that the contrary was true. If the official Church persecuted these heresies with such great fury it was because they represented, at least in part, the interests of the poor classes. An author of the Fourth Century writes of Constantinople: "This city," he says, "is full of slaves and craftsmen who are all of them profound theologians and preach in the shops and in the streets. Ask a man to change a piece of money for you and he will tell you wherein the Son is different from the Father. Ask another the price of a loaf of bread; he will reply that the Son is lower than the Father. Should you inquire if your bath is ready, you will be told that the Son was created out of nothing."

As we have seen, Christianity was originally the ideology of the poor Jewish masses. The first churches were formed around the synagogues. The Judo-Christians had their own Gospel which was called the Gospel according to the Hebrews. But probably the Judo-Christians disappeared quite rapidly in the great Christian community. They were assimilated into the great mass of converts. After the Third Century, epoch of the great expansion of Christianity, we hear no more of the Jewish community of Alexandria. It is probable that the majority of Alexandrine Jews entered the bosom of the Church.[86] The Alexandrine church for a certain time acquired hegemony within the new religion. At the Nicean Council, it played a leading role relative to the other Christian communities.

But while the poor layers of Judaism ardently embraced the teachings of Jesus, the same was not true of the ruling and commercial classes. On the contrary, they vigorously persecuted the primitive communist religion. Later, when Christianity became the religion of the great proprietors, when its initial anti-plutocratic tendencies were limited to trade and usury, obviously even then opposition to it by the well-to-do Jewish classes could have lost

---

[86] Schubart, *op. cit.*, p. 46.

none of its sharpness. On the contrary, Judaism became more and more conscious of its own role. Despite the decline of the Empire, the role of trade was far from ended. The ruling classes still needed luxury products from the East. If the Jews played an important role in trade in preceding epochs, they now became practically the sole intermediaries between the East and the West. "Jew" became more and more the synonym for "merchant."

The triumph of a natural economy and of Christianity thus allowed the completion of the selective process which transformed the Jews into a commercial class. Toward the end of the Roman Empire, there certainly still existed groups of Jews whose primary occupation was agriculture or cattle raising: in Arabia, Babylonia, North Africa. The Jews had certainly not disappeared in Palestine, far from it. Contrary to the opinion of idealist historians and ideologists, the Palestinian Jews were not dispersed to the four corners of the earth by the Romans. We have seen that the Diaspora had other roots. In 484, the emperors had a great deal of difficulty in suppressing a violent revolt of Samaritan peasants. At the beginning of the Seventh Century, "the Jews attacked Tyre, devastating its environs."[87] In 614, the Jewish battalions of Tiberiad, Nazareth and Galilee assisted the Persian king in conquering Jerusalem where a host of the inhabitants were slaughtered. Even in the time of the Mohammedan invasion, the Jews, according to Caro, constituted the bulk of the Palestinian population.[88]

The Mohammedan conquest produced the same effects there that it did in all conquered countries. The subjugated population was progressively assimilated by the conquerors. Just as Egypt completely lost its own character under Mohammedan rule, so

---

[87] Samuel Krauss, *Studien zur Byzantisch-Jüdischen Geschichte*, Leipzig, 1914, p. 29.

[88] Georg Caro, *Sozial - und Wirtschaftgeschichte der Juden im Mittelalter und der Neuzeit*, Frankfurt, 1924, p. 117.

Palestine was definitively despoiled of its Jewish character. Even today certain rites of Arab peasants in Palestine recall their Jewish origin. In other countries as well, the Jewish agricultural or pastoral groups were subjected to strong assimilationist pressure and succumbed sooner or later; and that is the essential phenomenon more and more discernible through historical evolution. Only the Jewish communities with a clearly defined commercial character, numerous in Italy, in Gaul, in Germany, etc., proved capable of resisting all attempts at assimilation. What remains of the pastoral Jewish tribes of Arabia or the Jewish farmers of North Africa? Nothing but legends. As against this, the Jewish commercial colonies of Gaul, Spain and Germany developed and flourished.

One can only say, therefore, that if the Jews have been preserved, it was not *despite* their dispersion but *because* of it. If there had been no Diaspora prior to the fall of Jerusalem, if the Jews had remained in Palestine, there is no reason to believe that their fate would have been different from that of all the other nations of Antiquity. The Jews, like the Romans, the Greeks, the Egyptians, would have been mixed up with the conquering nations, would have adopted their religion and their customs. Even if the present inhabitants of Palestine would have continued to bear the name of Jews, they would have had as little in common with the ancient Hebrews as the inhabitants of Egypt, Syria and Greece have with their ancestors of Antiquity. All the peoples of the Roman Empire were carried away in its fall. Only the Jews have been preserved because they brought into the barbarian world, which followed upon the Roman, vestiges of the commercial development which had chacterized the ancient world. After the Mediterranean world was dismembered, they continued, among themselves, to link its scattered parts together.

D. THE JEWS AFTER THE FALL OF THE ROMAN EMPIRE

It is consequently the transformation of the Jewish nation into a class which is at the bottom of the "preservation of Judaism." In the epoch of the ruin of the Roman Empire, their commercial role continued to gain in importance. "While the Jews had already participated in world commerce prior to the fall of the Roman Empire, they attained even greater prosperity after its end."[89] It is probable that the Syrian merchants referred to in the same period were also Jews. Such a confusion was common in Antiquity. Ovid, for example, speaks of the "day unsuited to business, on which every week falls the festival celebrated by the Syrians of Palestine."[90]

"In the Fourth Century, the Jews belonged to the well-to-do and wealthy layers of the population... Chrysostome states that the Jews possessed large sums of money and that their Patriarchs assembled immense treasures. He speaks of the wealth of the Jews as if it were a fact well known to his contempories."[91]

For many centuries, the Jews continued to be the sole commercial intermediaries between the East and the West. Spain and France progressively became the centers of Jewish life. The Arab postmaster in Spain, "Ibn-Kordadbeh, in the *Book of Routes*

---

[89] Lujo Brentano, *Eine Geschichte der Wirtschaftlichen Entwicklung Englands*, Jena, 1927-1929, vol. I, p. 363.

[90] Even if these Syrians were not Jews, it is a fact that they are no longer referred to in the Carolingian epoch. It is possible that they became assimilated with the Jewish commercial communities, if they did not completely disappear for other reasons. In the Carolingian epoch, "Jew" is a perfect synonym for "merchant."

[91] Rabbiner Dr. Leopold Lucas, *Zur Geschichte der Juden im Vierten Jahrhundert*, Berlin, 1910, pp. 31-35. "At Antioch, St. John Chrysostome... shows [the Jews] as occupying the highest commercial positions in the city, causing a cessation of all business when they celebrated their holidays." Jannet, *op. cit.*, p. 137.

(857-874), mentions the Radamite Jews who 'speak Persian, Roman, Arab and the Frankish, Spanish and Slav languages. They voyage from the Occident to the Orient, and from the Orient to the Occident, now by land and now by sea. They bring from the Occident eunuchs, women slaves, boys, silk, furs and swords. They embark in the land of the Franks, on the Western sea and sail to Farama (Pelustum) . . . They proceed to Sind, India and China. On returning they are laden with musk, aloes, camphor, cinnamon and other products of Eastern lands. Some set sail for Constantinople in order to sell their merchandise there; others repair to the country of the Frank.' "[92]

"Theodolf's verses relating to the wealth of the Orient doubtless referred to the goods imported by the Jews. Spain is further mentioned in the text of a Formula of Louis the Pious, with reference to the Jew Abraham of Saragossa.... The Jews therefore, were the purveyors of spices and costly fabrics. But we see from Agobard's texts that they also dealt in wine. And on the banks of the Danube they traded in salt. In the Tenth Century, the Jews possessed salt mines near Nuremberg. They also traded in arms, and exploited the treasuries of the churches. But their great specialty. . . was their trade in slaves. Some of these slaves were sold in the country but the majority were exported to Spain.... 'Jew' and 'merchant' become synonymous terms."[93]

Thus it is stated in an edict of King Louis: "Merchants, that is to say Jews and other merchants, from wherever they come, from this country or other countries, must pay a just tax both for slaves and for other merchandise, just as has been the custom under other kings."[94] According to Brutzkus, the name Radamites

---

92 Henri Pirenne, *Mohammed and Charlemagne, op. cit.*, p. 258.

93 *Ibid.*, pp. 258-260.

94 Dr. Julius Brutzkus, "Trade Relations of the West European Jews with Medieval Kiev," *Writings on Economics and Statistics*, J. Lestschinsky, Ed., Berlin, 1928, vol. I, p. 70.

which a section of the Jewish merchants had, comes from the river Rhodan [Rhone], from which their ships sailed. In various chronicles the designation of "nautae rhodanici" is also to be found.[95]

There can be no doubt that in the Carolingian period, the Jews were the principal intermediaries between the East and the West. Their already dominant position in trade in the epoch of the decline of the Roman Empire was excellent preparation for this role. Then "they were treated as equals of the Roman citizens... The poet Rutilius complained that the vanquished nation was oppressing the conquerors."[96]

In the middle of the Fourth Century, Jewish traders had located themselves at Tongres and Tournai. The bishops had the best relations with them and strongly encouraged their trade. In 470 Apollinaris Sidonius requested the Bishop of Tournai to receive a certain Jew favorably, in view of the fact that "these people generally did a very fine business."[97]

In the Sixth Century, Gregory of Tours speaks of colonies of Jews at Clermont-Ferrand and at Orleans. Lyons similarly had a large population of Jewish traders at this time.[98] The Archbishop of Lyons, Agobard, complains in *De Insolentia Judaeorum* that the Jews were selling Christian slaves in Spain. A monk of St. Gallen in the Eighth Century mentions a Jew living in the country of the Franks who brought precious things from Palestine.[99]

---

[95] *Ibid.*, p. 69.

[96] Georg Bernhard Depping, *Les Juifs dans le Moyen Age*, Paris, 1845, pp. 17-18.

[97] Salomon Ulmann, *Histoire des Juifs en Belgique*, Antwerp, [192-?], pp. 9-10.

[98] Pirenne, *Les Villes au Moyen Age*, *op. cit.*, p. 21.

[99] Ignaz Schipper, *Anfänge des Kapitalismus bei den Abendländischen Juden in Früheren Mittelalter*, Vienna, 1907, pp. 19-20.

It is consequently obvious that in the first centuries of the Middle Ages the Jews in France were primarily traders.[100] In Flanders, where the Jews lived from the Norman invasions up to the first Crusade, trade was lodged in their hands.[101] "Towards the end of the Ninth Century, there was a large Jewish community at Huy. The Jews occupied an important position there and had a flourishing trade.... In 1040, at Liège, trade was in their hands."[102] In Spain, "all foreign trade was exploited by them. This trade extended over all the country's provisions: wine, oil, minerals. Cloth and spices reached them from the Levant. The same was true in Gaul."[103]

The Jews of Poland and Little Russia also came to Western Europe in order to sell slaves, furs and salt there and to buy all kinds of cloth. We read in a Hebraic source of the Twelfth Century that the Jews purchased large quantities of Flemish cloth on the Rhenish markets in order to trade them in Russia for furs. Jewish trade between Mainz and Kiev, according to Pirenne, "the most important tradepost of the Southern plain" was very intensive.[104]

There was certainly an important trading colony of Jews at Kiev in this period, since we read in a chronicle of 1113 that "in order to prevail upon Monmaque [Constantine IX, Emperor of the Orient] to come to Kiev as soon as possible, the inhabitants of this city let him know that the population was prepared to pillage the Boyars [feudal lords] and the Jews."[105]

---

[100] H. E. Sée, *Esquisse d'une Histoire Economique et Sociale de la France*, Paris, 1929, p. 91.

[101] Verhoeven, *Algemeene Inleiding tot de Belgische Historie.* Quoted by Ullmann, *op. cit.*, p. 8.

[102] Ullmann, *op. cit.*, pp. 12-14.

[103] I. Bédarride, *op. cit.*, p. 55.

[104] Brutzkus, "Trade Relations of the West European Jews with Medieval Kiev," *op. cit.*, p. 71.

[105] *Ibid.*, p. 72.

The Arabian traveler Ibrahim Al Tartuahi similarly attests to the scope of Jewish trade between Europe and the Orient. He writes, in 973, on visiting Mainz: "It is marvelous to find, at such a distant point in the West, spices originating in the most remote East." In accounts of the travels of the Spanish Jews des Gorionides, Quasvini and Abraham Ibn Jakov, of the Tenth Century, mention is made of the price of wheat at Cracow and Prague; also of salt mines belonging to Jews.[106] According to Gumplowicz, the Jews were the sole intermediaries between the shores of the Baltic and Asia. An old document thus characterizes the Khazars, a Mongol tribe of the Caspian Sea which became converted to Judaism: "They have no slaves to the land because they buy everything by means of money."[107] Itil, the capital of the Khazars, was a great commercial center, the starting point for the transport of goods eventually ending up at Mainz.

The convert Herman relates, in an autobiographical work, that while he was still a Jew, he travelled regularly when he was twenty years old (about 1127) between Cologne and Mainz in the pursuit of commercial matters, for "all Jews are engaged in trade" (siquidem omnes judaei negotiationi inserviunt).

The words of R. Elieser Ben Natan are also characteristic of the period: "trade —but that is our principal means of subsistence."[108]

The Jews constituted "the only class to make its living by trading. At the same time, thanks to the contacts which they

---

[106] Schipper, *Anfänge des Kapitalismus bei den Abendländischen Juden in Früheren Mittelalter*, *op. cit.*, p. 23.

[107] Dr. J. Brutzkus, "History of the Jewish Mountaineers in in Daghestan (Caucasia)," *Yivo Studies in History*, Wilno, 1937, vol. II.

[108] Ignaz Schipper, *Jewish History*, Warsaw, 1930, vol. II, p. 47.

maintained among themselves, they constituted the only economic link which survived... between East and West."[109]

The situation of the Jews in the first half of the Middle Ages was therefore extremely favorable. The Jews were considered as being a part of the upper classes in society and their juridical position was not perceptibly different from that of the nobility. Under Charles the Bald, the Pistensian Edict punished the sale of impure gold or silver by the whip when serfs or those liable to forced labor were involved and by a money fine when the culprits were Jews or free men.[110] "The Jews of the earlier period filled a great need in the general economy which for a long time could not be filled by anybody else, namely, the need for carrying on a professional trade in goods."[111]

Bourgeois historians generally do not see any great difference between ancient or medieval trade and usury and the capitalism of our epoch. Nevertheless, there is at least as great a difference between capitalism and medieval business (and the usury to which the latter is linked) as there is between the great capitalist proprietor working for the market and the feudal lord; between the modern proletarian and the serf or slave. In the epoch of the commercial prosperity of the Jews the prevailing mode of production was feudal. Essentially it was use values that were produced and not exchange values. Each domain was self-sufficient. Only certain luxury products: spices, precious goods, etc., were objects of ex-

---

[109] Pirenne, *Mohammed and Charlemagne, op. cit.*, p. 174.

[110] The Jews were even better protected than the nobles by the Privilege of Speyer of Henry IV (1090). The Polish chronicler of the Twelfth Century, Vincenti Kadlubek, informs us that the same penalty, the "septuaginta," which was set for *lèse-majesté* or for blasphemy, was applied to assassins of Jews. In 966, the Bishop of Verona complained that in conflicts between clerics and Jews, the former were punished by fines that were triple those which the Jews had to pay.

[111] Roscher, *op. cit.*, p. 16.

change. The lords yielded a portion of the gross products of their lands for the rare merchandise coming from the Orient.

Feudal society, based on the production of use values, and "capitalism," in its commercial and usurious primitive form, do not exclude one another but complement each other. "An independent and prevailing development of capital in the shape of merchants' capital signifies that production is not subject to capital... *The independent development of merchants' capital stands therefore in an inverse ratio to the general development of society.*"[112]

"So long as merchants' capital promotes the exchange of products between undeveloped societies, commercial profit does not only assume the shape of outbargaining and cheating, but also arises largely from these methods. Leaving aside the fact that it exploits the difference in the prices of production of the various countries (and in this respect it tends to level and fix the values of commodities), those modes of production bring it about that merchants' capital appropriates to itself the overwhelming portion of the surplus-product, either in its capacity as a mediator between societies, which are as yet largely engaged in the production of use-values and for whose economic organization the sale of that portion of its product which is transferred to the circulation, or any sale of products at their value, is of minor importance; or, because under those former modes of production, the principal owners of the surplus-product, with whom the merchant has to deal, are the slave holder, the feudal landlord, the state (for instance, the Oriental despot), and they represent the wealth and luxury which the merchant tries to trap..."[113]

Whereas modern commercial or bank capital is, from an economic standpoint, only an appendage to industrial capital and

---

[112] Karl Marx, *Capital, op. cit.*, vol. III, p. 386. My emphasis.
[113] *Ibid.*, vol. III, p. 389.

appropriates only a part of the surplus value created in the process of capitalist production, commercial and usury capital realizes its profits by exploiting differences in the costs of production of various countries and by taking for itself a portion of the surplus value extorted by the feudal lords from their serfs. "It is always the same goods into which money is converted in the first phase and which, in the second phase, is converted into more money."[114]

The Jewish merchant did not invest money in production as the merchant of the great medieval cities does several centuries later. He does not purchase raw materials; nor finance the draper artisans. His "merchants' capital is... merely the intervening movement between extremes not controlled by it and between premises not created by it."[115]

Lending at interest, usury, is closely linked to commerce. If accumulated wealth in the hands of the feudal class implies luxury and the trade which serves to procure it, luxury, in its turn, becomes the distinctive hallmark of wealth. In the beginning, accumulated surplus product allows the lord to acquire spices, Oriental cloths, silks; later, all these products become the attributes of the ruling class. The cloth begins to make the monk. And when regular income does not allow the proprietor class to lead the kind of life which has become habitual, it must borrow. A second personage is added to the merchant: the usurer. Generally, in this period the second personage is identical with the first. Only the merchant has the necessary cash for the rich noble wastrel. But it is not alone the lord who has recourse to the usurer. When the king has to assemble an army immediately and the normal revenue from taxation is inadequate, he is compelled to go to the man with the cash. When the peasant, be-

---

[114] *Ibid.*

[115] *Ibid.*, vol. III, p. 388.

cause of a bad harvest, an epidemic, or the overwhelming burden of taxes, forced contributions and compulsory service, can no longer meet his obligations; when he has eaten up his seed, when he can no longer replace his worn-out tools, he must borrow his requirements from the usurer.

The treasury of the usurer is therefore indispensable to a society based on a natural economy; it constitutes the reserve on which society draws when various accidental circumstances intervene. "Interest-bearing capital, or usurer's capital, as we may call it in its ancient form, belongs like its twin brother, commercial capital, to the antediluvian forms of capital, which long precede the capitalist mode of production and are found in the most diverse economic formations of society."[116]

Often the kings and great lords pawned their tax revenues with the Jews. And it is in this way that we see Jews appearing in the role of tax farmers, tax collectors.[117] The finance ministers of the kings of the early Middle Ages were often Jews. In Spain, up to the end of the Fourteenth Century, the great Jewish bankers were also tax farmers. In Poland, the "kings entrusted to the Jews the important functions

---

[116] *Ibid.*, vol. III, p. 696.
"That the German Jews made loans on security even before the first crusade is incontestable. When Bishop Herman of Prague, in 1107, pawned five magnificent church draperies for the sum of 500 silver marks with the Jews of Regensburg, it is hard to believe that this was the first credit operation of its kind.. Moreover, a Hebrew document bears out that loans against security were customary for the German Jews of this period. But at this time, credit did not as yet constitute an independent profession; it was tightly linked up with commerce." Caro, *op. cit.*, p. 197.

[117] "The bankers also took charge of collecting the income of large seigniorial estates; they acted, in a way, like stewards or comptrollers." Georges d'Avenel, *Histoire Economique de la Propriété, etc.*, Paris, 1894, vol. I., p. 109.

of the financial administration of their domains... Under Casimir the Great and Vladislav Jagiello, not only were the public taxes farmed out to the Jews, but also such important sources of revenue as the royal mint and salt mines. Thus, for example, we know that in the second half of the Fourteenth Century, the 'Rothschild' of Cracow, Levko, the banker to three Polish kings, leased the famous salt mines of Wieliczka and Bochnia, and that he was also administrator of the mint at Cracow."[118]

So long as a natural economy reigned, the Jews were indispensable to it. It is its decline which gives the signal for persecutions against the Jews and will for a long time exert an adverse influence on their situation.

---

[118] Schipper, *Jewish History, op. cit.*, vol. IV, p. 224.

CHAPTER III

THE PERIOD OF THE JEWISH USURER

Up to the Eleventh Century, the economic regime reigning in Western Europe is characterised by the absence of commodity production. The few cities which survived from the Roman era primarily fulfill administrative and military functions. All production is destined solely for local consumption and the seignorial domains, being sufficient to themselves, enter into contact with the wide world solely through Jewish merchants who brave its strange places.[1] The commercial role played by Europeans could only be passive in character. But with time and with the continuous growth in the importation of Oriental goods, there is an incentive to produce directly for exchange. The development of trade thus stimulates native production. The production of use values progressively gives way to the production of exchange values.

Not all native products are desired by the Orient. The production of exchange values first develops in those places where a set of conditions exists for the manufacture or extraction of certain goods especially prized abroad: *Monopoly Products*. Such were the woolens of England, the cloths of Flanders, the salt of Venice,

[1] "The manorial domain must contain in itself all that is necessary for life. It must so far as possible buy nothing from without and must not call for external aid. It is a small world in itself and must be sufficient to itself." N. D. Fustel de Coulanges, *Histoire des Institutions Politiques de l'Ancienne France*, Paris, 1888-1892, vol. IV, p. 45.

copper from Dinant, etc. In these favored places, rapidly develop those "specialized industries, the products of which were at once beyond their place of origin."[2]

Trade advances from the passive to the active stage and Florentine fabrics leave to conquer the wide world. As they are much sought after, these products are at the same time the source of enormous profits. This rapid accumulation of wealth is the basis for an accelerated development of a native merchant class. Thus, "salt became a potent weapon in the hands of the Venetians for attaining wealth and for holding peoples in subjection. From the very beginning, these islanders had made a salt in their lagoons which was much sought after by all the peoples situated on the Adriatic and which brought Venice trading privileges, concessions, and advantageous treaties."[3]

So long as Europe lived under a regime of natural economy the initiative in commercial traffic belonged to merchants from the Orient, principally the Jews. Only some peddlers, some lowly suppliers to the chateaux of the nobles and the clergy, succeed in freeing themselves from the humble mass of serfs bound to the soil. But the development of native production makes possible the rapid formation of a powerful class of native merchants. Emerging from the artisans, they gain control over them by taking over the distribution of raw materials.[4] Contrary to trade as

---

[2] Henri Pirenne, *Belgian Democracy, Its Early History, op. cit.*, p. 91. "Copper from Dinant and Flemish cloths, owing to a merited reputation appear to have expanded beyond the narrow confines of the city market." Maurice Ansiaux, *Traité d'Economie Politique*, Paris, 1920-1926, vol. I., p. 267.

[3] Geo. Bernhard Depping, *Histoire du Commerce entre le Levant et l'Europe, op. cit.*, vol. I., p. 182.

[4] "...Among the weavers, who sometimes work for distant markets, we see merchants becoming differentiated from the mass of artisans: these are the cloth merchants..." Sée, *Esquisse d'une Histoire Economique et Sociale de la France, op. cit.*, p. 102.

conducted by the Jews, which is clearly separate from production, native trade is essentially based on industry.

Everywhere industrial development marches hand in hand with expansion of trade. "Venice had the advantage of being simultaneously one of the greatest commercial cities of the world and one of the most industrial. Its fabrics were of immense service to its traders in their relations with the Orient.... Venice and its neighboring cities were full of all kinds of fabrics."[5] "In Italy, as in Flanders, the maritime commerce, and the inland commerce which was its continuation, resulted in the activity of the seaports: Venice, Pisa and Genoa in the South; Bruges in the North. Then, behind the seaports, the industrial cities developed: on the one hand, the Lombard communes and Florence; on the other, Ghent, Ypres and Lille, Douai, and further inland, Valenciennes, and Brussels."[6]

The woolen industry became the basis of the greatness and prosperity of the medieval cities. Cloths and fabrics constituted the most important goods in the fairs of the Middle Ages.[7] In that is to be seen the profound difference between medieval capitalism and modern capitalism: the latter is based on a tremendous revolution in the means of production; the former reposed solely on the development of the production of exchange values.

The evolution in exchange of medieval economy proved fatal to the position of the Jews in trade. The Jewish merchant importing spices into Europe and exporting slaves, is displaced by respectable Christian traders to whom urban industry supplies the principal products for their trading. This native commercial class collides violently with the Jews, occupants of an outmoded eco-

---

[5] Depping, *op. cit.*, vol. I, pp. 184-185.

[6] Pirenne, *A History of Europe*, *op. cit.*, p. 227.

[7] Max Weber, *General Economic History*, *op. cit.*, p. 155.

nomic position, inherited from a previous period in historical evolution.

The growing contradiction between "Christian" and Jewish trade therefore leads to the opposition of two regimes: that of exchange economy as against natural economy. It was consequently the economic development of the West which destroyed the commercial function of the Jews, based on a backward state of production.[8]

The commercial monopoly of the Jews declined in the degree that the peoples, whose exploitation had fed it, developed. "For a number of centuries the Jews remained the commercial guardians of the young nations, to the advantage of the latter and not without open recognition of this advantage. But every tutelage becomes burdensome when it continues longer than the dependence of the ward. Entire nations emancipate themselves from the tutelage of other nations, even as individuals used to, only by means of struggle."[9]

With the development of exchange economy in Europe, the growth of cities and of corporative industry, the Jews are progressively eliminated from the economic positions which they had occupied.[10] This eviction is accompanied by a ferocious struggle

---

[8] Roscher states: "It might well be said that medieval policy toward the Jews is almost the reverse of the general economic trend." *The Status of the Jews in the Middle Ages*, *op. cit.*, p. 14.

[9] *Ibid.*, p. 20. "The rule that the independent development of merchants' capital is inversely proportioned to the degree of development of capitalist production becomes particularly manifest in the history of the carrying trade..." Marx, *Capital*, vol. III, p. 387.

[10] Aloys Schulte, in his *Geschichte des mittelalterlichen Handels und Verkehrs zwischen Westdeutschland und Italien* (Leipzig, 1900, p. 152), claims that the Jews did not try to establish connections with the artisans as the Christian entrepreneurs did, and losing their commercial position as a result of this, they had to engage exclusively in credit. This observation is highly interesting. It shows the essence of the problem: the link of Christian trade with industry and the lack of this tie on the part of Jewish trade.

of the native commercial class against the Jews. The Crusades, which were also an expression of the will of the city merchants to carve a road to the Orient, furnished them with the occasion for violent persecutions and bloody massacres of the Jews. From this period on, the situation of the Jews in the cities of Western Europe is definitely compromised.

In the beginning, the economic transformation reaches only certain important urban centers. The seignorial domains are very little affected by this change and the feudal system continues to flourish there. Consequently, the career of Jewish wealth is still not ended. The seignorial domains still offer an important field of action to the Jews. But now Jewish capital, primarily commercial in the preceding period, becomes almost exclusively usurious. It is no longer the Jew who supplies the lord with Oriental goods but for a certain time it is still he who lends him money for his expenses. If during the preceding period "Jew" was synonymous with "merchant," it now begins increasingly to be identified with "usurer."[11]

It is self-evident that to claim, as do most historians, that the Jews began to engage in lending only after their elimination from trade, is a vulgar error. Usurious capital is the brother of commercial capital. In the countries of Eastern Europe, where the Jews

---

[11] In a study devoted to the Jews of a German city, Halberstadt, Max Köhler states that from the Thirteenth Century on, "the most important profession of the Jews of Halberstadt appears to have been usury." Max Köhler, *Beiträge zur Neueren Jüdische Wirtschaftsgeschichte, Die Juden in Halberstadt und Umgebung bis zur Emanzipation,* Berlín, 1927, p. 2. Heinrich Cunow tells us in *Allgemeine Wirtschaftsgeschichte,* (*op. cit.*, vol. III, p. 45): "Although the economic conditions of the nobility were becoming worse all the time, its military games, its orgies, its festivals, its magnificent tourneys... did not fail to expand in the Fourteenth Century. Poor nobles also considered it their duty to take part in them. As the necessary monetary prerequisites for this show were lacking to them, they went into debt with the Jews whose principal occupation was lending at interest...."

were not evicted from commerce, we encounter, as we shall see later, a considerable number of Jewish usurers.[12] In reality, the eviction of the Jews from commerce had as a consequence their entrenchment in one of the professions which they had already practiced previously.

The fact that Jews at different periods may have held landed property cannot serve as a serious argument in favor of the traditional thesis of Jewish historians. Far from constituting a proof of the multiplicity of the occupations of the Jews, Jewish property must be considered as the fruit of their usurious and commercial operations.[13]

In the business books of the French Jew Heliot of Franche-Comté, who lived at the beginning of the Fourteenth Century, we find vineyards mentioned among his properties. But what clearly emerges from these books is that these vineyards did not constitute the basis of an agricultural profession for Heliot but were the product of his mercantile operations. When in 1360, the king of France had again invited the Jews into his territory, the

---

12 The example of Poland again proves how infantile are the customary schema of Jewish historians who attempt to explain the commercial or usurious function of the Jews on the basis of persecutions. Who then had forbidden the Jews of Poland from becoming agriculturalists or artisans? Long before the first attempts of the Polish cities to struggle against the Jews, all commerce and all banking in that country already lay in their hands.

13 This false conception of Jewish historians finds its counterpart in the proposition according to which the Jews had to abandon their "agricultural profession" because of legal bans. It is incorrect "to assert that the Jews were forbidden to own land. Wherever we find Jews doing business in the medieval cities, they are likewise the owners of their own houses. Moreover they often possessed larger pieces of land in the territory of the city. Truthfully speaking, it does not appear that they cultivated these lands anywhere. As soon as land came into their hands as security, they tried to sell it. It was not because they were forbidden to keep it but simply because they had no desire to do so. We do often find in the records, however, that vineyards, orchards, flax fields, etc. belonged to Jews. The products of these lands could easily be sold." Cunow, *op. cit.*, vol. III, p. 112.

representative of the Jews, a certain Manasé, raised the problem of royal protection for the vineyards and cattle which would pass into the hands of the Jews as unredeemed securities. In Spain, in the time of great theological disputes between Jews and Christians, the latter blamed the Jews for having become wealthy as a result of their "usurious" operations. "They have taken possession of fields and of cattle... They own three-fourths of the fields and lands of Spain."[14]

The passage of property of the nobility into the hands of the Jews was a common phenomenon in this epoch. Such was the village of Strizov, in Bohemia, which had belonged to two nobles and was assigned in payment of debts to the Jews Fater and Merklin (1382). The village Zlamany Ujezd, in Moravia, was allotted to the Jew Aron de Hradic; the village Neverovo, in Lithuania, was assigned to the Jew Levon Salomic, etc.

So long as the landed property of the Jews constituted solely an object of speculation for them, it could only have an extremely precarious character because the feudal class very early succeeded in imposing a ban upon mortgaging real properties with the Jews.

It was altogether different wherever a genuine economic and social mutation took place: in those places where the Jews abandoned business in order to become real landowners. Sooner or later, they necessarily also changed their religion.

At the beginning of the Fifteenth Century, a Jew named Woltschko, having become the proprietor of several villages, the king of Poland exerted every effort to lead him to "acknowledge his blindness and to enter the holy Christian religion." This fact is significant, for the kings of Poland carefully protected the Jewish religion. They would never have thought of converting Jewish

[14] Schipper, *Jewish History, op. cit.*, vol. I, p. 127.
"The Jews formed a social class very powerful because of the riches gained in industry, commerce and particularly banking operations." Rafael Ballester y Castell, *Histoire de l'Espagne*, Paris, 1928, p. 154.

merchants or bankers to Christianity. But a Jewish landowner in the Middle Ages could only be an anomaly.

This is equally true as regards the Christian usurer. This problem naturally has nothing in common with the banalities on racial peculiarities. Clearly it is foolish to claim, with Sombart, that usury constitutes a specific trait of the "Jewish race." Usury, which as we have seen plays an important role in precapitalist societies, is almost as old as humanity and has been practiced by all races and nations. It is enough to recall the leading role played by usury in Greek and Roman societies.[15]

But to pose the question in this way means to invert the conditions of the problem. It is not by the "innate" capacities or the ideology of a social group that we must explain its economic position. On the contrary, it is its economic position which explains its capacities and its ideology. Medieval society is not divided into lords and serfs because each of these groups originally possessed specific qualifications for the economic role which it was to play. The ideology and capacities of each class formed gradually as a function of its economic position.

The same is true of the Jews. It is not their "innate" predisposition for commerce which explains their economic position but it is their economic position which explains their predisposition to commerce. The Jews moreover constitute a very heterogeneous racial conglomeration. In the course of their history, they have absorbed a multitude of non-Semitic ethnic elements. In England, the "monopoly of usury brought them such wealth that some Christians undoubtedly went over to Judaism in order to participate in the Jewish monopoly in lending."[16]

---

[15] "The virtuous Brutus lent money in Cyprus at eight-and-forty per cent as we learn from the letters of Cicero." Adam Smith, *The Wealth of Nations*, Modern Library Edition, p. 94.

[16] Brentano, *Eine Geschichte der Wirtschaftlichen Entwicklung Englands, op. cit.*, vol. I, p. 366.

Judaism therefore consists rather of the result of a social selection and not of a "race having innate predispositions for commerce." But the primacy of the economic and social factor does not exclude —far from it— the influence of the psychological factor.

As it is infantile to see the economic position of Judaism as the result of the "predispositions of the Jews," just so it is puerile to consider it as the fruit of persecutions and of legal bans against exercising other professions than commerce or usury. "In numerous writings on the economic life of the Jews in the Middle Ages, it is stated that they were excluded, from the very beginning, from artisanry, from traffic in goods, and that they were prohibited from possessing land property. That is only a fable. In fact, in the Twelfth Century and in the Thirteenth Century, living in practically all of the great cities of Western Germany, they dwelt among the Christians and enjoyed the same civil rights as the latter.... At Cologne, during an entire period, the Jews even possessed the right to compel a Christian, who had a claim to make against a Jew, to appear before Jewish judges in order to have the matter adjudged according to Hebraic law.... It is just as false to assert that the Jews could not be admitted into the artisan guilds. True, several guilds did not admit what were termed 'Jewish children' as apprentices but this was not the case for all the guilds. The existence of Jewish goldsmiths and silversmiths, even in the period when the guild rules become far more severe, is sufficient proof of this. There were certainly few Jewish blacksmiths, masons and carpenters among the artisans of the Middle Ages, but Jewish parents who gave their children into apprenticeship in these trades were very rare. Even the guilds which excluded the Jews did not do so out of religious animosity or racial hated but because the trades of usury, and peddling were reputedly 'dishonest'.... The guilds excluded the children of Jewish business people engaged in usury or peddling, in the same way that they did not accept the sons of simple laborers, carters and boatsmen, barbers and weavers of linen into their ranks."[17]

Feudal society was essentially a caste society. It desired that everyone "should remain in his place."[18] It fought usury by Christians just as it made it impossible for the bourgeois to attain nobility, and just as it disdained the noble who lowered himself to the practice of a trade or to engaging in business.

In 1462 the doctor Han Winter was driven from the city of Nordlingen because he practiced usury through the intermediary of a Jew. Thirty years later, in the same city, a bourgeois named Kinkel was placed in the pillory and driven from the city for having practiced the "Jewish profession." The synod of Bamberg, in 1491 threatened to drive every Christian practicing usury, either by himself or through the intermediary of Jews, out of the Christian community. In 1487, in Silesia, it was decreed that every Christian practicing usury would be placed in the hands of the royal tribunal and punished in exemplary fashion.

So long as the feudal structure remains solid, the attitude of Christian society toward loans at interest does not change. But the deep-seated economic mutations which we have examined previously transform the conditions of the problem. Industrial and commercial development elevate banking to an indispensable role

---

[17] Cunow, *op. cit.*, vol. III, pp. 110 ff.

[18] If it is puerile to think that feudal society, whose principle was that "everyone should remain in his place," transformed "Jewish agriculturalists" into merchants, it is obvious, however, that legal prohibitions, themselves the fruit of economic conditions, played a certain role in confining the Jews within trade. This is above all true in periods when as a result of economic changes, the traditional situation of the Jews became compromised. Thus, for example, Frederick the Great was not in favor of the Jews exercising manual professions. He wanted "everyone to remain in his profession; that the Jews be aided in the exercise of commerce but that the other professions should be left to Christians."

in economy. The banker advancing funds to the merchant or the artisan becomes an essential element in economic development.

The treasury of the usurer, in the feudal era, fulfills the role of a necessary but absolutely *unproductive* reserve. "The most characteristic forms, in which usurers' capital exists in time antedating capitalist production, are two.... The same forms repeat themselves on the basis of capitalist production, but as mere subordinate forms. They are then no longer the forms which determine the character of interest-bearing capital. These two forms are: First, usury by lending money to extravagant persons of the higher classes, particularly to landowners; secondly, usury by lending money to the small producer who is in possession of his own means of employment, which includes the artisan, but more particularly the peasant, since under precapitalist conditions, so far as they permit of independent individual producers, the peasant class must form the overwhelming majority."[19]

The usurer makes loans to the feudal lords and to the kings for their luxuries and their war expenditures. He lends to the peasants and the artisans in order to allow them to pay their taxes, rents, etc.... The money loaned by the usurer does not create surplus value; it merely allows him to take possession of a portion of the surplus product which already exists.

The function of the banker is altogether different. He contributes directly to the production of surplus value. He is productive. The banker finances great commercial and industrial ventures. Whereas credit is essentially *consumer* credit in the feudal era, it becomes credit of *production* and of *circulation* in the era of commercial and industrial development.

There is consequently a fundamental difference between the usurer and the banker. The first is the credit organ in the feudal era, whereas the second is the credit organ in the era of exchange

[19] Marx, *Capital, op. cit.*, vol. III, pp. 697-698.

economy. Ignoring this fundamental distinction leads almost all historians into error. They see no difference between the banker of Antiquity, the Jewish banker of England of the Eleventh Century and Rothschild or even Fugger. "Newman... says that the banker is respected while the usurer is hated and despised, because the banker lends to the rich, whereas the usurer lends to the poor. (J. W. Newman, *Lectures on Political Economy,* London, 1851, p. 44.) He overlooks the fact that *the difference of two modes of production and of the corresponding social orders intervenes here* and the matter is not exhausted by the distinction between rich and poor."[20]

Of course this distinction becomes really obvious in the capitalist epoch properly so-called. But "the money lender stands in the same relation to him [the merchant] in former stages of society as he does to the modern capitalist. This specific relation was felt also by the Catholic universities. 'The universities of Alcala, of Salamanca, of Ingolstadt, of Freiburg in the Breisga, Mayence, Cologne, Treves one after another recognized the legality of interest on money for *commercial loans.*' "[21]

In the measure that economic development continues, the bank conquers ever more solid positions while the Jewish usurer increasingly loses ground. He is no longer to be found in the prosperous commercial cities of Flanders because the Jews, "unlike

---

[20] *Ibid*, p. 698. My emphasis.

[21] *Ibid*, p. 697. My emphasis.

"In the same period, the famous theologian Medina, developing a premise which is also found in St. Thomas, acknowledges the play of supply and demand as a natural mode of determining the proper price. The *Trinus Contractus*, that marvel of juridical analysis which justifies the charging of interest in *business loans* when the money is really used as capital, is then admitted by the Italian and Spanish canonists, more enlightened than those of France, or rather *situated in a more advanced social milieu.*" Jannet, *op. cit.*, p. 284. My emphasis.

the Lombards, *only practiced placement at interest and did not play the role of intermediaries in commercial operations.*"[22]

After their elimination from commerce, a process which is accomplished in Western Europe in the Thirteenth Century, the Jews continue to develop the business of usury in regions not yet reached by exchange economy.

In England, in the period of King Henry II (second half of the Twelfth Century) they are already involved up to the hilt in usury. They are generally very rich and their clientele is composed of the great landed proprietors. The most famous of these Jewish bankers was a certain Aaron of Lincoln, very active at the end of the Twelfth Century. King Henry II alone owed him 100,000 pounds, a sum equal to the annual budget of the Kingdom of England at this time.

Thanks to the extremely high rate of interest —it fluctuated between 43 and 86 per cent— a large number of estates of the nobility had passed into the hands of the Jewish usurers. But they had powerful associates and—exacting ones. If the kings of England supported the business of the Jews, it was because it constituted a very important source of revenue for them. All loans made with the Jews were registered in the *Scaccarium Judaeorum* [Exchequer of the Jews] and were assessed a tax of 10 per cent in behalf of the royal treasury. But this legal contribution was far from sufficient for the kings. Any pretext was good enough for despoiling the Jews and the income from their usury continually contributed to enlarging the royal treasury. It was particularly bad for the Jews to have the kings as important debtors. The rich banker Aaron of Lincoln found this out in 1187 when the King of England confiscated his property.

The dispossessed nobility would avenge itself by organizing

---

[22] Pirenne, *Histoire de Belgique*, Brussels, 1902-1932, vol. I, p. 251. My emphasis.

massacres of the Jews. In 1189, the Jews were massacred in London, Lincoln and Stafford. A year later, the nobility, led by a certain Malebys, destroyed the Scaccarium Judaeorum of York. The notes were solemnly burned. The Jews, besieged in the chateau, committed suicide. But the king continued to protect the Jews even after their death... He demanded payment to himself of the sums due the Jews, by virtue of the fact that the Jews were the "slaves of his treasury." Special employees were ordered by him to make an exact list of all the debts.

At the beginning of the Thirteenth Century, the king granted a "Magna Carta" to the nobility which brought certain improvements in the sphere of loans. Nevertheless, in 1262 and in 1264, new disturbances broke out against the Jews. In 1290, the entire Jewish population of England, that is to say almost 3,000 people, was expelled and its property confiscated.

The economic situation of the Jews of France, far more numerous than the English (100,000), was not perceptibly different from that of the English Jews. "With the accession of Philip Augustus (1180) and in the first years of his reign, the Hebrews were rich and numerous in France. Learned rabbis had been attracted to the synagogue of Paris, which, on the solemn entry of Pope Innocent at St. Denis in 1135 had already figured among the corporations of the capital at the time of the passage of the Pontiff. According to the historian Rigord, they had acquired almost half of Paris.... Their credits were spread throughout villages, cities and suburbs, everywhere. A great number of Christians had even been expropiated by the Jews because of debts."[23]

It is mainly in Northern France that the Jews were engaged in usury. In Provence during the Thirteenth Century, Jewish participation in trade was still very important. The Jews of Marseilles were in regular business relations with Spain, North Africa, Sicily

---

[23] Depping, *Les Juifs dans le Moyen Age, op. cit.*, pp 132-133.

and Palestine. They even owned ships, and like their ancestors of the Carolingian epoch, they imported spices, slaves, etc.

But these are only vestiges from a previous period. Usury appears to constitute the principal economic function of the Jews of France in the Thirteenth Century. A notary was appointed in each city for dealings in loans. The interest rate rose to 43%. Up to the statute of Melun (1230) which prohibited the Jews from making loans on real property, the principal clients of the Jewish bankers were the princes and lords. At the beginning of the Twelfth Century, the Jew Salomon of Dijon was the creditor of the greatest cloisters of France. The Count of Montpellier owed a Jew by the name of Bendet the sum of 50,000 sous. Pope Innocent III, in a letter to the king of France, expresses indignation at the fact that the Jews are taking possession of church property, that they are seizing lands, vineyards, etc.

While the economic position of the Jews of France is similar to that of the English Jews, their political situation is different. Power, which was far more divided, placed them in the hands of a multitude of princes and lords. The Jews were subjected to a host of levies and taxes which enriched the powerful. Various means were utilized in order to extract the maximum of money from the Jews. Mass arrests, ritual trials, expulsions, all of these were used as pretexts for enormous financial extortions. The kings of France expelled and admitted the Jews a number of times in order to seize their property.

The social and economic position of the Jews in Moslem Spain is not known with accuracy. There is however not the shadow of a doubt that they belonged to the privileged classes of the population. "Arriving in Granada," writes a certain Isak de Alvira, "I saw that the Jews here occupy leading positions. They have divided up the capital and the province. These accursed ones are everywhere at the head of the administration. They are engaged in the collection of taxes and live in luxury while you, Moslems, are clad in rags." In Christian Spain, in Castile, the Jews are bankers, tax farmers, quartermasters to the king. Royalty protects them as its economic and political supporters. The interest rate, lower than in other countries, is 33-1/3% at the beginning of the Twelfth Century. In a great many Cortes the nobility has struggled for a reduction in the rate of interest but has always met with the resistance of the kings. It was solely in the reign of Alphonse IX that the nobility achieved some concrete results in this sphere.

A similar situation arose in Aragon. Jehuda de Cavallera is a characteristic example of a great Jewish "capitalist" of the Thirteenth Century. He leased salt mines, coined money, supplied the army and possessed great estates and great herds of cattle. It was his fortune that made possible the construction of a battle fleet for the war against the Arabs.

The economic backwardness of Spain made it possible for the Jews to preserve their commercial positions longer than in England or in France. Documents of the Twelfth Century mention Jews of Barcelona who made voyages as far as the Bosphorus. In 1105, Count Bernard III granted a monopoly in the importation of Sicilian slaves to three Jews, merchants and proprietors of ships at Barcelona. We must await the Fourteenth Century, when Barcelona, according to Pirenne, will be "transformed into an enormous store and workshop," before the Jews are completely expelled from trade. Their situation then declined to such an extent that they were compelled to pay taxes in order to be able to pass through this city. "The unfortunate Israelites, far from being merchants at Barcelona, entered it like merchandise."[24]

Jewish usury took on such dimensions in Aragon that serious movements against the Jews arose among the nobility and the bourgeoisie.

---

[24] Depping, *Les Juifs dans le Moyen Age*, *op. cit.*, p. 387.

In Germany, the primarily commercial period extends up to the middle of the Thirteenth Century. The Jews bring Germany into relations with Hungary, Italy, Greece and Bulgaria. The slave trade flourishes up to the Twelfth Century. Thus, we are reminded in the customhouse tariffs of Walenstadt and of Coblenz that Jewish slave merchants had to pay four denars for each slave. A document of 1213 says of the Jews of Laubach "that they were extraordinarily wealthy and that they conducted a great trade with the Venetians, the Hungarians and the Croats."

From the Thirteenth Century on, the importance of the German cities grows. As elsewhere, and for the same reasons, the Jews are eliminated from commerce and turn towards the banking business. The center of gravity of Jewish usury is concentrated in the nobility. The Acts of Nuremberg show the average debt contracted with the Jews rose to 282 gulden among the city people and 1672 among the nobles. The same is true of the 87 notes of Ulm which belonged to Jewish banking houses. Of the 17,302 gulden which they covered, 90% belonged to noble debtors. In 1344, the Jewish banker Fivelin loaned the Count of Zweibrücken 1090 pounds. The same Fivelin, in collaboration with a certain Jacob Daniels, loaned 61,000 florins to the King of England, Edward III, in 1339.[25]

In 1451, Emperor Frederick III asked Pope Nicolas V for

---

[25] Bücher tells us in his book *Bevölkerung von Frankfurt am Main im XIV und XV Jahrhundert* (quoted by Cunow *op. cit.*, vol. III, p. 46) "Among the debtors to the Frankfort Jews, we find a large part of the nobility of Wetterau, Pfalz, Odenwald, etc., represented.... The Archbishop of Mainz also owed the Jews money.... It is primarily the nobility that is heavily indebted. There were few lords in the area around Frankfort whose notes and pledges were not to be found in the Jewish quarter.... Certain Christian bourgeois of Frankfort and the neighboring cities had also contracted 'Jewish debts' (as the report of the city council expresses itself on this subject) but the greatest part of the 279 notes with which the city council was concerned were obligations of nobles."

a privilege in behalf of the Jews, "so that they could live in Austria and there make loans at interest to the great convenience of the nobility." In the Thirteenth Century, in Vienna, the Jews Lublin and Nzklo are engaged in the important functions of "finance administrators of the Austrian Duke" *(Comites camarae ducis austriae)*.

But this state of affairs could not continue indefinitely. Usury slowly destroyed the feudal regime, ruined all classes of the population, without introducing a new economy in place of the old. In contrast to capital, usury is essentially conservative. "Both usury and commerce exploit the various modes of production. They do not create it but attack it from the outside. Usury tries to maintain it directly in order to exploit it ever anew..."[26] "Usury centralizes money wealth, where the means of production are disjointed. *It does not alter the mode of production* but attaches itself to it as a parasite, and makes it miserable. It sucks its blood, kills its nerve and compels production to proceed under even more disheartening conditions... Usurer's capital uses capital's method of exploitation without its mode of production."[27] Despite this destructive effect, usury remains indispensable in backward economic systems. But there it becomes an important cause of economic stagnation, as can be seen in many Asiatic countries.

If the burden of the usurer becomes more and more unbearable in Western Europe, it is because it is incompatible with the new economic forms. Exchange economy penetrates rural life. Industrial and commercial development of the cities deals a blow to the old feudal system in the country. A vast market opens up to agricultural products, which leads to a decided recession in the old forms of servitude, and of rents based on the natural economy. "Hardly anywhere, save in regions which were difficult of access,

---

[26] Marx, *Capital, op. cit.*, vol. III, p. 716.

[27] *Ibid.*, p. 700. My emphasis.

or very remote from the great commercial movements, did serfdom retain its primitive form. Everywhere else, if it did not actually disappear, it was at least mitigated. One may say that from the beginning of the Thirteenth Century the rural population, in Western and Central Europe, had become or was in process of becoming a population of free peasants."[28]

Everywhere in Western Europe and in part in Central Europe, the Twelfth, Thirteenth and Fourteenth Centuries are the epoch of the development of Jewish usury. But economic evolution brings about its rapid decline. The definitive expulsion of the Jews took place at the end of the Thirteenth Century in England; at the end of the Fourteenth Century in France; at the end of the Fifteenth Century in Spain. These dates reflect the difference in the speed of economic development within these countries. The Thirteenth Century is an epoch of economic flowering in England. For Spain it is the Fifteenth Century which is the high point of the process wherein the Spanish Kingdoms "developed their commerce and added to their wealth. Sheep began to cover the countryside, and in the trade with the North of Europe Spanish began to compete with English wool. The exports of wool to the Low Countries were considerably increased, and sheep-farming began to give Castile its characteristic aspect and to enrich the nobility. There was also an increasing trade with the North in iron from Bilboa, olive oil, oranges and pomegranates."[29]

Feudalism progressively gives way to a regime of exchange. As a consequence, the field of activity of Jewish usury is constantly contracting. *It becomes more and more unbearable because it is less and less necessary.* The more money becomes abundant as a result of the more intensive circulation of goods, the more pitiless becomes the struggle against an economic function which could

[28] Pirenne, *A History of Europe, op. cit.*, p. 237.

[29] *Ibid.*, pp. 491-492.

hardly find economic justification except in a time of economic immobility, when the treasury of the usurer constituted an indispensable reserve for society.

Now the peasant begins to sell his products and to pay his lord in money. The nobility, in order to satisfy its growing luxury requirements is interested in freeing the peasantry, and in everywhere replacing fixed rent in kind by rent in money. "The transformation of rent in kind into money rent, taking place sporadically, then on a more or less national scale, requires a considerable development of commerce, of city industry, of the production of commodities in general, and with them of the circulation of money."[30]

The transformation of all classes of society into producers of exchange values, into owners of money, raises them unanimously against Jewish usury whose archaic character emphasizes its rapacity. The struggle against the Jews takes on increasingly violent forms. Royalty, traditional protector of the Jews, has to yield to the repeated demands of congresses of the nobility and the bourgeoisie. Besides, the monarchs themselves are increasingly compelled to dig into the treasuries of the bourgeoisie, a class which soon monopolizes the most important portion of mobile wealth. In the eyes of the kings the Jews, as a source of revenue become less interesting (leaving out of consideration the fact that expulsion of the Jews was always an extremely profitable operation).

It is in this fashion that the Jews were progressively expelled from all the western countries. It was an exodus from the more

---

[30] Marx, *Capital, op. cit.*, vol. III. p. 926.

"This transformation of customs into money rent corresponds to the growth of mobile property wealth.... money becomes the readiest hallmark of wealth and begins to be preferred to natural products in evaluating the revenues of landed property. A similar evolution is noted in other countries and particularly in England where it is even more pronounced..." Sée, *Esquisse d'une Histoire Economique et Sociale de la France, op. cit.*, pp. 61-62.

developed countries to the more backward ones of Eastern Europe. Poland, deeply mired in feudal chaos, became the principal refuge of Jews driven out of every other place. In other countries, in Germany, in Italy, the Jews still survived in the less developed regions. At the time of the travels of Benjamin of Tudela, there were practically no Jews in commercial centers such as Pisa, Amalfi, Genoa. On the other hand, they were very numerous in the most backward parts of Italy. Even in the Papal States, conditions were far superior for Jewish trade and banking than in the rich mercantile republics of Venice, Genoa and Florence.

Mercantile economy therefore expelled the Jews from their last strongholds. The Jew, "banker to the nobility," was already completely unknown in Western Europe toward the end of the Middle Ages. Here and there, small Jewish communities succeeded in maintaining themselves in certain secondary economic functions. The "Jewish banks" were no longer anything but pawn-shops where it is poverty which is the borrower.

The collapse was a total one. The Jew became a petty usurer who lends to the poor of town and country against pledges of petty value. And what can he do with the securities which are not redeemed? He must sell them. The Jew became a petty peddler, a dealer in second-hand goods. Gone forever was his former splendor.

Now begins the era of the ghettos[31] and of the worst perse-

---

[31] Contrary to a rather widespread conception, the ghetto is a rather recent institution. It was not until 1462 that the Jews of Frankfort were enclosed in a ghetto. "There never was a question of such a measure in the Middle Ages. On the contrary, the Jews could select their living quarters freely and could go anywhere in the whole city at any time." Georg Ludwig Kriegk, *Frankfurter Bürgerzwiste und Zustände im Mittelalter*, Frankfort, 1862, p. 441.

We must not confuse Jewish quarters with ghettos. While the former are known in various epochs of Jewish history, the latter constitute an institution born of the period when the Jew becomes a

cutions and humiliations. The picture of these unfortunates bearing the badge of the wheel and ridiculous costumes, paying taxes like beasts for passing through cities and across bridges, disgraced and rejected, has been implanted for a long time in the memory of the populations of Western and Central Europe.

RELATIONS OF THE JEWS WITH OTHER CLASSES IN SOCIETY

The evolution of the social and economic situation of the Jews was a determining influence upon the relations between them and other social classes. In the era of their economic apogee, they are solicitously protected by kings and nobles. Their relations with the peasants are not of great importance. As against this, the relations of the Jews with the bourgeois class were hostile from the latter's very entry upon the historic scene.

Eliminated from commerce, Jewish "capital" takes refuge solely in usury. This new situation brings about a change in the attitude of the nobility and royalty toward the Jews. The lords, finding themselves obliged to defend their threatened properties, often pass over to a pitiless struggle against the usurers who are ruining them. The kings continue to "protect the Jews," but in reality they make use of the Jews to siphon off the resources of the country for their own profit. But so long as exchange economy has not yet penetrated into the rural sphere, the situation of the Jews still remains relatively tolerable.

It is only when the countryside begins to be "capitalized," when lords and peasants begin to produce more and more for the market, when money begins to conquer an increasingly wider

"petty usurer." Thus, in Poland, the ghetto constitutes the exception and not a rule. This did not prevent Hitlerite barbarism from "returning" the Polish Jews to the ghettos.

field of action, that all classes in society find themselves in agreement in persecuting and expelling the Jews. The victory of an economy based on money is also the defeat of the former "money-man." Eliminated from their role as bankers to the nobility, some Jews still succeed in hanging on within "pores" of the economy. Becoming pawn-brokers, old clothes merchants, peddlers and second-hand dealers, they eke out a miserable existence in dark ghettos, butt of the hatred and disdain of the people. Increasingly the Jews come into contact only with the poor, the artisans and the peasants. And often the anger of the people, despoiled by the kings and the lords and compelled to pledge their last belongings among the Jews, turns against the walls of the ghetto. The lords and rich bourgeois who utilize the Jews in order further to exploit the people often take advantage of these riots to pillage the "slaves of their treasury."

A. ROYALTY AND THE JEWS

When the enemy of the Jews, Gonzalo Matiguez, offered the king of Castile three million pieces of gold on condition that he would expel the Jews, the Bishop Don Gil replied to him: "The Jews are a treasure to the king, a veritable treasure! And you, you want to drive them out.... You are then no less an enemy of the king than you are of the Jews...." Again, in 1307, following upon a resolution of the Castilian priests against Jewish usury, the king prohibits raising any difficulties for the Jews. "The Jews," states a decree on this subject, "belong to the king to whom they pay taxes; and that is the reason why it is impossible to permit any limitation whatever on their economic life, because this would be prejudicial to the royal treasury."

In Poland, royal protection took on unusual proportions in this epoch. Thus, in 1504, the Polish king, Alexander, declares that he acts towards the Jews as befits kings and the mighty, who should not distinguish themselves solely by their tolerance to Christians, but also to the followers of other religions."[32]

Another Polish monarch, King Casimir Jagiello, similarly states that "he acts in accordance with the principle of tolerance imposed by divine law."

The reason for this attitude is not difficult to understand. The Jews constituted a source of considerable revenue for the kings. For example, in Spain, it was Jewish financiers, the Ravia brothers, who made it possible for the Castilian kings to bring the war against the Moors to a successful conclusion. Other Jewish bankers supported the Spanish kings in their struggle against the nobility. A special fiscal organization, constituted for the collection of Jewish taxes, functioned in several countries. In England, the Scaccarium Judaeorum permitted the registration of all Jewish business affairs and the recovery of loans was effected through its agency. It was directed by a committee of seven members, three of whom were Jews, two Christians and two appointees of the king. Each credit operation brought in ten per cent to the royal treasury.

It goes without saying that royalty could not remain content with such a meager share. So appropriate measures, such as extraordinary confiscations, made up for the deficiency in normal taxes.

Juridically, the Jews were "Kammerknechte," slaves of the royal treasury, and in countries where political power was extremely divided up, they were slaves of the treasuries of the lords.

---

[32] The principle of religious tolerance is preached at the end of the Middle Ages in one of the most backward countries of Europe. Isn't this rather embarrassing to idealist historians who view the whole Jewish problem through the prism of religious persecutions?

To fill the cashboxes of the mighty, this became their reason for existing.[33]

In Anglo-Saxon law it is stated: *"Ipsi Judaei et omnia sua regis sunt,"* that is to say, the Jews and all their property belong to the king. The law of North Spain is expressed in the same way: "The Jews are slaves of the king and belong forever to the royal treasury."[34]

The system was one of grandiose simplicity. The Jews despoiled the lords and the kings fleeced the Jews. But in order to fleece them, it was essential to keep them there. That is why the kings protected the Jews and encouraged their ventures with all the means in the royal power.

But while the king, in his capacity as representative of the State, was interested in protecting the Jews, we must not forget that he was, at the same time, a great lord and consequently one of their great debtors.

In this role he was obviously tempted to put an end to their undertakings, which always constituted a fruitful operation. Whereas, on the part of the lords of lesser importance, the will to free themselves from their debts and to satisfy their greed was checkmated or restrained precisely by the protection which royalty

---

[33] "Among nations to whom commerce and manufactures are little known, the sovereign, upon extraordinary occasions, can seldom draw any considerable aid from his subjects. It is in such countries, therefore, that he generally endeavors to accumulate a treasure, as the only resource against such emergencies." A. Smith, *op. cit.*, p. 414. It was to the Jews, "servi camarae," that fell the function of filling this treasury.

[34] A German interpretation of this condition does not lack a certain flavor: "In gratitude to Joseph Flavius who had cured his son, the Emperor Vespasian resolved to protect the Jews, and Titus, after the ruin of the second temple, welcomed many Jews whom he reduced to slavery. From that time on, the Jews are slaves of the state and it is as such that they should be considered in the German State, since the German kings are successors of the powerful emperors of ancient Rome."

accorded the Jews, the "Great King-Lord" obviously had no such external barriers to surmount.

"Two souls therefore inhabited his body." In his role as king, he fought the demands of nobility and the bourgeoisie and opposed the massacres and expulsions of the Jews; in his role as the greatest landed proprietor, he himself had the greatest interest in the persecutions directed against the Jews.

The means which the kings could use in order to "extract" money from their Jewish slaves were very varied. First there was the mass arrest. The Jews were imprisoned under any pretext and were not liberated until they handed over rather large sums of money. By this method, in 1180, the king of France, Philip II, extorted 150,000 marks from the Jews. Count Alphonse of Poitiers on a similar occasion "collected" 20,000 pounds.

Still other methods were available. The Jews were accused of poisoning wells and using the blood of Christians in their religious ceremonies (the ritual trial). In 1321, the Jews of France were fined 150,000 pounds for poisoning wells.

Finally, the most successful operation of this kind consisted of expelling the Jews, confiscating their goods and later readmitting them in consideration of the payment of enormous sums. In 1182, Philip Augustus throws all the Jews out of his kingdom and confiscates all their real property. He lets them return 15 years later and receives a "gift" of 150,000 marks for this "act of charity." Again, in 1268, the king of France decrees that all Jews must leave France and their treasuries are to be confiscated. Soon after negotiations are begun with his "servi camarae" and the order is subsequently rescinded in consideration of substantial gifts.

The expulsion of the Jews in 1306 brought the king of France 228,460 pounds, an enormous sum for the period. Invited anew to return in 1315, the Jews pay 22,500 pounds for this new favor.

But some six years later, they find themselves compelled again to take the path of exile.

The history of the Jews of France and of Languedoc ends in 1394 by their definitive expulsion, accompanied by the usual sequel: confiscation of all their goods.

These proceedings are not limited to France. In 1379, the Austrian princes imprisoned all the Jews found in their territories; the latter suceeded in getting free only at an enormous price. The same princes profited from anti-Jewish agitation among the peasants in 1387 by making the Jews pay 16,000 marks.

The attitude of the kings and princes toward the Jews therefore appears somewhat contradictory. But it is determined in the last analysis by economic development. Wherever the Jews play an indispensable role in economic life, wherever exchange economy is only weakly developed, state interests impel the kings to protect the Jews, to defend them against all their enemies. Thus, in Poland, royalty always appears as their firmest protector.

In the more developed countries, where usury is no longer anything but an anachronism, the kings have far fewer scruples about pillaging the Jews. Soon the sole important financial power will be that of bourgeoisie, basing itself on the development of economy, and in the eyes of the king the Jews will lose all interest. What are the "Jewish bankers" compared to financiers like the Fuggers, the Medicis? Here is what Schipper says in regard to the importance of these "Jewish bankers": "As regards the importance of the capital of the Jewish bankers of Italy, we have only found two really rich families among the Jewish capitalists. But what were they in comparison with such magnates as the Medicis who, around 1440, possessed half a million florins, or Agostino Chigi, who in 1520, left 800,000 ducats!" Jewish bankers had at their disposal only several thousand florins.

It goes without saying that under these conditions the Jews

could no longer be of interest to the kings. The era of the great Jewish magnates who supported the royal power against its domestic and foreign enemies was definitely closed. "The increasing expenditure which war imposed upon the state or the princes compelled the latter to find some new means of replenishing their treasuries; for now that bands of mercenaries and fleets were playing a greater part in warfare, it was becoming more costly than ever. The old sources of revenue were insufficient... Consequently, the only thing to be done was to apply to the Third Estate —that is, to the cities— and to ask them to open their purses."[35]

The decline of the economic position of the Jews, produced by the "capitalization" of economy, resulted in the loss of the protection which the kings and princes had accorded them. The kings became actively associated in the persecutions and pillaging of the Jews.

B. THE NOBILITY AND THE JEWS

In the early Middle Ages, the Jews were indispensable to the nobles in their capacity as principal suppliers of Oriental products. Later on, the noble wastrel, living without foresight, needed the Jews as a money reserve always ready to satisfy his caprices. For many a powerful lord the Jew was, as he was for the kings, an important source of revenue. In the epoch when royalty had not yet asserted its complete authority over the nobility, frequent conflicts broke out between princes, lords and kings for possession of the Jews.[36]

---

[35] Pirenne, *A History of Europe, op. cit.*, p. 390.

[36] "The Jew was such a fruitful and wonderful thing to exploit that every prince sought to have as many of them as possible. There were the king's Jews and those of the lords... Philip the Handsome,

In the Twelfth Century, there was much talk about the suit between the Countess Blanche and King Philip Augustus over the Jew Kresslin who had fled from the domain of the Countess in order to take refuge in the lands of the king.

"After the manner of the kings, the barons appropriated the Jews; a baron would say 'my Jews' just as he said 'my lands' when he counted up his income. This property was in fact very remunerative....

"Thibaud, Count of Champagne, was as certain as King Philip of his property right over the Jews who lived in his domains. In 1198 the two concluded an agreement in which each promised not to detain the other's Jews."[37]

The practice of agreements on the subject of the Jews spreads rapidly in the Thirteenth Century. Instead of having to engage in long suits, the kings and princes agreed to surrender to each other the Jews who took refuge on their territories. Such an agreement reached in 1230 states that the king as well as the princes preserve their rights in the Jews "who are like slaves" (Judaeus tamquam proprius servus).

"Later on, we see Jews put on the auction block after a fashion. Philip IV buys all the Jews of the county of Valois from his brother, the Count of Valois, after having had a suit against him concerning 43 Jews whose property he claimed. He also buys from him a Jew of Rouen who was good for 300 pounds quarterly."[38]

"Whereas the Prince Electors have the right within their domains to exploit all mines of gold, silver, tin, iron as well as salt mines, therefore be it also granted them the right to admit

---

in 1299, bought all the Jews of the county of Valois from his brother for 20,000 pounds." G. d'Avenel, *op. cit.*, vol. I, p. 111.

[37] Depping, *Les Juifs dans le Moyen Age, op. cit.*, p. 174.

[38] Bédarride, *op. cit.*, p. 219.

and to possess Jews." This is the wording of a "golden bull" of the German emperor in the year 1356.

Presently the German cities, prospering increasingly, will dispute the right to possess Jews with the kings and princes. Just as between royalty and the princes, so also an agreement will be reached with the cities which will thus acquire an important share of the profits accruing from the exploitation of the Jews.

It goes without saying that all those who thus profited from Jewish usury could only be hostile to the conversion of the Jews to Christianity. So true is it that religion is only a reflection of an economic function, that conversion of Jews to Christianity automatically led to the abandonment of their profession by the converts. "The conferences convoked by the new converts always led to violent conversions of a certain number of Jews, even if they did not win over the rabbis who participated in the discussions. This reached a point where the lords, and the bishops themselves, whose Jews were thus being taken from them and who were thus being deprived of the income which they received from them, complained to the king on a number of occasions. The Bishop of Palencia, following a conference convoked by a converted Jew, Jehuda-Mosca —a conference which had led to the conversion of a large number of Jews— prayed the king to come to his aid, in view of the fact that his resources were going to be greatly reduced."[39]

The English King William II, who went so far as to farm out the revenues of vacant Episcopal seats to the Jews, compelled converted Jews to return to Judaism in order not to lose the profits which he drew from them. In order to prevent the conversion of Jews, another English King, Henry II, decreed that the goods of Jews embracing Christianity, would be attached by the

---

[39] *Ibid.*, p. 205.

Crown, to make up for the losses in revenues that the Jews would have brought the king if they had not been converted.[40]

By this we can see the naiveté of our idealist historians who imagine that all the efforts of Christianity were in the direction of converting the Jews and who believe that all the sufferings of the Jews must be explained by the resistance which they made to these efforts. So long as the economic function represented by Judaism was necessary, there was opposition to their religious assimilation which also meant their economic assimilation. It is solely when Judaism became superfluous economically that it had to assimilate or disappear.

It was, of course, only a tiny part of the nobility which profited from Jewish usury. For the majority of feudal lords, the Jew was a direct cause of their ruin. For the king or the prince to be able to despoil the Jews, it was necessary that the majority of the nobles should groan under the weight of their debts.

Compelled thus to surrender to the Jews a portion of the surplus value which they extorted from the peasants, it was obvious that the nobles would endeavor to retake it from them at the first opportunity. The indebtedness of the nobles to the Jewish usurers contained the germs of bloody conflicts.

In 1189, there were anti-Jewish excesses in a number of English cities: at London, Lincoln, etc.

A year later occurred the tragedy of York. The indebted knights of the Yorkshire Jews, goaded on by a certain Malebys, attacked the Jews and the Scaccarium Judaeorum. The notes found in the Scaccarium were solemnly burned and the Jews who

---

[40] Brentano, *Eine Geschichte der Wirtschaftlichen Entwicklung Englands, op. cit.*, vol. I., p. 369. "...A custom was introduced of confiscating the effects of those Jews who embraced Christianity.... this confiscation was a species of the right of amortization, to recompense the prince, or the lords, for the taxes levied on the Jews, which ceased on their embracing Christianity." Montesquieu, *Spirit of the Law*, Cincinnati, 1873, vol. II, p. 42.

took refuge in the chateau were besieged. The affair ended by a mass suicide of the besieged Jews. The customary sequel was not lacking: the king took over the notes held by the suicides, since the Jews were the slaves of his treasury. The anti-Jewish massacres at London in 1264, which counted 550 victims, had also been organized by landed proprietors indebted to the Jews. The same was true about the anti-Jewish riots in other cities. Thus, at Canterbury, it began by an attack against the Scaccarium Judaeorum.

All over Europe assemblies of the nobility are unceasing in their protest against Jewish usury. Their various demands best characterize the position of the feudal lords relative to the Jews.

In the second half of the Thirteenth Century, the Castilian Cortes submit the three following demands to the king:

1. Regulation of Jewish credit operations and limitations on the interest rates demanded by usurers;
2. Proscription of hereditary rights in the possession of lands by Jews;
3. A reform of the financial administration and elimination of Jewish functionaries and comptrollers.

These will be the classical demands of the nobility in all the countries of Europe. They aim to limit the portion of surplus value that the nobility is compelled to turn over to the Jews, to prevent the latter from becoming landed proprietors and from seizing control of the state apparatus.

It was not until the Fourteenth Century that the Spanish nobility achieved its first results in this sphere. In 1328 King Alphonse IX reduced the rate of interest to 25% and canceled one-fourth of all Jewish credits. In 1371, there was another amputation of the credits. The occasions were not few in which the Aragon Cortes raised their voices against the high rate of interest paid to the Jews, notably in 1235, 1241, 1283, 1292 and 1300.

The Cortes of Portugal complain of Jewish usury in 1361 as becoming an increasingly unbearable yoke upon the population.

"In the circles of the Spanish nobility and rich patrician class the Jews were hated because of their state functions, where they showed themselves to be servile instruments of royalty, as well as because of the great tax and impost farming by which the Jewish magnates unceasingly augmented their fortunes."[41]

In Poland also, the demands of the nobility and the clergy against Jewish usury became more and more pressing. An ecclesiastical congress, held in 1420, demanded measures by the king against "great Jewish usury." In 1423, Vladislav Jagiello promulgated the Statute of Warta which forbade the Jews to lend on mortages. In 1454, the Statute of Nieszawa limited the validity of Jewish credit to three years. The seyms of the nobility succeeded in banning the Jews from access to state employment.

The Polish nobility pursued the same objectives as the Spanish nobility: limitation of the interest rate, safeguarding of its properties, elimination of Jews from state employment.

Political reasons join with economic causes for the hostility which the nobility nurses against the Jews. "In 1469 the Cortes protest against the admission of Jews to tax farming and against the protection with which the kings surround them. Ritual trials and massacres come to the support of the pressures exerted by the nobility upon royalty."[42]

The Jews were, in fact, solid supports of royal absolutism which was above all directed against the nobility. The surplus

---

[41] Schipper, *Jewish History, op. cit.*, vol. II, p. 133.

[42] Sometimes the Jews also go over to the offensive. In 1376 the banker Jekl employs bands of mercenaries against noble debtors who have refused to pay their debts. His son engages mercenaries with a view to launching an attack against Nuremburg, the council of this city having confiscated his houses.

value surrendered to the Jews by the nobles aided in forging their chains.

The small barons hated the Jews as creditors, the great ones saw in them one of the principal financial resources on which the king's independence of them rested.

The financial support furnished the kings by the Jews was indispensable to them in their struggle against the nobility as well as in their opposition to the growing demands of the cities. It was the Jews who first permitted the kings to maintain costly armies of mercenaries which begin to take the place of the undisciplined hordes of the nobility. These armies first served foreign policy. Thus, in Spain, it was in large part Jewish finance which allowed the kings to defeat the Arabs. "In 1263, the Jewish banker Jehudah de Cavallera loans the king [of Aragon] a great sum which permits him to equip a flotilla against the Arabs. In 1276, Cavallera amasses funds for an army which fights the Arabs at Valencia."[43]

But what is more serious in the eyes of the nobility and augments the list of its grievances, is the support that the Jews furnish royalty in the struggle which it is conducting against the feudal lords.

We have already spoken of the Ravia brothers who supplied the royal army with money and arms during the domestic wars which the king conducted against the insurgent nobles of Catalonia. The nobility could not forgive the Jews for that. The Ravia brothers fell victims of assassins as did so many of their successors.

Generally speaking the struggle of the nobility against the Jews was far less radical than that of the bourgeoisie. Different social contents influenced the intensity and forms of struggle of each class. Whereas the landed proprietor still had need of the usurer and sought simply to limit the field of his activity, the

[43] Schipper, *Jewish History*, *op. cit.*, vol. I, p. 144.

bourgeois and even the bourgeoisified noble resented him more and more as an intolerable barrier.

C. THE BOURGEOISIE AND THE JEWS

The commercial monoply of the Jews was one of the greatest obstacles that the nascent bourgeoisie had to surmount. Destruction of the commercial domination of the Jews was the precondition for its own development.

It was not a question of a struggle between two national or religious groups for commercial supremacy but a conflict between two classes each representing a different economic system. The apparent national competition is only a reflection here of the transition from feudal economy to exchange economy. The Jews ruled commerce in the epoch when "the great proprietors bought works of refinement and objects of luxury of great price against large quantities of the raw materials from their lands."[44] The industrial development of Western Europe put an end to their monopoly.[45]

In struggling against the Jews, the native traders were rising

---

[44] "The inhabitants of trading cities, by importing the improved manufactures and expensive luxuries of richer countries, afforded some food to the vanity of the great proprietors, who eagerly purchased them with great quantities of the rude produce of their own lands. The commerce of a great part of Europe in those times accordingly, consisted chiefly in the exchange of their own rude for the manufactured produce of more civilized nations." A. Smith *op. cit.*, p. 380.

[45] "So long as raw materials were the principal product for export by England, foreign commerce was in the hands of foreign traders and merchants of the market place (Stapelkaufleute).... *This changed in the degree that the English began themselves to process their raw materials especially wool. Now [English] merchants began to seek outlets for the ready sale of their manufactured goods,* 'the merchant adventurers.'" Brentano, *Eine Geschichte der Wirtschaftlichen Entwicklung Englands, op. cit.*, vol. II, p. 139. My emphasis.

up against an outmoded economic function which appeared more and more as an intolerable exploitation of the country by foreigners.

The relations of the merchant class with the Jews after the eviction of the latter from commerce underwent a profound modification. Jewish credit was essentially consumers' credit. It was not to the Jewish bankers that the traders had recourse for their business. Great banking houses like the Medicis, the Chigis, the Fuggers, developed in the great cities. Later, when exchange economy will have penetrated into the rural domains, the Jewish usurers will be crowded out by these great invading Christian banks. Just like precapitalist commerce, which exchange economy drives out of the cities, the usurer is dislodged by the penetration of capitalism into the feudal domain.

Altogether different will be the position of the great merchants towards the Jews when the latter, upon the decline of their economic role, will no longer be anything but petty usurers lending to artisans and small shopkeepers. The Jew no longer appears in that period as a competitor of the rich trader or banker; he concerns them insofar as he is an interesting source of profit and insofar as he is a means for weakening the popular classes with whom he is engaged in continuous struggle. The great merchants will now dispute with the kings and lords for the Jews. It is above all in Germany that the cities pass over to a general offensive to take possession of the profits which the "royal" Jew procured for the princes.

The "royal" Jew is increasingly divided up from the second half of the Thirteenth Century on. The German cities, already flourishing in this period, begin to demand a share of him also. Their determined struggle against the feudal lords had enabled them to conquer a series of liberties such as autonomous courts and the right of administration. They now turn their attention to the "royal" Jew; they strive to tear him out of the hands of the lords and of the emperor.

The city of Cologne, in 1252, secures from its archbishop the right to a third of the taxes collected from the Jews in the city. The bishop of Worms, in 1293, allows the city council to admit and to tax Jews.[46] "On March 7, 1456, the bishop Burchard pawns the Jews of Halberstadt for three years with the council of this city."[47]

The "royal" Jew is conquered:
by Mainz, in 1259;
by Regensburg, at the end of the Thirteenth Century;
by Nuremberg, in 1315;
by Speyer, in 1315;
by Zurich, in 1335;
by Frankfort, in 1337;
by Strasbourg, in 1338, etc.

The struggle of these three forces: the nobility, the emperor and the cities ends up in a compromise upon the backs of the Jews.

They will pay:

a) to the emperor:
    1) a normal tax (in 1240 the Jews paid one-fifth).
    2) a gold pfennig which every Jew or Jewess possessing more than 20 gulden had to pay;

b) to the nobility:
    1) an annual tax;
    2) an extraordinary tax;

---

[46] Schipper, *Jewish History, op. cit.*, vol. II, p. 35.
[47] Köhler, *op. cit.*, p. 3.

c) to the cities:

a special tax, the amount of which is set for each Jew, at the time when he receives his "letter of citizenship" (Bürgerbrief).

Numerous taxes and extraordinary imposts were added to those listed above. Methods similar to those which we have encountered in other European countries were employed to extort as much money from the Jews as possible. Popular and peasant riots similarly constituted unique occasions for getting lush payments from the Jews for the protection that was granted them.

The growth of the power of the cities augmented their power over the Jews. "In 1352," according to an authorization by the emperor to the city of Speyer, "the Jews inhabiting our city will belong to us exclusively, will be our property in body and goods."

An agreement of 1352 stipulates that the city of Frankfort must pay the emperor half of the profits that it collects from the Jews. At Nuremberg, the emperor's share rose as high as two-thirds.

The class struggle having as its object the division of the profits derived from the exploitation of the Jews, often turned against the latter. "The bishop of Cologne," states a chronicle of this city, "wished to have a perpetual monopoly of the profits from the 'royal' Jew. That is the reason why the Jews were driven out of this city forever." The Jews "of the emperors" were badly treated by the princes, those of the princes by the bourgeoisie.

D. RELATIONS OF THE JEWS WITH THE ARTISANS AND PEASANTS

In the measure that usury became the principal occupation of the Jews, they entered increasingly into relations with the popular masses and these relations worsened all the time.[48] It was not luxury needs but the direst distress which forced the peasant or the artisan to borrow from the Jewish usurer. They pawned their working tools which were often indispensable to assure their livelihood. It is easy to understand the hatred that the man of the people must have felt for the Jew in whom he saw the direct cause of his ruin, without perceiving the emperor, the prince or the rich bourgeois, who became richer thanks to the Jewish usurer. It is in Germany above all, where Jewish usury took on its most "popular" form, principally in the Fourteenth and Fifteenth Centuries, that the hatred of the Jews manifested itself most, a hatred which ended in anti-Jewish massacres and in the "burning" of Jews (Judenbrand).

"Many instances of Jewish persecutions in the Middle Ages were first and foremost efforts to destroy the letters of credit which were in their possession and are, therefore, to be viewed as a barbarous method of meeting a financial crisis, as a medieval form of what we of the present time would call a social revolution."[49]

The first large scale riots against the Jews took place between 1336 and 1338. They were led by the publican Cimberlin, the "king of the poor," and from Alsace they spread into Bavaria, Austria and Bohemia. But it was above all during the years of the "Black Death," between 1348 and 1350, that fanaticism joined with hatred and made terrifying ravages. At Strasbourg, it was the guilds that preached annihilation of the Jews. But the city council, on which sat a patrician majority, which drew large profits from usury, refused to give its consent. Bourgeois such as Conrad von Winterbourg, the rich Sturm and the wealthy artisan

---

[48] See quotation from *Capital*, vol. III, p. 700 previously given on p. 150.

[49] Roscher, *op. cit.*, p. 24.

Schwarber, made speeches in favor of the Jews. Nevertheless the guilds did not abandon their anti-Jewish demands. The matter was finally left to a congress which was to meet in 1343 and in which representatives of the church, the nobility and the cities were to take part. The demands of the guilds were supported by the church and by the lords, who were anxious to rid themselves of their debts.[50] Following this, the Jews were declared outside the pale of the law and the burning of Jews spread throughout Alsace.

At Mainz and at Cologne, the patricians tried to protect the Jews but were submerged by the popular wave. A city chronicle of Augsburg relates the following: "In 1384, the bourgeois of Nedlingen having massacred all the Jews of Nedlingen, took possession of their goods. The debtors of the Jews, among them the Count of Etingen, were freed of their debts. The pledges and notes of the Count were returned to him. All this was done by the mob against the will of the city council."

The peasant revolts were accompanied by massacres of Jews. In 1431, the armed peasants of the Pfalz marched against Worms and demanded that the city council hand over the Jews to them, "in view of the fact that they had ruined them and taken away their last shirt." The council opposed these demands since its members were the ones who profited most from Jewish usury. The lords entered into negotiations with the council in order to obtain the cancellation of accumulated interest bearing down upon the impoverished peasants.

The anti-Jewish riots in Catalonia and in the Balearic Islands

---

[50] The attitude of the nobility is probably explained by the fact that the wealthy bourgeoisie had succeeded in getting possession of the "royal" Jew and as a consequence the interests of the lords coincided with those of the popular masses of the cities as against the patricians.

bear the same character. The peasants, living in great poverty and heavily indebted to the Jews because of the burden of taxes, revolt in order to free themselves from their debts. They burn the judicial archives.

CHAPTER IV

THE JEWS IN EUROPE AFTER THE RENAISSANCE

A. THE JEWS IN WESTERN EUROPE AFTER THE RENAISSANCE. THE THESIS OF SOMBART.

The discovery of the new world and the tremendous current of exchange that followed upon it sounded the death-knell of the old corporative feudal world. Mercantile economy reached a higher stage, smashing the remnants of previous periods and preparing, by the development of manufacture and rural industry, the bases of industrial capitalism. The place of the old centers of corporative industry and medieval trade, fallen into decay, was taken over by Antwerp, which became the commercial center of the world for a certain period.

Everywhere, although at different times and in different forms, the decline of the economy producing use values was accompanied by the decay of the economic and social function of the Jews. An important number of the Jews was compelled to leave the countries of Western Europe in order to seek refuge in the countries where capitalism had not yet penetrated, principally in Eastern Europe and in Turkey. Others became assimilated, fused with the Christian population. This assimilation was not always easy. Religious traditions long survived the social situation which had been their foundation. For centuries the Inquisition struggled mercilessly and barbarously against Jewish traditions which persisted among the mass of converts.

The Jews who penetrated into the merchant class acquired a

certain notoriety under the name of "new Christians," principally in America and also at Bordeaux and Antwerp. In the first half of the Seventeenth Century, all the great sugar plantations in Brazil were in the hands of Jews. By the decree of March 2, 1768, all registers concerning new Christians were destroyed; by the law of March 24, 1773, "new Christians" were made equal before the law with "old Christians."

In 1730, Jews possessed 115 plantations out of 344 at Surinam. But contrary to previous epochs, the activity of the Jews in America no longer had a special economic character; it was in no ways distinguished from the activity of Christians. The "new Christian" merchant was little different from the "old Christian" merchant. The same was true of the Jewish plantation owner. And this is also the reason why juridical, religious and political distinctions rapidly disappeared.

In the Nineteenth Century, the Jews in South America no longer constituted more than a handful.[1] Assimilation of the Jews proceeded just as rapidly in France and in England. The rich merchant Jews of Bordeaux, of whom it was said that they "possessed entire streets and had large trade," felt themselves completely integrated into the Christian population. "Those who are acquainted with the Portuguese Jews of France, Holland, England, know that they are far from having an unconquerable hatred for all the peoples who surround them, as Mr. Voltaire says, but on the contrary they believe themselves so identified with these peoples that they consider themselves a part of them. Their Portuguese or Spanish origin has become a pure ecclesias-

---

[1] In the Nineteenth Century "there were hundreds of Jewish merchants, landed proprietors, and even soldiers scattered throughout the vast republics of what once was Spanish South America, but they now knew hardly anything of the religion of their fathers." Martin Philippson, *Neueste Geschichte des Jüdischen Volkes*, Leipzig, 1907, p. 226.

tical discipline."[2] The assimilated Jews of the West acknowledged no relationship with the Jews still living under the conditions of feudal life. "A Jew of London as little resembles a Jew of Constantinople as the latter does a Chinese Mandarin. A Portuguese Jew of Bordeaux and a German Jew of Metz have nothing in common." "Mr. Voltaire cannot ignore the delicate scruples of the Portuguese and Spanish Jews in not mixing with the Jews of other nations, either by marriage or otherwise."[3]

Alongside the Spanish, French, Dutch and English Jews, whose complete assimilation is proceeding slowly and surely, we still find Jews in Western Europe, primarily in Italy and in Germany, who inhabit ghettos and are mostly petty usurers and peddlers. This is a sorry remnant of the former Jewish merchant class. They are reviled, persecuted, subject to innumerable restrictions.

It was on the special basis of the rather important economy role played by the first category of Jews that Sombart presented his famous thesis on "The Jews and Economic Life."[4] He has himself summarized it in these terms: "The Jews promote the economic flowering of countries and cities in which they settle; they lead the countries and cities which they abandon to economic decay." "They are the founders of modern capitalism." "There would be no modern capitalism, no modern culture without the dispersion of the Jews in the countries of the North." "Israel passes over Europe like the sun: at its coming new life bursts forth; at its going all falls into decay."

---

[2] In England "certain Spanish Jews converted to Christianity... Some families which later became famous throughout the world thus abandoned Judaism: the Disraelis, Ricardos, Aguilars. Other Sephardic families were slowly assimilated by English society." Heinrich Hirsch Graetz, *Histoire Juive*, vol. VI, p. 344.

[3] *Lettres de Quelques Juifs*, 5th Edition, 1781. Quoted by Sombart, *The Jews and Modern Capitalism, op. cit.*, p. 348.

[4] See Sombart, *The Jews and Modern Capitalism, op. cit.*, chap. 2

This is the way, in rather poetic fashion as we can see, that Sombart presents his thesis. And here are the proofs adduced in its support:

1. "The first event to be recalled, an event of world-wide import, is the expulsion of the Jews from Spain (1492) and from Portugal (1495 and 1497). It should never be forgotten that on the day before Columbus set sail from Palos to discover America (August 3, 1492) 300,000 Jews are said to have emigrated from Spain..."

2. In the Fifteenth Century, the Jews were expelled from the most important commercial cities of Germany: Cologne (1424-1425), Augsburg (1439-1440), Strasbourg (1438), Erfurt (1458), Nuremberg (1498-1499), Ulm (1499), Regensburg (1519). In the Sixteenth Century, the same fate befell them in a number of Italian cities; they were driven out of Sicily in 1492, from Naples in 1540-1541, from Genoa and Venice in 1550. Here as well the decline of these cities coincides with the departure of the Jews.

3. The economic development of Holland at the end of the Sixteenth Century is marked by a great rise of capitalism. The first Portuguese Marranos settled at Amsterdam in 1593.

4. The brief flowering of Antwerp as the center of world trade and as a world Exchange coincides exactly with the arrival and departure of Marranos.

These arguments, essential to the Sombart thesis, are very easily refuted:

1. It is absurd to see in the simultaneity of the departure of Christopher Columbus "to discover America" and the expulsion of the Spanish Jews a proof of the decline of the countries which they left. "Not only did Spain and Portugal not fall into decline in the Sixteenth Century, under Charles V and Emanuel, but on the contrary they reached their historical apogee at that time.

Even at the beginning of the reign of Philip II, Spain is still the foremost power in Europe and the wealth of Mexico and Peru which flowed to it was immeasurable."[5]

This first Sombartist proof is based on a crying falsehood.

2. The very figures which he supplies on the redistribution of the Jewish refugees coming from Spain aids in demolishing his thesis. According to him, out of 165,000 exiles, 122,000 or 72% emigrated to Turkey and into Moslem countries. Consequently it is there that the "capitalist spirit" of the Jews should have produced the most important effects. Is it necessary to add then, that while we can speak of a certain economic rise in the Turkish Empire under Suleiman the Magnificent, that country remained the least accessible to capitalism up to a very recent period, so that the rays of the sun there proved to be... very cold? It is true that a rather important number of Jews (25,000) settled in Holland, at Hamburg and in England, but can we concede that the same cause produced diametrically opposite effects?

3. The coincidence which Sombart perceives in the decline of the German cities is easily explained by reversing the causal relation. The ruin of these cities was not provoked by the measures taken against the Jews; these measures were on the contrary the effect of the decline of these cities. On the other hand, the prosperity of other cities was not the result of Jewish immigration but it was the latter which naturally directed itself toward prosperous cities. "It is obvious that the relation of cause and effect is contrary to that presented by Sombart."[6]

A study of the economic role of the Jews in Italy and Germany at the end of the Fifteenth and Sixteenth Centuries fully confirms this viewpoint. It is clear that the pawnshops, the busi-

[5] Brentano, *Die Anfänge des Modernen Kapitalismus, op. cit.*, p. 163.

[6] Brentano, *Ibid.*, p. 165.

ness of Jewish usurers, were endurable so long as the economic situation of these cities was relatively good. Every worsening of the situation rendered the burden of usury more intolerable and the anger of the population vented itself first of all against the Jews.

4. The example of Holland does not, it is true, weaken the thesis of Sombart but neither does it reinforce it. Even if we admit that its prosperity was favored by the arrival of the Marranos, we are not thereby authorized to make it its cause. And how can we explain, if we base ourselves on this criterion, the decline of Holland in the Eighteenth Century? It appears, moreover, that the economic role of the Jews in Holland is exaggerated. Sayous says, in connection with the Dutch East India Company, whose importance to the prosperity of Holland was decisive: "The Jews have in any case no role whatsoever in the formation of the first genuinely modern stock corporation, the Dutch East India Company; they subscribed barely 0.1% of its capital and played no important role in its activity during the ensuing years."[7]

Is it necessary to continue? Must it be shown that the important economic development of England took place precisely after the expulsion of the Jews? "If the causal relation established by Sombart were true, how explain that in Russia and in Poland, where the southern people from the 'desert' have been most numerous for centuries, their influence on the northern peoples produced no economic flowering whatever?"[8]

The theory of Sombart is consequently completely false.[9]

---

[7] André Sayous, "Les Juifs," *Revue Economique Internationale*, March 1932 p. 526.

[8] Brentano, *Die Anfänge des Modernen Kapitalismus*, *op. cit.*, pp. 165-166.

[9] "Mr. Sombart's book on the Jews suffers from an endless sequence of serious errors; one might call it the rigorous development of a paradox by a man having the genius for portraying things

Sombart claims that he is portraying the economic role of the Jews, but he does so in a completely impressionistic way, rearranging history to suit his theory. Sombart presents a thesis on the Jews and economic life in *general,* but deals solely with a very limited part of their history. Sombart builds a theory on the Jews in *general* and on economic life, but he limits himself to a minority of Western Jews, of Jews on the road to complete assimilation.

In reality, even if the role of the Western Jews had been such as Sombart presents, he would still have had to make an abstraction from it in order to understand the Jewish question in the present period. Without the influx of Eastern Jews into Western Europe in the Nineteenth Century, the Western Jews would long ago have been absorbed in the surrounding milieu.[10]

One more observation regarding the theory of Sombart: If the Jews constituted such an economic boon; if their departure provoked the economic decay of cities and countries, how explain their continuous persecution in the late Middle Ages? Can this be explained by religion? But then, why was the position of the Jews so solid in Western Europe in the early Middle Ages and in Eastern Europe up to the Nineteenth Century? How explain the prosperity of the Jews for long centuries in the most backward countries of Europe, in Poland, in Lithuania; the powerful protection accorded them by the kings? Can the difference in the situation of the Jews be explained by the difference in the intensity of religious fanaticism? But then how can we concede

---

with a great sweep. Like every paradox, it does not consist solely of false ideas; its part relating to the present period deserves to be read, although it very often deforms the characteristics of the Semitic people. Its historical portion in every case is almost ridiculous... Modern capitalism was born and first developed at the moment when the Jews, rejected almost everywhere, were in no condition to become its precursors." Sayous, *op. cit.*, p. 533.

[10] See Chapter VI.

that religious fanaticism should be most intense precisely in the most developed countries? How can we explain that it was precisely in the Nineteenth Century that anti-Semitism developed most strongly in Poland?

The question then is to seek the causes for the existence of differences in the intensity of religious fanaticism. And thus we are brought back to the duty of studying economic phenomena. Religion explains anti-Jewish persecutions like a soporific explains sleep. If the Jews had really played the role that Sombart attributes to them, it would be very difficult to understand why the development of capitalism was such a mortal blow to them.[11]

It is consequently inaccurate to regard the Jews as founders of modern capitalism. The Jews certainly contributed to the development of exchange economy in Europe but their *specific* economic role ends precisely where modern capitalism starts.

B. THE JEWS IN EASTERN EUROPE UP TO THE NINETEENTH CENTURY

At the dawn of the development of industrial capitalism, Western Judaism was on the road to disappearance. The French Revolution, by destroying the last juridical obstacles which stood in the way of assimilation of the Jews, only gave sanction to an already existing situation.

But it is certainly not by chance that at the same time that the Jewish question was being extinguished in the West, it re-

---

[11] In history "the position of the Jews during the Middle Ages may be compared sociologically with that of an Indian caste in a world otherwise free from castes... Hardly a Jew is found among the creators of the modern economic situation... This type was Christian and only conceivable in the field of Chistianity. The Jewish manufacturer, on the contrary, is a modern phenomenon." Max Weber, *op. cit.*, pp. 358-360.

bounded with redoubled violence in Eastern Europe. In the period when the Jews in Western Europe were being massacred and burned, a large number of Jews had sought refuge in the countries where capitalism had still not penetrated. At the beginning of the Nineteenth Century, the inmense majority of Jews inhabited the East of Europe, principally the former territory of the monarchist republic of Poland. In this paradise of a carefree *Shlachta* (petty nobility), the Jewish commercial class had found a large field of activity. For long centuries, the Jew was a merchant, usurer, publican, steward to the noble, an agent for everything. The small Jewish cities, submerged in a sea of peasant villages, often themselves adjoining the chateaux of the Polish feudal lords, represented exchange economy within a purely feudal society. The Jews were situated, as Marx states, in the pores of Polish society. This situation lasted as long as the social and political organization of Poland remained static. In the Eighteenth Century, following upon political confusion and economic decay, Polish feudalism found itself fatally stricken. Along with it the secular position of the Jews in Eastern Europe was shaken to its foundations. The Jewish problem, close to vanishing in the West, flared up violently in Eastern Europe. The flame, close to extinction in the West, received renewed vitality from the conflagration which arose in the East. The destruction of the economic position of the Jews in Eastern Europe will have as a consequence a massive emigration of Jews into the world. And everywhere, although in different forms and under different guises, the flood of Jewish immigrants coming from Eastern Europe will revitalize the Jewish problem. It is in this respect that the history of the Jews of Eastern Europe has certainly been the decisive factor in the Jewish question in our epoch.

The commercial relations of the Jews of Eastern Europe, of Bohemia, Poland, and Little Russia, date from the Carolingian era. The trading circuit that the Jews had established during the early Middle Ages between Asia and Europe became extended in this way across the fields of Poland and the plains of the Ukraine. Like their coreligionists, the Radamites, the Eastern Jews exchanged the precious products of Asia, spices and silks, for the raw materials of Europe. They constituted the sole commercial element in a purely agricultural society. In the Carolingian era, the economic regime of all Europe being practically the same, the role of Eastern Judaism was similar to that of Western Judaism. It is only later that their history will enter upon completely different paths.

Accounts of the travels of Ibrahim Ibn Jakob (965) testify to the considerable development of Jewish trade at Prague in the Tenth Century. The Jews came there from the Far East and from Byzantium, bringing different kinds of precious merchandise and Byzantine money, and there bought wheat, tin, and furs. In a document of 1090, the Jews of Prague are depicted as traders and money-changers, possessing large sums of silver and gold; they are depicted as the richest merchants among all peoples. Jewish slave merchants, as well as other Jewish traders coming from the Far East and traversing the frontier in caravans, are also mentioned in documents of 1124 and 1226. The interest rate among the Jewish bankers of Prague, whose operations were very extensive, fluctuated between 108 and 180%.[12] The chronicler Gallus states that in 1085, Judith, the wife of Prince Ladislag Herman of Poland, strove to buy back some Christian slaves from Jewish merchants. Excavations undertaken in the past century have helped bring to light the great economic importance of the Jews in Poland in this period. Polish money has been discovered bearing Hebraic characters and dating from the Twelfth and Thirteenth Centuries. This fact in itself proves that Polish trade

---

[12] Schipper, *Jewish History, op. cit.*, vol. II, pp. 77-81.

was in the hands of the Jews. The Tartar invasions of the Thirteenth Century must certainly have had some influence on the Russian and Polish Jews, but as early as 1327, there is a privilege conferred by the Polish King Vladislav Lokietek, involving Hungarian Jewish merchants coming to Cracow. Far from diminishing, Jewish trade in Poland only takes on greater extension in the course of succeeding centuries.

Just as in Western Europe, development of trade went together with an expansion of usury. Here also, the nobility, principal client of the Jewish usurers, strove to obtain restrictions on Jewish usury, as against the kings who favored it —"for the Jews, in their capacity as slaves of the treasury, must always have money ready for our service." In the seym of 1347, the nobility, desiring to limit the interest rate which had reached 108%, collided with the firm resistance of royalty.

In 1456, King Casimir Jagiello, proclaims that in protecting the Jews he is inspired by the principle of tolerance which is imposed upon him by divine law. In 1504, the Polish King Alexander declares that he acts towards the Jews as befits "kings and the powerful who distinguish themselves not only by tolerance towards worshippers of the Christian religion but also towards the adherents of other religions."

Under such auspices, the affairs of Jews could not help but prosper. In the Thirteenth, Fourteenth and Fifteenth Centuries, Jewish usurers succeeded in taking possession of a portion of the lands belonging to the nobles. In 1389, the Jew Sabetai becomes proprietor of a section of the Cawilowo domain. In 1390, the Cracow Jew Iosman receives the property of Prince Diewiez of Pszeslawic as security. In 1393, the Posen Jew Moschko takes possession of the Ponicz manor. In 1397, the lands of the Abiejesz manor are pledged with the Posen Jew Abraham. These lands of the nobles are allotted to the Jews with complete property rights.

Thus, in the last cited example, the noble having attacked the possessions transmitted to Abraham, the tribunal confirms the right of possession of the Jew and punishes the aggressor with a heavy fine. In 1404, the verdict of a tribunal declares that three villages pledged with the Jew Schmerlin of Cracow, are transmitted to him with complete property rights and forever (cum omnibus juribus utilitatibus dominio, etc. in perpetuum).

The most important "bankers" lived in Cracow, residence of the kings. Their principal debtors were in effect the kings, the princes, the voyevode (governors) and the archbishops. Thus Casimir the Great borrowed the enormous sum of 15,000 marks from Jewish bankers. King Louis of Hungary owed the usurer Levko of Cracow 30,000 gulden at one time, 3,000 gulden at another. King Vladislav Jagiello and the queen, Jadwiga, also owed him substantial sums.

Levko was not only a great banker; he was also a wholesale farmer for the kingdom. He leased the Mint and coined its money; and the salt mines of Wieliczka and of Bochnia were also farmed out to him. He owned houses at Cracow, as well as a brewery. Just like the great patricians, he was honored with the title of "vir discretus."

The usury of the great Jewish bankers such as Miesko, Jordan of Posen, and Aron, who succeeded in amassing immense properties and took possession of villages and lands, raised a storm of protest among the nobility. The Statute of Warta (1423) greatly restricted Jewish usury. Thus, in 1432, the Jew Alexander, with whom the villages Dombrowka and Sokolow and a part of their living inventory had been pledged, was forced to return these properties to his debtor by decision of the tribunal, the Statute of Warta having proscribed loans on real property.

The Jews and the kings did not readily resign themselves to this situation. A fierce struggle enabled them to abolish the

Statute of Warta. The bankers were able to expand their sphere of operation. Thus, in 1444, the King pledged his palace at Lemberg to the banker Schina. This usurer also had among his clients Prince Szwidrigiella, the voyevoda Chriczka, who had pledged the village of Winiki with him, etc.

But neither did the nobility accept defeat. It returned continuously to the charge and succeeded in forcing the king to promulgate the Statute of Nieszawa in 1454, with harsher provisions than the Statute of Warta. Nevertheless, and this fact is sufficient to show the fundamental difference which existed in this sphere between Poland and Western Europe, the most Draconian laws were not able to end Jewish usury. Starting with 1455, we even witness a rebirth of the banking trade mainly as a result of the immigration of Jews from Moravia and Silesia, as well as from other countries. From 1460 on, the records of Cracow testify to such an extensive revival of usurious transactions that this period is reminiscent of the epoch of Levko and of Schmerlin. The richest banker is a certain Fischel who had married the female banker Raschka of Prague and who furnished funds to the Polish king, Casimir Jagiello, as well as to his sons, the future kings Albrecht and Alexander. Whereas the nobility of Western Europe, thanks to the penetration of exchange economy and to an abundance of money, succeeded in ridding itself everywhere of Jewish usury, the persistence of feudal economy in Eastern Europe made the nobility powerless on this terrain. Jewish banking survived all proscriptions.

The backward state of the country also fettered the evolution which we have observed in the countries of Western Europe: the eviction of Jews from commerce and their confinement within usury. The bourgeois class and the cities were only beginning to develop. The struggle of the bourgeoisie against the Jews remained in an embryonic state and did not achieve any decisive results. The artisans oppressed by Jewish usury, joined ranks with the traders. Here also, the sooner a province developed, the sooner arose conflicts with the Jews. In 1403, at Cracow, and in 1445 at Bochnia, artisans incite massacres of Jews. But the struggles were only episodic and nowhere ended with the elimination of the Jewish element. On the contrary, in the Sixteenth and Seventeenth Centuries, their situation is only strengthened and Jewish commerce continues to flourish.

In the second half of the Fourteenth Century, we hear of a "syndicate" of three Lemberg Jews, Schlomo, Czewja and Jacob, formed with a view to furnishing Italian merchandise to the city council of Lemberg. At the beginning of the Fifteenth Century, Jews are provisioners of the royal court. In 1456, the starosta of Kamieniec Podolsky confiscates Oriental merchandise worth 600 marks from Jewish merchants coming to Poland from the commercial centers of the Black Sea. The Byzantine and Italian Jews of Capha made numerous trips to Poland. The Jew Caleph Judaeus of Capha passed great quantities of Oriental goods through the customhouse of Lemberg. Even after the destruction of the Italian colonies in the Black Sea (1475) the Jews continued to maintain relations with the Orient. From 1467 on, the Jew David of Constantinople regularly supplied Lemberg with Oriental goods. There is even mention of a renewal of the slave trade in Little Russia from 1440 to 1450. Russian law books recount an interesting fact in 1449: A slave belonging to a Jew Mordecai of Galicia having fled, his owner sues in the courts for his return.

The Jewish merchants of Capha and Constantinople came only to the great fairs of Lemberg and Lublin. To these also came the Jews dispersed throughout the Russian and Polish cities and market towns in order to purchase Oriental goods and spread them throughout the districts which they inhabited. These Jewish merchants travelled the roads running from Lemberg and Lublin through Little and Greater Poland up to the Silesian frontier.

The Jews also crossed this frontier and conducted a very lively trade with Bohemia and Germany. Letters from 1588 inform us that hides and furs were brought from Cracow to Prague and that money was loaned at interest and against pledges.

The fair of Lublin served as the commercial meeting place between the Jewish merchants of Poland and of Lithuania. The Jewish merchants exported hides, furs, timber, honey from Lithuania, and at the Lublin fair they bought spices coming from Turkey and manufactured goods originating in Western Europe. Records of the city of Danzig mention Jewish merchants from Lithuania who exported timber, wax, furs, hides, etc., during the period 1423 to 1436.

The position of Lithuanian Judaism was still more favorable than that of the Polish Jews. Until the Union of Lublin (Union of Poland and Lithuania), the Lithuanian Jews enjoyed the same rights as the entire free population. In their hands lay big business, banking, the customhouses, etc. The farming of taxes and customs brought them great wealth. Their clothes glittered with gold and they wore swords just like the gentry.

Records of the Lithuanian chancellery show that in the period from 1463 to 1494 the Jews had leased almost all the customs offices of the Duchy of Lithuania: Bielek, Bryansk, Brchiczin, Grodno, Kiev, Minsk, Novgorod, Zhitomir. Some documents from the years 1488 and 1489 mention certain Jews of Trock and of Kiev as exploiting the Grand Duke's salt mines. In the same period, we begin to meet Jews in the role of publicans, a profession which in the Polish and Little Russian village goes hand in hand with the trade of usury.

The strengthening of the anarchy of the nobles in Poland necessarily affected the situation of the Jews. In the Sixteenth

Century, their position remains very solid but they pass more and more from royal control to that of the large and small feudal lords. The decline of the royal power makes its protection less effective and the Jews themselves seek less brilliant but surer protectors. King Sigismund complains to the seym of 1539: "The aristocracy of our kingdom wants to monopolize all the profits of the Jews inhabiting the market towns, villages, and manors. It demands the right to judge them. To that we reply: If the Jews themselves resign the privileges of an autonomous jurisdiction which the kings our forefathers granted them and which have also been confirmed by us, they do in fact abandon our protection, and no longer drawing profit from them, we have no reason whatever to impose our kindnesses on them by force."

It is obvious that if the Jews now declined these "kindnesses," it was because royalty no longer had any degree of real power in this country dominated by the nobles.

In the Sixteenth Century, the situation of the Jews became stronger. They received anew all the rights against which attempts had been made in the preceding century. Their economic position improved. The growing power of the nobility (Poland became an electoral kingdom in 1569) deprived them of the protection of the kings but the feudal lords did everything to stimulate their economic activity. The traders, lenders at interest, stewards of the noble manors, with their inns and breweries, were extremely useful to the feudal lords who passed their time abroad in luxury and idleness. "The small towns located on the estates of the nobility were full of shops, of inns, of eating and drinking places, as well as of artisans. The Jew enjoyed absolute freedom if he only succeeded in ingratiating himself into the favor of his lord or 'Poritz.' "[13]

---

[13] Graetz, *Popular History of the Jews*, New York, 1919, vol. V, p. 10.

The economic situation of the Jews was in general very good but their subordinate position to the nobility sapped the basis of the highly developed Jewish autonomy which had existed in Poland. "Circumstances were such at that time that the Jews of Poland could form a state within a state."[14]

With their special religious, administrative and juridical institutions, the Jews constituted a *special* class there enjoying a special internal autonomy.

A decree of Sigismund August (1551) established the following bases for the autonomy of the Jews of Great Poland: The Jews had the right to choose, upon general agreement among themselves, rabbis and judges who were to administer them. The coercive power of the State could be put at their disposal.

Each Jewish city or market town had a community council. In large centers, the community council consisted of 40 members; in small ones, of ten members. The members of this council were elected by a system of double voting.

The activity of the council was very extensive. It had to raise taxes, administer the schools, institutions, decide economic questions, engage in administering justice. The power of each council, called a Kahal, extended to the Jews of the surrounding villages. The councils of the large cities had authority over the small communities. In this way community unions were created, the Galil.

We have already spoken of the Vaad Arba Aratzoth which was the General Assembly of the Jewish councils of Poland (of four countries, Great Poland, Little Poland [Cracow], Podolia [Galicia-Lemberg], and Volhynia), which met at regular intervals and constituted a veritable parliament.

In the Seventeenth Century, the foundations of Jewish autonomy began to rock. This coincided with the worsening of the sit-

---

[14] *Ibid.*, vol. V, p. 28.

uation of Polish Judaism as it began to feel the disagreeable effects of the anarchy that Polish feudal society was passing through. The partial change in the situation of the Jews, arising from the lessening of royal authority, had as result the placing of the Jews in greater contact than previously with the great mass of the bonded population. The Jew, becoming the steward of the noble or a publican, was hated by the peasants equally with or even more than the lords, because he was the one who became the principal instrument for their exploitation. This situation soon led to terrible social explosions, above all in Ukrainia, where the authority of the Polish nobility was weaker than in Poland. The existence of vast steppes permitted the formation of Cossack military colonies where fleeing peasants could prepare their hour of vengeance.

"The Jewish steward strove to draw as much as possible from the manors and to exploit the peasant as much as possible. The Little Russian peasant bore a deep hatred for the Polish landed proprietor, in his double role as foreigner and noble. But he hated even more, perhaps, the Jewish steward with whom he was in continuous contact and in whom he saw at one and the same time the detestable representative of the lord and a 'non-Christian' who was foreign to him both by his religion and his way of life."[15]

The tremendous Cossack revolt of Chmielnicki in 1648 results in completely erasing 700 Jewish communities from the face of the earth. At the same time the revolt demonstrates the extreme feebleness of the anarchic Polish kingdom and prepares its dismemberment. From 1648 on, Poland never ceases to be the prey to invasions and domestic troubles.

With the end of the old feudal state of things in Poland the privileged position of Judaism is likewise finished. Massacres

[15] Graetz.

decimate it; the anarchy which rules the country makes any normal economic activity impossible.

The worsening of the situation of the Jews weakens the old ideological bases of Judaism. Poverty and persecution create a propitious terrain for the development of mysticism. Study of the Kabbala begins to replace that of the Talmud. Messianic movements like that of Sabbatai Zebi take on a certain dimension.

It is also interesting to recall the conversion of Frank and his adherents to Christianity. "The Frankists demanded that they be given a special territory because they did not want to exploit the peasants and live from usury and the exploitation of taverns. They preferred to work the land."[16]

These movements did not take on very great dimensions because the position of Judaism was not as yet definitely compromised. It is only toward the close of the Eighteenth Century that Polish feudal society really begins to cave in under the combined blows of internal anarchy, economic decay and foreign intervention. It is then that the problems of emigration and of passing over to other professions ("productivization") begin to be posed for Judaism.

---

[16] Graetz.

CHAPTER V

EVOLUTION OF THE JEWISH PROBLEM IN THE NINETEENTH CENTURY

At the beginning of the Nineteenth Century, the immense majority of Jews was concentrated in the backward countries of Eastern Europe. In Poland at the time of the partition of the country there were over a million Jews. According to the Russian census of 1818, the social composition of Eastern Judaism was the following:

	BUSINESSMEN	ARTISANS	FARMERS
Ukrainia	86.5%	12.1%	1.4%
Lithuania and White Russia	86.6%	10.8%	2.6%
Together	86.5%	11.6%	1.9%

The percentage of artisans and farmers indicates the beginning of the social differentiation of Judaism. But in a general way, the structure of Eastern Judaism had not yet undergone any important changes; it remained what it had been for many centuries. Certain travellers' stories by soldiers who participated in the Russian campaign of Napoleon constitute invaluable testimony relative to the life of the Jews at the beginning of the Nineteenth Century. "Many of them," says von Furtenbach, "farm out and manage seignorial manors and exploit taverns. Everything is in their hands. They lend money to lords and peasants and they go to purchase merchandise at Leipzig."[1] Another soldier, the Frenchman Puybusque, in his *Lettres sur la Guerre en Russie* (Paris, 1818), supplies interesting information on the role of the Jews in the economic life of the country: "They were the intermediaries between the peasants and the lords. The lords farmed out the taverns to them and compelled them to sell only drinks made in their manors. On the occasion of festivals, baptisms, burials, marriages, the peasants were compelled to buy at least a bucket of whiskey. The Jews sold them on credit but exacted heavy interest. They intervened in all the commercial operations of the country. They were also bankers." The author relates that constant business relations linked the Polish Jews to their brothers in Germany. They had their own postal service and were informed about stock exchange quotations everywhere in Europe.[2]

The author of *Journey of the Moscovite Officer V. Bronevsky from Trieste to Constantinople in 1810* states: "Poland should in all justice be called a Jewish kingdom... The cities and towns are primarily inhabited by them. Rarely will you find a village without Jews. Jewish taverns mark out all the main roads... Apart from some rare manors which are administered by the lords themselves, all the others are farmed out or pledged to the Jews. They possess enormous capitals and no one can get along without their help. Only some few very rich lords are not plunged up to the neck in debt with the Jews."[3] "The Jews in the villages," writes Kamanine in *l'Archive de la Russie Méridionale et Occidentale*, "restrict themselves to farming [leasing] mills, liquor shops and taverns. There is hardly a village without its Jewish 'farmer.' Such is the

[1] F. von Furtenbach, *Krieg gegen Russland und Russische Gefangenschaft*, Leipzig, 1912, pp. 101ff, 204ff.

[2] *Yivo Studies in History*, Wilno, 1937, vol. II, p. 521.

[3] Quoted by Dubnow in "On the Economic History of the Jews in Russia," *Writings on Economics and Statistics* (Yiddish). J. Lestschinsky, editor, Berlin, 1928, vol. I, p. 92.

extent of this that the census often confuses the idea of farmer with that of Jew and links the profession to the nationality or to the religion. Instead of writing 'there is no Jew in the village,' they write: 'there is no "farmer" in the village.' "[4]

Nevertheless, while believing that they were describing the present, these various authors were no longer painting anything but the past. The secular situation of Judaism in Eastern Europe was, very slowly it is true, being swept away in the current of capitalist economy. Even before substituting itself for the old, the new regime was breaking it. The decay of feudalism preceded its replacement by new capitalist forms. "The numerical growth of the Jews demanded new and greater means of subsistence while the old economic positions were vanishing... The Jews, adapted for centuries to a natural economy, felt the ground slipping beneath their feet... In that earlier undeveloped economy they had been the middlemen and had held a virtual monopoly of trade... The process of capitalization in Russia and in Poland now led the landed proprietors to attend personally to various branches of production and to drive the Jews out of them. Only a small section of rich Jews could find a favorable field of action in this new situation."[5]

On the other hand, the immense majority of Jews, consisting of petty merchants, publicans and peddlers, suffered greatly from this new state of things. The old trade centers of the feudal epoch declined. New industrial and commercial cities supplanted the small towns and fairs. A native bourgeoisie began to develop.

"The economic situation of the Jewish masses had become so critical, even before the partition of Poland, that questions of

---

[4] Quoted by Jacob Lestschinsky, *The Development of the Jewish People in the Last 100 Years* (Yiddish), Berlin, 1928, p. 55.

[5] S. B. Weinryb, *Neueste Wirtschaftsgeschichte der Juden in Russland und Polen*, Breslau, 1934, pp. 5-8.

the transformation of the social structure of the Jews and of their emigration became posed automatically."[6] Emigration was possible in this period only within the boundaries of the states into which Poland had been divided. The Jewish masses strove to leave the decadent and backward regions of the former aristocratic kingdom with the continually declining possibilities for subsistence, in order to seek new occupations in the more developed sections of the Empires which had inherited Poland. As early as 1776 and 1778 several Polish Jewish communities ask the Russian government for permission to emigrate to Russia. "At the beginning of the Nineteenth Century, a large stream of emigration is going from former Poland towards Russia."[7] The same was true of the regions annexed by Prussia and Austria. The Jews headed for Berlin, for Vienna, for all the centers in which the pulse of a new economic life was beating, where commerce and industry offered them vast openings. "Jewish emigration from Podolia, Volhynia, White Russia and Lithuania, towards Russia, that of Posnan and Polish Jews to England and even to America, all prove that the Jews of Eastern Europe were looking for countries of immigration as early as the first half of the Nineteenth Century."[8]

This desire for expatriation went hand in hand with attempts to make the Jews into "useful citizens," to adapt them to the new situation by making them artisans and farmers. The Polish "Great Seym" of 1784-1788, already had the problem of the "productivization" of the Jews on its agenda.[9] All the governments which had inherited a section of Polish Judaism considered its social structure as an anomaly. Attempts were made to transform the Jews

---

[6] Lestschinsky, *op. cit.*, p. 25.

[7] *Ibid.*, p. 28.

[9] *Ibid.*, p. 30.

[8] *Ibid.*, p. 29.

into factory workers. Premiums were granted both to artisans who hired Jewish apprentices and to the Jews who became apprentices.[10]

Thousands of Jews were also colonized in certain regions of Russia. Czar Alexander I encouraged this colonization. Despite great difficulties at the start, these villages succeeded in becoming acclimated in the long run.

"Two processes characterize the development of the Jewish people in the course of the last century: the process of emigration and the process of social differentiation... The decay of the feudal system and of feudal property and the rapid growth of capitalism in Central and Eastern Europe created new sources for subsistence, but in a far greater measure they destroyed their positions as intermediaries, by which the greatest part of the Jewish people lived. These processes forced the Jewish masses to change their living places as well as their social appearance; forced them to seek a new place in the world and a new occupation in society."[11]

At the beginning of the Nineteenth Century, the process of "productivization" is still only in its opening phase. On the one hand, the decline of feudal economy is proceeding rather slowly and the Jews are still able to hang on to their old positions for a long time; on the other hand, the development of capitalism is still clothed in quite primitive forms and a great number of Jews find a vast field for occupations in trade and in artisanry.[12] They

---

[10] *Ibid.*, pp. 32-34.

[11] *Ibid.*, p. 1.

[12] The struggle between "Haskalah" (the movement for emancipation) and orthodoxy, between those who wanted to transform the economic life of Judaism as well as its cultural life as against the supporters of old traditions, is a reflection of the antagonism between the new Jewish bourgeoisie profiting from capitalist development and tending towards complete assimilation and the old feudal layers attached to their ancient mode of existence. This struggle continues throughout the entire course of the Nineteenth

played a role as very active commercial agents for young capitalist industry and contributed to the capitalization of agriculture.

In general we may consider that Jewish penetration into capitalist society took place up to the end of the Nineteenth Century. Towards the end of the Nineteenth Century, however, substantial masses of Jews were compelled to leave Eastern Europe.

The annual average of Jewish emigration was:

1830 to 1870	4,000 to 5,000
1871 to 1880	8,000 to 10,000
1881 to 1900	50,000 to 60,000
1901 to 1914	150,000 to 160,000

During the first period, which extends up to 1880, we witness primarily an internal migration directed towards the great cities. From 1830 to 1880, when annual emigration did not exceed 7,000, the Jewish people increased from 3,281,000 to 7,763,000. Consequently, this substantial natural increase was in the main absorbed within the countries inhabited by the Jews. But what an extraordinary change takes place, beginning with 1881 and even more so after 1901, when Jewish emigration reaches the truly impressive figure of 150,000 to 160,000 per annum! What were the causes for this change?

The process of capitalization of Russian economy was accelerated by the reform of 1863. Agriculture began to produce increasingly for the market. The bonds of serfdom and of feudal restrictions became looser; social differentiation progressed rapidly in the village. A section of peasants became transformed into well-to-do farmers; another section became proletarianized. Cap-

---

Century and ends in the defeat of the assimilationists. This defeat is due not so much to the solidity of the old economic forms as to the fragility of the new ones.

italization of agriculture had as effect the opening of an important domestic market for means of production (machines, etc.) and for articles of consumption.

Capitalist production in agriculture means in effect the following: 1. Division of labor within agriculture due to the specialization of its branches. 2. A growing demand for manufactured products by the enriched peasants and by the proletarianized mass which has only its labor power to sell and must purchase its subsistence. 3. Agricultural production for the market necessitates a more and more extensive use of machines, and this develops industry in the means of production. 4. Growth in production of the means of production brings with it a continuous increase of the proletarian mass in the cities, and this contributes also to enlarging the market for means of consumption.

These vast possibilities within the domestic market gave the Jewish masses, crowded out of their former economic positions, the opportunity to integrate themselves into capitalist economy. Workshops and small industries experienced a great expansion.

Whereas the non-Jewish blacksmith or peasant found his way into the factory or the mine, the Jewish proletarianized masses flowed into small industries producing consumers' goods.[13]

But there is a fundamental difference between the transformation of the peasant or blacksmith into a steelworker and the transformation of a Jewish merchant into an artisan or garment worker. Capitalist development of the branches of heavy industry is accompanied by a *change in the material conditions of production.* Not only do the means of production change their destination but they also change their *form.* The primitive tool becomes the perfected modern machine. The same is not true of the means of consumption. Clothing, whether it be produced for

---

[13] This process is analyzed later in the chapter.

the maker's own use or for the local or world market, does not change its appearance. The same is not true of the tool which is transformed into the ever increasingly perfected machine and which *requires the investment of increasingly greater capital.*

In order to undertake the manufacture of machines, it is necessary, from the very beginning, to have a large capital. This is explained, especially in the beginning, by the length of the working period, the "number of consecutive working days required in a certain branch of production for the completion of the finished product."[14] "According as the working period required by the specific nature of the product, or by the useful effect aimed at, is short or long, a continuous investment of additional circulating capital (wages, raw and auxiliary material) is required..."[15]

It is for this reason that from its very beginning production of the means of production has taken place in the capitalist form of large factories, whereas the production of means of consumption can continue to be carried out in the same artisan workshops as before.

It is only much later that the great factory crowds out the workshop and its outmoded methods of work in this latter sphere as well. This follows upon the invention of perfected machines which then invade the sector of the means of consumption. It is, consequently, the growth of fixed capital which here plays a dominant role.[16] In this way conditions of production in these two main sectors of economy are brought to the same level. "Whether a steam-engine transfers its value daily to some yarn, which is the product of a continuous labor-process, or for three months to the

---

[14] Marx, *Capital, op. cit.*, vol. II, p. 262.

[15] *Ibid.*, vol. II, p. 264.

[16] The long persistence of the system of home industry has its basis in the slightness of the fixed capital which it requires. See Max Weber, *op. cit.*, p. 160.

locomotive, which is the product of a continuous process, is immaterial for the investment of the capital required for the purchase of the steam-engine.... In either case, the reproduction of the steam-engine may not take place until after twenty years."[17]

The liberation of the peasants in Russia had created a big market for manufactured products. Instead of an economy still largely feudal, the production of exchange values becomes established. Russia begins to become the granary of Europe. Cities, centers of trade and industry, rapidly develop. The Jews leave the small towns en masse in order to settle in the great urban centers, where they contribute heavily to the development of trade and artisan industry (means of consumption). In 1900, out of 21 important cities in Poland, Jews are an absolute majority in 11 of them. Migration of the Jews into the large cities is accompanied by a social differentiation which shakes the traditional bases of Judaism.

But the development of the means of production sector brings about a mechanization of agriculture and light industry. Machines begin to compete fiercely with the small Jewish artisan workshops. Towards the end of the last century, a great mass of non-Jewish workers migrates to the great cities where the rhythm of increase in the Jewish population is falling off and even coming to a complete halt.[18] Jewish artisan industries, which developed because of the expansion of the domestic market, succumb for the

---

[17] Marx, *Capital, op. cit.*, vol. II, p. 263.

[18] "In the Nineteenth Century, the increase in the Jewish population in the cities of Poland was greater than that of the non-Jewish population. Towards the end of the last century, in the period when large-scale industry was created and when great masses of non-Jewish workers migrated to the cities, the rhythm of Jewish population increase slowed down and in places the movement came to a complete halt." Congrès Juif Mondial, Départment Economique, *La Situation Economique des Juifs dans le Monde*, Paris, 1938, pp. 215-216.

most part because of the mechanization and modernization of industry.

It was difficult for the Jewish artisan to compete with the peasant masses flowing in from the country, who had a very low standard of living and were accustomed to hard physical labor from earliest times. Of course, in some places Jewish workers, surmounting all difficulties, also found a place in mechanized industries, but for the most part they had to take the path of exile at the end of the Nineteenth and beginning of the Twentieth Century. The process of transformation of the Jewish precapitalist merchant into a craft worker is crossed by another process, that of the elimination of the Jewish worker by the machine.[19]

This last process influences the first. The Jewish masses, crowded out of the small towns are no longer able to become proletarianized and are forced to emigrate. Herein, in large part lies the explanation of the enormous growth in Jewish emigration at the end of the Nineteenth and beginning of the Twentieth Century. Whereas dissolution of the old feudal economy and creation of the domestic market had *similar* effects on the Jewish and non-Jewish masses, industrial mechanization and concentration produced opposite results. From that also arise certain different tendencies in Jewish emigration from those of general emigration. Jewish emigration is relatively late and continues to increase, whereas the reverse is often the case for general emigration. For example, in Germany annual emigration, which fluctuated between 100,000 and 200,000 persons from 1880 to 1892, never exceeded 20,000 at the beginning of the Twentieth Century.

---

19 A similar phenomenon can also be seen in the rural sphere. "In those districts where agricultural capitalism is developed most, this process of introducing wage labor, simultaneously with the introduction of machinery, cuts across another process, namely the wage workers are squeezed out by the machines." Lenin, "The Development of Capitalism in Russia," *Selected Works*, vol. I, p. 275.

This heavy drop in German emigration is explained by the tremendous economic development of Germany in this period.

The phenomenon of the elimination of the Jews from industry leads us quite naturally to the subject of the Jewish proletariat.

The confinement of the Jewish working class in consumer goods industries undoubtedly constitutes one of the most remarkable phenomena of the economic and social structure of the Jewish people. The fact that a tiny number of Jewish workers is involved in the initial phases of industrial production, whereas their percentage in the final phases is extremely high, strikingly characterizes what has become known as the Jewish anomaly. This economic base of the Jewish proletariat is not alone weak in itself; it is also continually contracted by technological development. The Jewish workers not only suffer the inconveniences inherent in craft industry, notably social weakness, seasonal employment, sharpening exploitation and bad working conditions, but they are increasingly driven out of their economic positions.

Capitalist economy is characterized by the uninterrupted growth of constant capital at the expense of variable capital, or to put this another way, by the increase in the importance of capital constituted by means of production and the decrease in the importance of capital which buys the form of labor. This economic process produces the familiar phenomena of elimination of the worker by the machine, of annihilation of the artisan workshop by the factory and of a decrease in the specific weight of the section of the class producing consumers' goods relative to the other section which is engaged in the manufacture of means of production.

Official economics thus characterizes this process:

"The one certain fact —and it is a very important one— is that the economic evolution of the past hundred or hundred and fifty years has operated in the direction of the increase in relative importance of fixed capital and the decrease in relative importance of circulating capital."[20]

The more primitive man is the more important is the work which allows him to satisfy his immediate needs. But the more humanity progresses, the more it turns first towards the tool, and later towards the machine which enormously increases its productive power. First the tool is an appendage to man, then man becomes an appendage to the tool.

This recollection of a rather well-known economic process serves but to underline its decisive importance in the specific situation of the Jewish working class and allows us to proceed immediately to our subject. The question which becomes posed immediately and which has not up to now received any attention is to find the historic cause or causes for this state of things.

In the substantial study dedicated to Jewish economy at the beginning of the Nineteenth Century which was undertaken by Lestschinsky in his book *The Development of the Jewish People in the Last* 100 *Years,* he writes as follows on the professional composition of Jewish and non-Jewish artisans in this period:

"The most superficial glance over this comparative statistical material is sufficient to note that those trades were in the hands of Jewish artisans which had the smallest chance of going over to factory production, whereas, precisely to the contrary, the professions most adapted to this transformation were widespread among non-Jewish artisans. In Galicia, non-Jews constituted 99.6% of the metalworkers, 99.2% of the weavers, 98.2% of the blacksmiths, 98.1% of the spinners (whereas, in sharp contrast, 94.3% of the tailors and 70% of the furriers were Jews). These first four trades were the labor foundation on which the textile and metallurgical

---

[20] Ansiaux, *op. cit.*, vol. I, p. 137.

industries were later constructed. Without these trained workers which large-scale industry inherited from artisanry, the birth of these industries would have been impossible... It is in this historic fact that the fundamental cause may lie for the weak penetration of large-scale industry by the Jews. It was no more than natural that the first workers' cadres in the metallurgical and textile plants should consist exclusively of non-Jews. And these compact masses of non-Jewish workers certainly had a natural attractive force for the non-Jewish populations which were closer to them from the religious, national, and psychological point of view, whereas, on the other hand, they repelled the Jewish mass which has remained foreign to them in every way up to this day."[21]

Lestschinsky's explanation contributes to clarifyng the problem with which we are engaged and shows us the first immediate cause for the specific professional structure of the Jewish working class. But in its turn, it places us before a new problem, or rather raises the old one to a new level. If we now clearly see the present Jewish worker as a descendant of the Eighteenth Century artisan, we must still find an explanation of the different professional composition of Jewish and non-Jewish artisans in that period. Why were the former primarily tailors and the non-Jewish artisans blacksmiths? Why were the latter to be found in trades linked with *production,* and the former confined to clothing, producing consequently for *consumption?* To pose the question in this way is practically to resolve it.

Natural economy which ruled Eastern Europe in this period was characterized by the almost exclusive production of use values and implied an almost complete absence of the division of labor (into trades).

Each family was self-sufficient or practically so, producing

---

[21] Lestschinsky, *op. cit.,* p. 60.

everything necessary for the satisfaction of its needs. Here is how Vandervelde describes this state of affairs:

"Each family is sufficient to itself or practically so: it is lodged in a house made of timber coming from the nearest forest, and obtains straw and mortar right on the spot. It warms itself exclusively and primarily with turf, heather, furze, dead wood gathered in the vicinity. It spins, weaves, transforms flax and hemp of its own harvesting into clothes; it feeds itself with its own wheat, potatoes, vegetables... it bakes its bread, makes its wine... or beer, dries its own tobacco, exchanges its eggs and butter against rare goods which it secures from without: candles, oil, ironware, etc. In short, it produces almost everything which it consumes and consumes all that it produces, selling only what is strictly necessary to meet very limited money expenses."[22]

The same could be said, with very little correction, regarding the feudal manor.

It is readily understandable that while such an economic system does not *absolutely* exclude professional specialization, the few trades that find a place within it are the products of quite exceptional conditions.

"We should consider the labors of the blacksmith and the potter as the first which rose to special professions because they demanded from the very beginning more skill and more specialized working equipment. Even among nomad peoples, special artisans devoted themselves to the iron trade."[23]

It is therefore easy to understand that even in the era of

---

[22] Emile Vandervelde, *L'Exode Rural et le Retour aux Champs*, Paris, 1903, p. 70.

[23] A. Menes, "Craft Industry among the Jews in Biblical and Talmudic Times," *Writings on Economics and Statistics* (Yiddish), J. Lestschinsky, editor, Berlin, 1928, vol. I, p. 65.

natural economy, the trades of blacksmith and of weaver[24] were spread throughout the villages and abounded in the cities, which, in Eastern Europe, were almost exclusively military and administrative centers.

"In Galicia, in Bucovina, in many parts of Hungary, Romania and Transylvania, as among the Yugoslav peoples, there were up to recent times no artisans other than blacksmiths."[25]

Non-Jewish artisanry in Eastern Europe was therefore the product of special causes which, in a society based on natural and not exchange economy, nevertheless requires an exchange of services.

Completely different was the point of departure of Jewish artisanry. *It was born in the specific conditions of the small Jewish town and produced for that town.*

But whoever speaks of the small Jewish town of the Eighteenth Century speaks of an agglomeration of small traders, publicans, bankers and intermediaries of all sorts.[26]

The Jewish artisan therefore did not work for the peasant *producers,* but for the merchants, the banker *intermediaries.* It is here that we must seek the fundamental cause for the specific

---

[24] The trade of weaver, like that of the blacksmith, demanded a special professional formation and early became separated from household economy. The weaver in the feudal era is a traveler who moves from one place to another, from one village to another, in pursuing his trade.

[25] Ansiaux, *op. cit.*

[26] All the Jews did not live in small towns, far from it, but their social role in the large cities or in the village was the same as in the small town. The latter, however, by its specific aspect, best characterized this social role. According to a governmental census in 1818, in Ukrainia and Byelo-Russia:

86.5% of the Jews were traders
11.6% of the Jews were artisans
1.9% of the Jews were farmers.

In Galicia, in 1820, 81% of the traders were Jews.

professional structure of the Jewish proletariat and of its ancestor, Jewish artisanry. The non-Jewish artisan did not produce articles of consumption for the peasant because, as we have seen, the latter was sufficient to himself in this regard. But that was precisely the principal occupation of the Jewish artisan, his clientele being composed of men devoted to trade in money and in goods, thus non-producers by definition. Alongside of the peasant, we find the non-Jewish blacksmith artisan; close to the money man, we find the Jewish tailor.[27]

The professional difference existing between the Jewish and non-Jewish artisans therefore derives in the last analysis from the difference in their spheres of activity.

It goes without saying that this explanation is necessarily schematic and like all schemas allows us to understand phenomena in their general aspect but cannot present the diversity of real life with complete exactness. But to try to reflect the latter with exactness and in detail would mean in turn to make it difficult to understand the general processes which derive from it. Sociology is therefore compelled to make a complete and continuous circuit: from reality to theoretical schema and the reverse. Those who reproach this method for not reflecting the entire diversity of life, have not completely understood this dialectical interdependence.

It should also be noted that the struggles which broke out in certain periods between Jewish and non-Jewish artisans appear to have been provoked by the *encroachment* of one section of artisans upon the sphere of activity of another and should not be attributed to some alleged national competition which was simply inconceivable in the feudal epoch because it

[27] Certain crafts, close to trade, were also often exercised by Jews. Such was the goldsmith's craft.

is prior to the formation of nations. "Nationality" is "a sentiment unknown to the heterogeneous society of the Middle Ages."[28]

By way of illustration, we quote this passage from an ancient chronicle of Prague, the *Ramschackie Chronik* of 1491: "Jews were forbidden to do work for Christians but they were all free to work for Jewish clients."

The city council of Prague also complains in the same period: "that the Jews pay no attention to the old privileges and ordinances whereby they are forbidden to work for Christians." "At Posen," states Graetz, "Jews were allowed to engage in certain trades, like that of tailoring, but only to satisfy their own needs and not for Christians."

It seems to me that we have thus traversed the causal chain leading from the present-day economic structure of the Jewish proletariat back to its origins. It is complete in this sense that it brings us back to the social problem of a more general order, which has already been explored: that of the social and economic function of the Jews in the precapitalist era.

---

[28] Pirenne, *Belgian Democracy, Its Early History, op. cit.*, p. 143.

CHAPTER VI

CONTRADICTORY TRENDS IN THE JEWISH PROBLEM DURING THE PERIOD OF THE RISE OF CAPITALISM

The French Revolution put the finishing touches to the course of the economic and social evolution of Judaism in Western Europe. The development of industrial capitalism will speed up the penetration of the Jews into the ranks of the bourgeoisie and their cultural assimilation. The triumphant march of the Napoleonic armies was the signal for Jewish emancipation everywhere. Napoleonic policy reflected the will of bourgeois society to assimilate the Jews completely. But in the regions still ruled by the feudal system, important difficulties surged across the road to emancipation. Thus, contrary to the Jews of Bordeaux, completely absorbed into the bourgeois class, the Alsatian Jews were little differentiated from their ancestors of the Middle Ages. The peasant riots against Jewish usury compelled Napoleon to promulgate exceptional laws against Alsatian Judaism. Bourgeois juridical norms proved inapplicable to a feudal state of society. The same was true of Poland where formal legality for all citizens before the law introduced by Napoleon was not applicable to Jews "for a period of ten years" —as the face-saving formula put it. It is necessary to add that the great mass of Polish Jews, led by fanatical rabbis, was resolutely opposed to emancipation. Except for a small layer of wealthy bourgeois, the Polish Jews in no way felt the need for civil equality.

But in general, from the beginning of the Nineteenth Century, Western Judaism enters on the road of complete assimilation. By the end of the Eighteenth Century, one half of the Jews of Berlin had become converted to Christianity in a period of 30 years. Those who remained faithful to the Jewish religion vigorously denied that they formed a distinct nation. "Without a land, without a state, without a language, there can be no nation, and that is why Judaism long ago ceased to constitute a nation," said Riesser, one of the representatives of the German Jews in the first half of the Nineteenth Century.[1] "We are Germans, and Germans only, in whatever concerns nationality," a Jewish professor of Berlin wrote somewhat later, in 1879.

Contrary to Western Europe, where their assimilation was favored by capitalism, in Eastern Europe capitalism uprooted the Jews from their secular economic positions. Thus, by provoking a flow of Jews towards the West with its left hand, it was destroying the accomplishments of its right hand. Waves of Eastern Jews continuously flowed towards the Western countries and instilled new life into the moribund body of Judaism.[2]

"Our great popular masses of the East, who are still rooted in Jewish tradition, or at least live in its atmosphere, form a barrier to the disappearance of Western Judaism... *Western Judaism no longer exists save as a reflection of Eastern Judaism.*"[3]

In order to understand the importance of the immigration

---

[1] S. M. Dubnow, *Die Neueste Geschichte des Jüdischen Volkes*, Berlin, 1920-1924, vol. II, p. 42.

[2] "The flow of Eastern Jews into Western Europe stopped and probably saved the Western Jews from the complete disappearance which was inevitable." Lestschinsky, *op. cit.*, p. 9.
"Without immigration from Eastern Europe, the small Jewish communities of England, France and Belgium would probably have lost entirely their Jewish character. Also German Jewry...." Ruppin, *op. cit.*, p. 63.

[3] Jacob Klatzkin *Poleme des Modernen Judentum*, Berlin, 1918, p. 46.

of Jews from Eastern Europe, it is sufficient to recall that in Vienna, at the beginning of the Nineteenth Century, there were only several hundred Jews, and that in the Twentieth Century, their number reached 176,000.

The massive emigration of Jews to Western Europe and mainly to America went hand in hand with a complete transformation of the territorial structure of Judaism. We know that the advance of capitalism was accompanied by an enormous extension of urban developments. From the middle of the Nineteenth Century on, the great centers of commercial and industrial life became a powerful attractive pole for the Jews.

The concentration of the Jewish masses in great cities was as obvious in the countries of immigration as in the regions from which the Jews originated. The Jews en masse forsook the little towns which had for centuries been the centers of their economic life and flowed either into the commercial and industrial cities of Poland and Russia, or towards the great cities of the Western world, Vienna, London, Berlin, Paris and New York. "Far into the Nineteenth Century the greater part of world-Jewry inhabited Eastern Europe, where in the absence of good means of communication small towns continued to offer opportunities to traders [and] during that period the Jews lived predominantly in small towns.... According to a statistical survey of the Polish provinces of Kiev, Volhynia and Podolia, made in the second half of the Eighteenth Century, there were in every village, on the average, seven Jewish inhabitants, *i. e.,* one Jewish family. But there were innumerable villages and very few towns; in East Galicia, therefore, 27% of the Jewish population lived in villages, and in West Galicia, even 43.1%.... Similar conditions prevailed in a few German states, for instance, in Hesse and Baden."[4]

This condition underwent a decisive change in the Twentieth

---

[4] Ruppin, *op. cit.*, pp. 31-33.

Century. Substantial Jewish masses became concentrated in the urban centers of the world.

In Russia, between 1847 and 1926, the Jewish population in communities numbering more than 10,000 multiplied eightfold. In 1847, there were only three Jewish communities comprising more than 10,000 people in the entire Russian Empire. There were 28 of these in 1897 and 38 in 1926 (in the old territory of Holy Russia).

The percentage of Russian Jews living in large communities was:

1847	5 %
1897	28.2%
1926	50.2%

Here are the corresponding figures for Germany:

1850	6 %
1880	32 %
1900	61.3%

More than three-quarters of American Jews are presently living in communities of more than 10,000 persons. The tremendous Jewish agglomerations of New York (two million), Warsaw (300,000 to 500,000), Paris, London, etc., bear witness to the fact that the Jews have become the "greatest urban people in the world." The concentration of the Jewish masses in the great cities undoubtedly constitutes one of the most important phenomena of Jewish life in the modern capitalist epoch.

We have already examined the difference between Jewish emigration up to 1880 and the exodus after that date. Up to 1880, the states inhabited by the Jews still offered vast possibilities for penetration into capitalist economy; migration was primarily internal. After this date, events are precipitous: feudal economy is smashed to bits and with it goes the ruin of the artisan branches of capitalism in which the Jews are very widely represented. The Jews begin to forsake their countries of origin in great masses.

"Between 1800 and 1880 the number of Jews in the United States, the main destination of Jewish emigrants, rose from a few thousands to 230,000 — which points to an average yearly immigration of about 2,000; between 1881 and 1899, the yearly average reached 30,000, and between 1900 and 1914, 100,000. Adding the emigration to other over-sea countries (Canada, the Argentine, South Africa, Palestine, etc.) and to Central and Western Europe, the total Jewish emigration from Eastern Europe during the years 1800 to 1880 must be put at about 250,000, *i. e.* a yearly average of about 3,000; for 1881-1899, at 1,000,000, and a yearly average of about 50,000; and for 1900-1914 at 2,000,000, and an average of 135,000. Percentually these figures place the East European Jews first among emigrant nations; about the middle of the period 1881-1914, their number in Russia, Galicia, and Romania amounted to about six and one-half millions, and measured by that figure, the emigrants formed about 46%. The corresponding Italian rate, which is otherwise the highest in Europe, was only 15% after the re-emigrants have been deducted —these were numerous among the Italians, but very few among the Jews."[5]

This great emigration was favored by the high birthrate of the Jews. Their number in the world rose as follows:

1825	3,281,000
1850	4,764,500
1880	7,663,000
1900	10,602,500
1925	14,800,500

[5] Ruppin, *op. cit.*, p. 45.

Between 1825 and 1925, the number of Jews multiplied five times, a rate of increase one and one-half times larger than that of the population of Europe.

"The number of Jews must certainly exceed 18 million at the present time. It is important to note that despite the high emigration figures, not only has the number of Jews in Eastern Europe not decreased but it has even greatly increased." "Judaism in Eastern Europe sent abroad almost four million persons in the course of the last thirty-five years and yet not only has the number of Jews in Eastern Europe not diminished during this period but it has greatly increased; it has gone from less than six to eight millions."[6]

Emigration contributed to the social differentiation of Judaism, a process which had made rapid progress in the course of the Nineteenth Century.

At least 90% of the Jews were agents and merchants at the beginning of the capitalist era. In the Twentieth Century, we can consider that in America we have almost two million Jewish proletarians, who are almost 40% of all the economically active Jews.[7]

---

[6] *Yiddishe Economic*, Wilno, January-February 1938, p. 11.

[7] The percentage of employees and workers was:

England	77 %	(1923)
U. S. A	75 %	(1920)
Belgium	73 %	(1910)
Germany	62 %	(1907)
France	48 %	(1906)
Poland	24.8%	(1921)
Russia	15 %	(1925)
Jews	35.8%	

Here is the professional division for all Jews in 1932:

Trade (including transportation, amusement, banking)	6,100,000	(38.6%)
Industry (including mining and artisanry)	5,750,000	(36.4%)
Liberal professions and administration ...	1,000,000	(6.3%)
Agriculture	625,000	(4%)
Part-time workers and domestics	325,000	(2%)
No trade (living from incomes, pensions, or charity)	2,000,000	(12.7%)
	15,800,000	

The number of Jewish workers, relatively low in the backward countries like Poland where it reaches about 25% of all persons economically active, reaches 46% in America. The professional structure of the Jewish working class still differs greatly from that of the proletariats of other peoples. Thus white collar workers form 30 to 36% of all Jewish wage earners, which is a proportion three to four times as great as among other nations. Agricultural workers, practically completely missing among the Jews, constitute from 15 to 25% of non-Jewish workers. Sixty to 70% of the Jews employed in industry are in reality worker-artisans (in Eastern Europe 80% of the proletarians work in shops and not in factories) whereas among the workers of other nationalities, 75 to 80% are factory workers. Finally, the Jewish workers are employed primarily in branches of consumer goods; non-Jewish workers in the same branches form only a small percentage of the proletariat as a whole.

Comparative statistics of the professional division of Jewish and "Aryan" workers will permit of an easier grasp of this phenomenon.

In several European countries	*Jews*	*Non-Jews*
Clothing	43.7	8.5
Food	11.0	9.5
Leather	10.5	1.7
Metallurgy	8.6	19.9
Lumber	7.9	6.9
Textiles	6.8	12.0
Building	4.2	15.2
Printing and paper	3.2	3.2
Others	3.8	22.1

In Poland (1931)[8]	*Jewish workers*	*Non-Jewish workers*
Artisanry	58.7	33.2
Business and transportation	18.7	12.5
Home work	9.2	1.9
Small industry	8.9	9.6
Medium and large industry	3.8	23.0
Mines	.4	8.4
Electricity, water, railroads	.3	8.9
Foundries		2.5

These statistics clearly show that the Jews are employed primarily in artisanry whereas non-Jewish workers, on the contrary, are concentrated mainly in heavy industry. Jews are relatively five times more numerous than non-Jewish workers in the clothing industry, but in metallurgy, the textile industry and building, non-Jewish workers are two or three times more numerous than Jewish workers.

[8] *Yiddishe Economic*, July-August, 1938, p. 317.

However, while the professional structure of the Jewish working class still differs greatly from that of the non-Jewish, poverty is driving them more and more to the penetration, despite all barriers, into professions which have been inaccessible to them up to now.

Some twenty years ago, when a great industrialist of Lodz was asked about the ban against Jewish workers in his factories, he replied: "I do not want to have two thousand partners in my business." But prior to this war [World War II], 15% of Jewish workers were operating machines.

Judaism has therefore undergone a very important transformation in the capitalist epoch. The people-class has become differentiated socially. But this process, while of considerable scope, is accompanied by a multitude of contradictory tendencies, which have not as yet allowed the crystallization of a stable form for Judaism in our period. It is far easier to say what Judaism has been than to define what it is.

In effect, the evolution of the Jewish question resulting from capitalist development has been thrust onto diametrically opposite paths. On the one hand, capitalism favored the economic assimilation of Judaism and consequently its cultural assimilation; on the other hand, by uprooting the Jewish masses, concentrating them in cities, provoking the rise of anti-Semitism, it stimulated the development of Jewish nationalism. The "renaissance of the Jewish nation," the formation of a modern Jewish culture, elaboration of the Yiddish language, Zionism, all these accompany the processes of emigration and of the concentration of Jewish masses in the cities and go hand in hand with the development of modern anti-Semitism. In all parts of the world, along all the roads of exile, the Jewish masses, concentrated in special quarters, created their own special cultural centers, their newspapers, their Yiddish schools. Naturally it was in the countries of greatest

Jewish concentration, in Russia, Poland, and the United States, that the national movement took on its greatest scope.

But the development of history is dialectical. At the same time that the bases for a new Jewish nationality were being elaborated all the conditions were likewise being created for its disappearance. Whereas the first Jewish generations in the countries of immigration still remained firmly attached to Judaism, the new generations rapidly lost their special customs and language.

"Among the East European immigrants to Western Europe, America and other non-European countries, Yiddish is still retained, at any rate in the first generation, though a large number of English words are introduced, so that it is growing into a dialect different from the Polish or Lithuanian Yiddish. The second generation speak both Yiddish and the language of the country, while the third no longer know Yiddish..."[9] "The Yiddish press in the United States developed strongly during the last fifty years because of the coming in of more than two million East European Jews who knew no English.... But of recent years, a marked decline has set in of the Yiddish press, immigration having stopped, while the younger generation is becoming Americanized."[10]

In 1920, according to official statistics, Yiddish was the mother tongue of 32.1% of American Jews; in 1930, of 27.8%. In Hungary, Yiddish disappeared almost completely. In the census of 1920, 95.2% declared Hungarian as their mother tongue, 4% German and .8% other languages.

Throughout the world: in 1900, 60.6% of the Jews spoke Yiddish; in 1930, 42.7% of the Jews spoke Yiddish.

During this same period that the use of Yiddish is declining, we witness a considerable growth in mixed marriages. The more

---

[9] Ruppin, *op. cit.*, pp. 289-290.

[10] *Ibid.*, p. 351.

highly developed the country, the more frequent are its mixed marriages.

In Bohemia, 44.7% of all marriages in which at least one party was Jewish were mixed marriages. As against this, the number of mixed marriages in sub-Carpathian Russia and Slovakia was insignificant.[11]

Ratio of mixed marriages between Jews and non-Jews to purely Jewish marriages:[12]

Berlin	1901-1904	35.4%
	1905	44.4%
Hamburg	1903-1905	49.5%
Trieste	1900-1903	61.5%
Copenhagen	1880-1889	55.8%
	1890-1899	68.7%
	1900-1905	82.9%

An increase in conversions is also noted. Thus in Vienna, the average of Jewish conversions went from .4% in 1870 to 4.4% in 1916-1920. However, the general weakening of religion removes most of the importance from this index.

---

[11] *Yiddishe Economic*, April-June, 1939, p. 176.

[12] Based on Ruppin, *op. cit.* Leon's operation on Ruppin's statistics here appears to be incorrect. We therefore append an abstract of Ruppin's table (pp. 319-320). Despite the differences. these confirm Leon's contention. *Tr.*

City	*Year or Period*	*To every 100 Jews entering marriage, mixed marriages were contracted by*
Berlin	1901-1904	15.06%
	1929	29.21%
Hamburg	1906-1910	24.30%
	1928	3.83%
Trieste	1900-1903	17.9 %
	1927	56.1 %
Copenhagen	1880-1889	21.84%
	1900-1905	31.76%

We thus see how precarious are the bases for the "national renaissance" of Judaism. Emigration, at first a powerful obstacle to assimilation and a "nationalization" factor of the Jews, rapidly changes into an instrument of fusion of the Jews with other peoples. The concentration of Jewish masses in the great cities, which thus became a sort of "territorial base" for the Jewish nationality, cannot long impede the process of assimilation. The atmosphere of the great urban centers constitutes a melting pot in which all national differences are rapidly wiped out.

While capitalism first created conditions for a certain Jewish "national renaissance," by uprooting millions of Jews, by tearing them from their traditional living conditions and concentrating them in large cities, it soon contributes to accelerating the process of assimilation. The development of Yiddish, for example, is followed by its rapid decline. Capitalist development, although at times in rather unexpected ways, ends with the fusion of the Jews among other peoples. But at the beginning of the Twentieth Century, the signs of capitalist degeneration become manifest. The Jewish question, which seems to be developing normally in the Nineteenth Century, rebounds with unprecedented sharpness as a result of the decline of capitalism. The solution of the Jewish question appears to be farther off than ever.

CHAPTER VII

THE DECAY OF CAPITALISM AND THE TRAGEDY OF THE JEWS IN THE TWENTIETH CENTURY

The primary merit of the capitalist regime lay in its tremendous expansion of the productive forces, its creation of a world economy, its permitting an unprecedented development of technology and science. As against the stagnation of the feudal world, capitalism presented an unparallelled dynamism. Hundreds of millions of people, immobilized up to then in a routinized, horizonless existence, suddenly found themselves drawn into the current of a feverish and intensive life.

The Jews lived within the pores of feudal society. When the feudal structure started to crumble, it began expelling elements which were, at one and the same time, foreign to it and indispensable to it. Even before the peasant had left the village for the industrial center, the Jew had abandoned the small medieval town in order to emigrate to the great cities of the world. The destruction of the secular function of Judaism within feudal society is accompanied by its passive penetration into capitalist society.

But if capitalism has given humanity certain tremendous conquests, only its disappearance can allow humanity to enjoy them. Only socialism will be able to lift humanity to the level of the material bases of civilization. But capitalism survives and all the enormous acquisitions turn more and more against the most elementary interests of humanity.

The progress of technology and science has become the progress of the science of death and its technology. The development of the means of production is nothing but the growth of the means of destruction. The world, become too small for the productive apparatus built up by capitalism, is constricted even further by the desperate efforts of each imperialism to extend its sphere of influence. While unbridled export constitutes an inseparable phenomenon of the capitalist mode of production, decaying capitalism tries to get along without it, that is to say, it adds to its disorders the disorder of its own suppression.

Powerful barriers impede the free circulation of merchandise and men. Insurmountable obstacles arise before the masses deprived of work and bread following the breakdown of the traditional feudal world. The decay of capitalism has not only accelerated the decomposition of feudal society but has multiplied a hundredfold the sufferings which resulted from it. The bearers of civilization, in a blind alley, bar the road to those who wish to become civilized. Unable to attain civilization, the latter are still less able to remain in the stage of barbarism. To the peoples whose traditional bases of existence it has destroyed, capitalism bars the road of the future after having closed the road of the past.

It is with these general phenomena that the Jewish tragedy of the Twentieth Century is tied up. The highly tragic situation of Judaism in our epoch is explained by the extreme precariousness of its social and economic position. The first to be eliminated by decaying feudalism, the Jews were also the first to be rejected by the convulsions of dying capitalism. The Jewish masses find themselves wedged between the anvil of decaying feudalism and the hammer of rotting capitalism.

A. THE JEWS IN EASTERN EUROPE

The entire situation of Judaism in Eastern Europe is explained by the combination of the decline of the old feudal forms and of the degeneration of capitalism. The social differentiation which took place in the village as a result of capitalist penetration brought about an influx into the cities of enriched as well as proletarianized peasants; the former wanted to invest their capital; the latter to offer their labor. But the openings for the placement of capital were as slight as those for work. Hardly born, the capitalist system already showed all the symptoms of senility. The general decay of capitalism manifested itself in crises and unemployment within the countries of Eastern Europe; by the closing of all the outlets for emigration outside their frontiers. Seven to eight million peasants were landless and almost without work in "independent" Poland. Placed between two fires, the Jews were exposed to the hostility of the petty bourgeoisie and the peasantry, who sought to find a place for themselves at the expense of the Jews. "Jewish positions are particularly threatened by the urban Polish bourgeoisie and by the rich peasants who seek a solution for their difficulties through a fierce economic nationalism, whereas the Polish working class suffering from permanent unemployment, seeks a remedy for its poverty through social liberation and puts its reliance upon economic and political solidarity rather than upon a sterile and murderous competition...."[1]

It is precisely in the regions which capitalism had most developed that a non-Jewish commercial class formed most rapidly. It is there that the anti-Semitic struggle was fiercest. "The decrease in the number of Jewish shops has been greatest in the

---

[1] Congrès Juif Mondial, *op. cit.*, pp. 246-247.

central provinces, that is to say, in a region where the population is purely Polish, where the peasants have attained a higher standard of living, where industry is more developed, which is very important for the material and intellectual situation of the village."[2]

Whereas in 1914, 72 percent of the stores in the villages were Jewish, this fell to 34 percent in 1935, that is to say, by more than one-half. The situation was better for the Jews in territories less developed economically. "The participation of Jews in commerce is more important in the most backard provinces," maintains Lipovski. "The eastern sections belonging to White Russians are, in all their relations —economic, intellectual and political— the most backward part of Poland. In these regions, the absolute majority of Jewish businessmen has increased by a third."[3] In 1938, 82.6 percent of the shops in the backward regions of Poland were in the hands of Jews.[4]

All of these facts are further proof that the destruction of feudalism is at the bottom of the Jewish question in Eastern Europe. The more backward a region is, the more easily are the Jews able to preserve their secular positions. But it is the general decay of capitalism which renders the Jewish question impossible of solution. The crisis and chronic unemployment make it impossible for the Jews to go into other professions, producing a frightful crowding in the professions which they follow and unceasingly augmenting anti-Semitic violence. The governments of the provincial nobles and large capitalists naturally endeavored to organize the anti-Jewish current and thereby divert the masses from their real enemy. "Resolve the Jewish question" became for them a synonym for the solution of the social question. In order

---

[2] *Ibid.*, p. 249.

[3] *Ibid.*, p. 249.

[4] *Yiddishe Economic*, September-October 1938, p. 437.

to make place for the "national forces," the state organized a systematic struggle for "dejudifying" all the professions. The methods of "Polanizing" business in Poland proceeded from simple boycotting of Jewish stores by means of propaganda, right up to pogroms and incendiarism. Here, by way of example, is a "victory bulletin" published June 14, 1936, in the governmental paper *Illustrowany Kurjer codzienny*: "One hundred and sixty Polish business positions were conquered during the first months of this year in the Madom district. At Przktyk alone (notorious pogrom city) 50 business licenses were purchased by Poles. All in all, 2,500 Polish business positions were conquered in the various districts."[5]

Jewish craftsmanship was no more tenderly handled by the Polish governments. Boycott, exorbitant taxes, Polish examinations (thousands of Jewish craftsmen did not know this language), contributed to grinding down the Jewish artisans. Deprived of unemployment relief, the craft proletariat was one of the most disinherited. The wages of Jewish workers were very low and their living conditions frightful (work day up to 18 hours).

The universities constituted the favorite arena for the anti-Semitic struggle. The Polish bourgeoisie exerted all its efforts to prevent Jews from entering the intellectual professions. The Polish universities became places of veritable pogroms, throwing people out of windows, etc. Well before Hitler's stars of David, the Polish bourgeoisie initiated ghetto benches in the universities. "Legal" measures, more circumspect but no less effective, rendered entry into the universities almost impossible for the Jewish youth, whose ancestral heritage had strongly developed their intellectual facul-

---

[5] At Warsaw in 1882, 79.3 percent of businessmen were Jews; in 1931, 51.4 percent of the business men were Jews. Jacob Lestschinsky, *Der Wirtschaftliche Zusammenbruch der Juden in Deutschland u. Polen*, Paris, 1938, p. 48.

ties. The percentage of Jewish students in Poland declined from 24.5 percent in 1923-1933 to 13.2 percent in 1933-1936.[6]

The same policy of excluding Jewish students was followed in Lithuania and Hungary. The percentage of Jewish students in Lithuania declined from 15.7 percent in 1920 to 8.5 percent in 1931; in Hungary, from 31.7 percent in 1918 to 10.5 percent in 1931. In general the situation of the Jews in Hungary had for centuries resembled in every way that of Poland.

In the country of great feudal magnates, the Jews for a long time played the role of an intermediary class between the lords and the peasants. "One of our correspondents reminds us that at the end of the Nineteenth Century, a certain Count de Palugyay had great trouble in avoiding expulsion from the National Club of the Hungarian nobility at Budapest, because he wanted to take charge personally of the industrial transformation of his agricultural products, particularly the distillation of alcohol and whiskey from potatoes; he had even gone so far as to take charge of their sale!

"The liberal professions were likewise not unaffected by this prejudice, which was as widespread among the high aristocracy as among the petty nobility. Shortly before the fall of the dual monarchy, a Hungarian magnate expressed his disgust of noble-

---

[6] In the period when Jewish and non-Jewish petty-bourgeois intellectuals represent Hitler as the sole responsible party for anti-Semitism in our time, in the period when the United Nations, among them Poland, lay claim to being defenders of the "rights of man" — recalling this fact will most certainly not be devoid of usefulness. Of course Hitler organized, in a premeditated way, the destruction of European Judaism, and personified capitalist barbarism in this sphere as in others. But the various more or less "democratic" governments which followed each other in Poland could not have learned very much from him. The disappearance of Hitler can change nothing fundamental in the situation of the Jews. A transitory improvement of their condition will in no wise alter the profound roots of Twentieth Century anti-Semitism.

men, who 'for money, examined the throats of individuals whom they did not know.' A natural consequence of this attitude was that the Jews formed the intermediary class between the peasantry and the nobility, particularly in the towns... Trade, and especially petty trade, was a Jewish matter in the eyes of the people.

"Even today, in the minds of the masses of the Magyar population, the shop, and in a general way everything connected with the exploitation of the shop, are thought of as Jewish, even if this shop has become an instrument of economic struggle against the Jews.

"Here is a story which strikingly illustrates this state of mind: A peasant woman sent her son on some purchasing errands. She wanted them taken care of at the semi-state-ized *Hangya* cooperative and not at a Jewish shop, so she said to him: 'Pista, go to the Jew; not to the Jew who is a Jew, but to the new shop.'"[7]

The process of elimination of the Jews from their economic positions took place in all of Eastern Europe. The situation of the Jewish masses became hopeless. A declassed youth, having no possibility of integrating itself into economic life, lived in black despair. Prior to the second war, 40 percent of the Jewish population of Poland had to resort to philanthropic institutions. Tuberculosis raged.

"Let us give the floor to correspondents of the Economic and Statistical Section of the Jewish Scientific Institute residing in regions where despair and the complete absence of a better future were stifling the Jewish youth. Here is what one wrote of Miedzyrzecze, province of Volhynia: 'The condition of the Jewish youth is very difficult, notably that of the sons and daughters of tradesmen who are without work because their parents do not require assistance. It is impossible to open new businesses. Seventy-five

---

[7] Congrès Juif Mondial, *op. cit.*, pp. 120-121.

boys and 120 young girls, aged 15 to 28 years, have no hope whatever of integrating themselves into the economic life of the country.' Of Sulejow (province of Lodz) we are in possession of a more detailed picture, which is characteristic of the small towns of Poland: 'Almost 50 percent of the children of Jewish business people work with their parents, but solely because they are unable to find another job. Twenty-five percent are learning some sort of trade and twenty-five percent are completely idle. Seventy percent of the children of artisans remain in the workshops of their parents even though the latter are almost without work and can very well get along without assistants. Ten percent are learning new trades... twenty percent have nothing to do. The sons of rabbis and of employees of Jewish communities are trying to attain a livelihood by learning a trade. The entire youth desires to emigrate, 90 percent to Palestine, but because of the limited number of emigration visas, their chances are slim. And yet they are ready to go to the North Pole or the South Pole, just so long as they can tear themselves out of this stagnation. More and more the youth is turning towards the crafts and the number of young people in business is on the decline.' "[8]

B. THE JEWS IN WESTERN EUROPE

The condition of Judaism, rendered hopeless in Eastern Europe by the combined decay of feudalism and capitalism —which created a stifling atmosphere filled with insane antagonisms —had repercussions of a certain worldwide character. Western and Central Europe became the theater of a frightful rise of anti-Semitism. Whereas the reduction in Jewish emigration, whose average annual rate declined from 155,000 between 1901 and 1914 to 43,657

---

[8] *Ibid.*, p. 254.

between 1926 and 1935, greatly aggravated the situation of the Jews in Eastern Europe, the general crisis of capitalism made even this reduced emigration an intolerable burden to the western countries.[9]

The Jewish question reached unprecedented sharpness not only in the countries of emigration but in the countries of immigration as well. Even before the first imperialist war, the mass arrival of Jewish immigrants created a strong anti-Semitic movement among the middle classes of several Central and Western European countries. We need only recall the great successes of the anti-Semitic Social-Christian Party at Vienna and of its leader, Lueger; the sweeping rise of anti-Semitism in Germany (Treitschke) and the Dreyfus Affair. Anti-Semitism showed its roots most clearly in Vienna, one of the great centers of Jewish immigration before the first imperialist war. The petty bourgeoisie, ruined by the development of monopoly capitalism and headed for proletarianization, was exasperated by the mass arrival of the Jewish element, traditionally petty-bourgeois and artisan.

After the first imperialist war, the countries of Western and Central Europe: Germany, Austria, France and Belgium, saw tens of thousands of Jewish immigrants, in tatters, lacking all resources, pour in from Eastern Europe. The seeming postwar prosperity permitted these elements to penetrate into all branches of business and artisanry. But even the Jewish immigrants who had penetrated into the plants did not remain there for long.

The long commercial past of the Jews weighed heavily on their descendants and the favorable postwar economic conditions brought about a perceptible process of de-proletarianization in Western Europe as well as in the United States. The Jewish workers retained their artisan position in the countries of immigration.

---

[9] *Yiddishe Economic*, July-August 1938, p. 353.

In Paris in 1936 out of 21,083 Jewish workers belonging to trade unions, 9,253 worked at home.

The economic catastrophe of 1929 threw the petty-bourgeois masses into a hopeless situation. The overcrowding in small business, artisanry and the intellectual professions took on unheard of proportions. The petty bourgeois regarded his Jewish competitor with growing hostility, for the latter's professional cleverness, the result of centuries of practice, often enabled him to survive "hard times" more easily. Anti-Semitism even gained the ear of wide layers of worker-artisans, who traditionally had been under petty-bourgeois influence.

It is consequently incorrect to accuse Big Business of having brought about anti-Semitism. Big Business only proceeded to make use of the elementary anti-Semitism of the petty-bourgeois masses. It fashioned it into a major component of fascist ideology. By the myth of "Jewish capitalism," Big Business endeavored to divert and control the anti-capitalist hatred of the masses for its own exclusive profit. The real possibility of an agitation against Jewish capitalists lay in the antagonism between monopoly capital and speculative-commercial capital, which Jewish capital was in the main. The relatively greater permeability of speculative capital (stock exchange scandal) allowed monopoly capital to channelize the hatred of the petty-bourgeois masses and even of a part of the workers against "Jewish capitalism."

C. RACISM

"Ideology is a process accomplished by the so-called thinker consciously, indeed, but with a false consciousness. The real motives impelling him remain unknown to him, otherwise it would not be an ideological process at all. Hence he imagines false or apparent motives."[10]

Up to now we have tried to understand the real bases of anti-Semitism in our time. But it is sufficient to consider the role played in the development of anti-Semitism by the wretched document fabricated by the Czarist Okhrana, *The Protocols of Zion,* to become aware of the importance of the "false or apparent motive forces" of anti-Semitism. In Hitlerite propaganda today, the real motivation of anti-Semitism in Western Europe —the economic competition of the petty bourgeoisie— no longer plays any role. On the contrary, the most fantastic allegations of the *Protocols of Zion* —"the plans of universal domination by international Judaism"— reappear in every speech and manifesto of Hitler. We must therefore analyze this mythical ideological element of anti-Semitism.

Religion constitutes the most characteristic example of an ideology. Its true motive forces must be sought in the very prosaic domain of the material interests of a class, but it is in the most ethereal spheres that its apparent motive forces are found. Nevertheless, the God, who launched the Puritan fanatics of Cromwell against the English aristrocracy and Charles I, was nothing but the reflection or symbol of the interests of the English peasantry and bourgeoisie. Every religious revolution is in reality a social revolution.

It is the unbridled development of the productive forces colliding against the narrow limits of consumption which constitute the true motive force of imperialism, the highest stage of capitalism. But it is the "race" which seems to be its most characteristic apparent force. Racism is therefore in the first place the ideological disguise of modern imperialism. The "race struggling

[10] Engels to Mehring, *Selected Correspondence of Marx and Engels,* New York, 1942, p. 511.

for its living space" is nothing but the reflection of the permanent necessity for expansion which characterizes finance or monopoly capitalism.

While the fundamental contradiction of capitalism, the contradiction between production and consumption, involves for the big bourgeoisie the necessity to struggle for the conquest of foreign markets, it compels the petty bourgeoisie to struggle for the expansion of the domestic market. The lack of foreign markets for the big capitalists proceeds hand in hand with the lack of domestic markets for the small capitalists. Whereas the big bourgeoisie struggles furiously against its competitors on the foreign market, the petty bourgeoisie combats its competitors on the domestic market not a whit less fiercely. "Racism" abroad is consequently accompanied by "racism" at home. The unprecedented aggravation of capitalist contradictions in the Twentieth Century brings with it a growing exacerbation of "racism" abroad as well as "racism" at home.

The primarily commercial and artisan character of Judaism, heritage of a long historical past, makes it Enemy Number One of the petty bourgeoisie on the domestic market. It is therefore the petty-bourgeois character of Judaism which makes it so odious to the petty bourgeoisie. But while the historical past of Judaism exercises a determining influence on its present social composition, it has effects no less important on the representation of the Jews in the consciousness of the popular masses. For the latter, the Jew remains the traditional representative of the "money power."

This fact is of great importance because the petty bourgeoisie is not only a "capitalist" class, that is to say, a repository "in miniature" of all capitalist tendencies; it is also "anti-capitalist." It has a strong, though vague, consciousness of being ruined and despoiled by Big Business. But its hybrid character, its inter-class position, does not permit it to understand the true structure of society nor the real character of Big Business. It is incapable of understanding the true tendencies of social evolution, for it has a presentiment that this evolution cannot help but be fatal for it. It wants to be anti-capitalist without ceasing to be capitalist. It wants to destroy the "bad" character of capitalism, that is to say, the tendencies which are ruining it, while preserving the "good" character of capitalism which permits it to live and get rich. But since there does not exist a capitalism which has the "good" tendencies without also possessing the "bad," the petty bourgeoisie is forced to dream it up. It is no accident that the petty bourgeoisie has invented "super-capitalism," the "bad" deviation of capitalism, its evil spirit. It is no accident that its theoreticians have struggled mightily for over a century (Proudhon) against "bad speculative capitalism" and defended "useful productive capitalism."[11] The attempt of Nazi theoreticians to distinguish between "national productive capital" and "Jewish parasitic capital" is probably the last attempt of this kind. "Jewish capitalism" can best represent the myth of "bad capitalism." The concept of "Jewish wealth" is in truth solidly intrenched in the consciousness of the popular masses. It is only a question of reawakening and giving "presence," by means of a well-orchestrated propaganda, to the image of the "usurious" Jew, against whom peasant, petty bourgeois and lord had struggled over a long period. The petty bourgeoisie and a layer of workers remaining under its sway are easily influenced by such propaganda and fall into this trap of "Jewish capitalism."

Historically, the success of racism means that capitalism has managed to channelize the anti-capitalist consciousness of the masses into a form that antedates capitalism and which no longer exists except in a vestigial state; this vestige is nevertheless still sufficiently great to give a certain appearance of reality to the myth.

---

[11] See the Proudhon Utopia of free credit.

We see that racism is made up of rather strange elements. It reflects the expansionist will of big capital. It expresses the hatred of the petty bourgeoisie for "foreign" elements within the domestic market as well as its anti-capitalist tendencies.

It is in its aspect as a capitalist element that the petty bourgeoisie fights its Jewish competitor, and in its anti-capitalist aspect that it struggles against "Jewish capital." Racism finally diverts the anti-capitalist struggle of the masses into a form that antedates capitalism, persisting only in a vestigial state.

But while scientific analysis permits us to reveal its component parts, racist ideology must appear as an absolutely homogeneous "doctrine." Racism serves precisely to cast all classes into the crucible of a "racial community" opposed to other races. The racist myth strives to appear as a whole, having only vague connections with its origins which are often very different. It endeavors to fuse its different elements together in perfect fashion.

Thus, for example, "foreign" racism, the ideological disguise of imperialism, is not compelled, in and of itself, to adopt a strong anti-Semitic coloration. But from the necessity of synchronization, it generally does take on this character. The anti-capitalism of the masses, first channelized in the direction of Judaism, is then carried over against the "foreign enemy," which is identified with Judaism. The "Germanic race" will find itself faced with the duty of fighting the "Jew," its principal enemy, in all his disguises: that of domestic Bolshevism and liberalism, of Anglo-Saxon plutocracy and of foreign Bolshevism. Hitler states in *Mein Kampf* that it is indispensable to present the various enemies under a common aspect, otherwise there is a danger that the masses will start thinking too much about the differences which exist among those enemies. That is why racism is a myth and not a doctrine. It demands faith, and fears reason like the plague. Anti-Semitism contributes most to cementing the different elements of racism.

Just as it is necessary to cast the different classes into *one single race*, so is it also necessary that this "race" have only a single enemy: "the international Jew." The myth of race is necessarily accompanied by its "negative" — the anti-race, the Jew. The racial "community" is built on hatred of the Jews, a hatred of which the most solid "racial" foundation is buried in history in a period when the Jew was in effect a foreign body and hostile to all classes. The irony of history wills that the most radical anti-Semitic ideology in all history should triumph precisely in the period when Judaism is on the road of economic and social assimilation. But like all "ironies of history" this seeming paradox is very understandable. At the time when the Jew was unassimilable, at a time when he really represented "capital," he was indispensable to society. There could be no question of destroying him. At the present time, capitalist society, on the edge of the abyss, tries to save itself by resurrecting the Jew and the hatred of the Jews. But it is precisely because the Jews do not play the role which is attributed to them that anti-Semitic persecution can take on such an amplitude. Jewish capitalism is a myth; that is why it is so easily vanquished. But in vanquishing its "negative," racism at the same time destroys the foundations for its own existence. In the measure that the phantom of "Jewish capitalism" disappears, capitalist reality appears in all its ugliness. The social contradictions, banished for a moment by the fumes of "racial" intoxication, reappear in all their sharpness. In the long run, the myth proves powerless against reality.

Despite its apparent homogeneity, the very evolution of racism allows to be clearly discerned the economic, social and political transformations that it strives to conceal. At the beginning, in order to arm itself for the struggle for its "living space," for imperialist war, Big Business must beat down its domestic enemy, the proletariat. It is the petty bourgeoisie and declassed proletarian elements that furnish it with its shock troops, capable of smashing the economic and political organizations of the proletariat. Racism, at the beginning, appears therefore as an ideology of the petty bourgeoisie. Its program reflects the interests and illusions of this class. It promises struggle against "super-capitalism," against the trusts, stock exchange, big department stores, etc. But as soon as Big Business has succeeded in smashing the proletariat, thanks to the support of the petty bourgeoisie, the latter becomes an unbearable burden to it. The program of preparation for war implies precisely the ruthless elimination of small business, a prodigious development of the trusts, an intensive proletarianization. This same military preparation necessitates the support or at least a kind of neutrality from the proletariat, the most important factor in production. Thus Big Business does not hesitate for a moment to violate its most solemn promises in the most cynical way and to strangle the petty bourgeoisie in the most brutal fashion. Racism now devotes itself to flattering the proletariat, to appearing as a radically "socialist" movement. It is here that the Judaist-capitalist indentification plays its most important role. The radical expropriation of Jewish capitalists has to fulfill the role of "collateral," of "endorser" of racism's anti-capitalist will to struggle. The anonymous character of the capitalism of the monopolies, in contrast to the generally personal (and often speculative commercial) character of Jewish businesses, facilitates this operation of spiritual swindling. The common man more readily sees the "real" capitalist, the businessman, the manufacturer, the speculator, than the "respectable director of a corporation" who is made to pass as an "indispensable factor in production." It is in this way that racist ideology reaches the following identifications: Judaism = capitalism; racism = socialism; a regulated war economy = a planned socialist economy.

It is undeniable that large layers of workers, deprived of

their organizations, blinded by the foreign political successes of Hitler, have allowed themselves to be taken in by racist mythology, just as was the case previously with the petty bourgeoisie. For the time being the bourgeoisie appears to have attained its objective. The furious anti-Jewish persecution extending throughout Europe serves to indicate the "definitive" victory of racism, the final defeat of "international Judaism."

D. THE JEWISH RACE

The racial "theory" now dominant is nothing but an attempt to establish racism "on a scientific basis." It is devoid of any scientific value. It is enough to observe the pitiful acrobatics which the racist theoreticians perform to demonstrate the relationship of the "Germans and the Nipponese" or the irrevocable antagonism between "the heroic German spirit" and the "commercial Anglo-Saxon spirit" in order to be completely convinced of this. The ramblings of a Montadon on "de-prostituting" the Jewish "ethnic entity" by... compelling the Jews to wear stars of David, are certainly not worth much. The real prostitution of certain "scholars" to racism presents an unusual spectacle of the decline of human dignity. But we see there only an end product of the complete decay of bourgeois science which had already, under democracy, lost its objectivity.

Racist stupidities must not however deter us from examining the extent to which it is necessary to speak of a Jewish race. The most superficial examination of the question leads us to the conclusion that the Jews constitute in reality a mixture of the most diverse races. It is evidently the Diaspora character of Judaism which is the fundamental cause of this fact. But even in Palestine, the Jews were far from constituting a "pure race." Leaving aside the fact that, according to the Bible, the Israelites brought a mass of Egyptians with them when they left Egypt and that Strabo considered them as descendants of Egyptians, it is enough to recall the numerous races which had established themselves in Palestine: Hittites, Canaanites, Philistines ("Aryans"), Egyptians, Phoenecians, Greeks and Arabs. According to Strabo, Judea was inhabited by Phoenecians, Egyptians and Arabs. The development of Jewish proselytism during the Greek and Roman era strongly accentuated the mixed character of Judaism. As early as 139 B. C., the Jews were driven out of Rome for having made proselytes there. The community of Antioch was composed in large part of proselytes. Proselytism continued even during subsequent eras. The compulsory conversion of slaves to Judaism, the conversion of the Khazars as well as of other races and tribes in the course of the long Diaspora, have been so many factors which have made a characteristic conglomeration of races out of Judaism.

At the present time there is absolutely no racial homogeneity between the Yemenite Jews, for example, and the Jews of Daghestan. The first are Oriental in type while the second belong to the Mongol race. There are black Jews in India, Ethiopian Jews (Falasha), "Troglodyte" Jews in Africa. However, this fundamental difference which exists, for example, betwen the Jews of Daghestan and the Yemenite Jews, does not exhaust the question. Actually nine-tenths of today's Jews are inhabitants of Eastern Europe or descendants of Jews from this area.

Is there a European-Oriental Jewish race? Here is how the anti-Semitic theoretician, Hans Günther, answers this question: "Eastern Judaism, which comprised close to nine-tenths of the Jews, consisting today of the Jews of Russia, Poland, Galicia, Hungary, Austria and Germany, as well as the largest part of the Jews in North America and a large part of Western European Jewry constitutes a racial mixture which we may designate as

Western Asiatic-Oriental-East Baltic-Eastern-Central Asiatic-Nordic-Hamitic-Negroid."[12]

According to research undertaken in New York of 4,235 Jews there were:

	Jews %	*Jewesses* %
Brunet types	52.62	56.94
Blond types	10.42	10.27
Mixed types	36.96	32.79

14.25 percent of Jews and 12.7 percent of Jewesses had what is called the Jewish nose, which is nothing else but the nose common to the peoples of Asia Minor, especially widespread among the Armenians. This nose is also common among the Mediterranean peoples as well as among the Bavarians (Dinaric race). These few observations permit us to see how stupid the concept of the "Jewish race" is. The Jewish race is a myth. On the other hand, it is correct to say that the Jews constitute a racial mixture that is different from the racial mixtures of most of the European peoples, especially the Slavs and Germans.

However, it is not so much the anthropological characteristics of the Jews which distinguish them from other peoples as their physiological, pathological and above all psychological characteristics.

It is primarily the economic and social function of Judaism throughout history which explains this phenomenon. For centuries the Jews were the inhabitants of cities, occupied in trade. The Jewish type is far more the result of this secular function than a racial characteristic. The Jews have absorbed a mass of heterogeneous racial elements but all these elements have been subjected to the influence of the special conditions in which the Jews lived,

---

[12] Hans Günther, *Rassenkunde des Jüdischen Volkes*, Munich, 1930, p. 191.

which, in the long run, ended up with the creation of the so-called "Jewish type." This is the result of a long selection, not racial but economic and social. The physical weakness, the frequency of certain illnesses like diabetes, nervous disorders, a specific body posture, etc., are not racial characteristics but are the result of a specific social position. Nothing is more ridiculous than to explain, for example, the Jews' penchant for trade or their tendency to abstract thinking on the basis of their race. Wherever the Jews are assimilated economically, wherever they cease to form a class, they rapidly lose all these characteristics. And so it happens that where the racist theoreticians thought they were face to face with a "genuine race," they were in reality only viewing a human community, whose specific characteristics are above all the result of the social conditions in which it lived for many centuries. A change in these social conditions must naturally bring with it the disappearance of the "racial characteristics" of Judaism.

E. ZIONISM

Zionism was born in the light of the incendiary fires of the Russian pogroms of 1882 and in the tumult of the Dreyfus Affair —two events which expressed the sharpness that the Jewish problem began to assume at the end of the Nineteenth Century.

The rapid capitalist development of Russian economy after the reform of 1863 made the situation of the Jewish masses in the small towns untenable. In the West, the middle classes, shattered by capitalist concentration, began to turn against the Jewish element whose competition aggravated their situation. In Russia, the association of the "Lovers of Zion" was founded. Leo Pinsker wrote *Auto-Emancipation,* in which he called for a return to Palestine as the sole possible solution of the Jewish question. In Paris, Baron Rothschild, who like all the Jewish magnates viewed with very little favor the mass arrival of Jewish immigrants in the western countries, became interested in Jewish colonization in Palestine. To help "their unfortunate brothers" to return to the land of their "ancestors," that is to say, to go as far away as possible, contained nothing displeasing to the Jewish bourgeoisie of the West, who with reason feared the rise of anti-Semitism. A short while after the publication of Leo Pinsker's book, a Jewish journalist of Budapest, Theodor Herzl, saw anti-Semitic demonstrations at Paris provoked by the Dreyfus Affair. Soon he wrote *The Jewish State,* which to this day remains the bible of the Zionist movement. From its inception, Zionism appeared as a reaction of the Jewish petty bourgeoisie (which still forms the core of Judaism), hard hit by the mounting anti-Semitic wave, kicked from one country to another, and striving to attain the Promised Land where it might find shelter from the tempests sweeping the modern world.

Zionism is thus a very young movement; it is the youngest of the European national movements. That does not prevent it from pretending, even more than all other nationalism, that it draws its substance from a far distant past. Whereas Zionism is in fact the product of the last phase of capitalism, of capitalism beginning to decay, it pretends to draw its origin from a past more than two thousand years old. Whereas Zionism is essentially a reaction against the situation created for Judaism by the combination of the destruction of feudalism and the decay of capitalism, it affirms that it constitutes a reaction against the state of things existing since the fall of Jerusalem in the year 70 of the Christian era. Its recent birth is naturally the best reply to these pretensions. As a matter of fact, how can one believe that the remedy for an evil existing for two thousand years was discovered only at the end of the Nineteenth Century? But like all nationalisms —and even more intensely— Zionism views the historic past in the light of the present. In this way, too, it distorts the present-day picture. Just as France is represented to French children as existing since the Gaul of Vercingetorix; just as the children of Provence are told that the victories that the kings of Ile de France won over their ancestors were their own successes, in the same way Zionism tries to create the myth of an eternal Judaism, eternally the prey of the same persecutions. Zionism sees in the fall of Jerusalem the cause of the dispersion, and consequently, the fountain-head of all Jewish misfortunes of the past, present and future. "The source of all the misfortunes of the Jewish people is the loss of its historic country and its dispersion in all countries," declares the Marxist delegation of the "Poale-Zion" to the Dutch-Scandinavian committee. After the violent dispersion of the Jews by the Romans, their tragic history continues. Driven out of their country, the Jews did not wish (oh beauty of free will!) to assimilate. Imbued with their "national cohesiveness," "with a superior ethical feeling," and with "an indestructible belief in a single God" (see the article of Ben-Adir on "Anti-Semitism" in the General Encyclopedia), they have resisted all attempts at assimilation. Their sole hope during these somber days which lasted two thousand years has been the vision of a return to their ancient country.

Zionism has never seriously posed this question: Why, during these two thousand years, have not the Jews really tried to return to this country? Why was it necessary to wait until the end of the Nineteenth Century for a Herzl to succeed in convincing them of this necessity? Why were all the predecessors of Herzl, like the famous Sabbatai Zebi, treated as false Messiahs? Why were the adherents of Sabbatai Zebi fiercely persecuted by orthodox Judaism?

Naturally, in replying to these interesting questions, refuge is sought behind religion. "As long as the masses believed that they had to remain in the Diaspora until the advent of the Messiah, they had to suffer in silence," states Zitlovski,[13] whose Zionism is moreover quite conditional. Nevertheless this explanation tells us nothing. What is required is precisely an answer to the question of why the Jewish masses believed that they had to await the Messiah in order to be able to "return to their country." Religion being an ideological reflection of social interests, it must perforce correspond to them. Today religion does not at all constitute an obstacle to Zionism.[14]

In reality just so long as Judaism was incorporated in the feudal system, the "dream of Zion" was nothing but a dream and did not correspond to any real interest of Judaism. The Jewish tavern owner or "farmer" of Sixteenth-Century Poland thought as little of "returning" to Palestine as does the Jewish millionaire in America today. Jewish religious Messianism was no whit different from the Messianism belonging to other religions. Jewish pilgrims who went to Palestine met Catholic, Orthodox and Moslem pilgrims. Besides it was not so much the "return to Palestine" which constituted the foundation of this Messianism as the belief in the rebuilding of the temple of Jerusalem.

All of these idealist conceptions of Zionism are naturally inseparable from the dogma of eternal anti-Semitism. "As long as the Jews will live in the Diaspora, they will be hated by the 'natives.'" This essential point of view for Zionism, its spinal column so to speak, is naturally given different nuances by its various currents. Zionism transposes modern anti-Semitism to all of history; it saves itself the trouble of studying the various forms of anti-Semitism and their evolution. However, we have seen that in different historical periods, Judaism made up part of the

---

[13] *Materialism and the National Question.*

[14] There is a religious Zionist bourgeois party, *Misrakhi*, and a religious Zionist workers' party, *poale-Misrakhi.*

possessing classes and was treated as such. To sum up [the idealist conception], the sources of Zionism must be sought in the impossibility of assimilation because of "eternal" anti-Semitism and of the will to safeguard the "treasures of Judaism."[15]

In reality, Zionist ideology, like all ideologies, is only the distorted reflection of the interests of a class. It is the ideology of the Jewish petty bourgeoisie, suffocating between feudalism in ruins and capitalism in decay. The refutation of the ideological fantasies of Zionism does not naturally refute the real needs which brought them into being. It is modern anti-Semitism, and not mythical "eternal" anti-Semitism, which is the best agitator in favor of Zionism. Similarly, the basic question to determine is: To what extent is Zionism capable of resolving not the "eternal" Jewish problem but the Jewish question in the period of capitalist decay?

Zionist theoreticians like to compare Zionism with all other national movements. But in reality, the foundations of the national movements and that of Zionism are altogether different. The national movement of the European bourgeoisie is the consequence of capitalist development; it reflects the will of the bourgeoisie to create the national bases for production, to abolish feudal remnants. The national movement of the European bourgeoisie is closely linked with the ascending phase of capitalism. But in the Nineteenth Century, in the period of the flowering of nationalisms, far from being "Zionist," the Jewish bourgeoisie was profoundly assimilationist. The economic process from which the modern nations issued laid the foundations for integration of the Jewish bourgeosie into the bourgeois nation.

It is only when the process of the formation of nations approaches its end, when the productive forces have for a long

[15] Adolf Böhm, *Die Zionistische Bewegung*, Berlin, 1935, vol. I, Chap. 3.

time found themselves constricted within national boundaries, that the process of expulsion of Jews from capitalist society begins to manifest itself, that modern anti-Semitism begins to develop. The elimination of Judaism accompanies the decline of capitalism. Far from being a product of the development of the productive forces, Zionism is precisely the consequence of the complete halt of this development, the result of the petrifaction of capitalism. Whereas the national movement is the product of the ascending period of capitalism, Zionism is the product of the imperialist era. The Jewish tragedy of the Twentieth Century is a direct consequence of the decline of capitalism.

Therein lies the principal obstacle to the realization of Zionism. *Capitalist decay —basis for the growth of Zionism— is also the cause of the impossibility of its realization.* The Jewish bourgeoisie is compelled to create a national state, to assure itself of the objective framework for the development of its productive forces, precisely in the period when the conditions for such a development have long since disappeared. The conditions of the decline of capitalism which have posed so sharply the Jewish question make its solution equally impossible along the Zionist road. And there is nothing astonishing in that. An evil cannot be suppressed without destroying its causes. But Zionism wishes to resolve the Jewish question without destroying capitalism, which is the principal source of the suffering of the Jews.

At the end of the Nineteenth Century, in the period when the Jewish problem was just beginning to be posed in all its sharpness, 150,000 Jews each year left their countries of origin. Between 1881 and 1925, nearly four million Jews emigrated. Despite these enormous figures, the Jewish population of Eastern Europe rose from 6 to 8 million.

Thus, even when capitalism was still developing, even when the countries across the ocean were still receiving immigrants, the

Jewish question could not even begin to be resolved (in the Zionist sense); far from diminishing, the Jewish population showed a bad penchant of wanting to grow. In order to begin to resolve the Jewish question, that is to say, in order to begin really to transplant the Jewish masses, it would be necessary for the countries of immigration to absorb at least a little more than the natural growth of Jews in the Diaspora, that is at least 300,000 Jews per year. And if such a figure could not be reached before the first imperialist war, when all the conditions were still favorable for emigration, when all developed countries such as the United States were permitting the mass entry of immigrants, then how can we think that it is possible in the period of the continuous crisis of capitalism, in the period of almost incessant wars?

Naturally there are enough ships in the world to transport hundreds of thousands, even millions of Jews. But if all countries have closed their doors to immigrants, it is because there is an overproduction of labor forces just as there is an over production of commodities. Contrary to Malthus, who believed that there would be too many people because there would be too few goods, it is precisely the abundance of goods which is the cause of the "plethora" of human beings. By what miracle, in a period when the world markets are saturated with goods, in a period when unemployment has everywhere become a permanent fixture, by what miracle can a country, however great and rich it may be (we pass over the data relating to poor and small Palestine), develop its productive forces to the point of being able to welcome 300,000 immigrants each year? In reality the possibilities for Jewish emigration diminish at the same time that the need for it increases. The causes which promote the need for emigration are the same as those which prevent its realization; they all spring from the decline of capitalism.

It is from this fundamental contradiction between the *neces-*

sity for and the *possibility of* emigration that the political difficulties of Zionism flow. The period of development of the European nations was also the period of an intensive colonization in the countries across the ocean. It was at the beginning and middle of the Nineteenth Century, in the golden age of European nationalism, that North America was colonized; it was also in this period that South America and Australia began to be developed. Vast areas of the earth were practically without a master and lent themselves marvelously to the establishment of millions of European emigrants. In that period, for reason that we have studied, the Jews gave almost no thought to emigrating.

Today the whole world is colonized, industrialized and divided among the various imperialisms. Everywhere Jewish emigrants come into collision at one and the same time with the nationalism of the "natives" and with the ruling imperialism. In Palestine, Jewish nationalism collides with an increasingly aggressive Arab nationalism. The development of Palestine by Jewish immigration tends to increase the intensity of this Arab nationalism. The economic development of the country results in the growth of the Arab population, its social differentiation, the growth of a national capitalism. To overcome Arab resistance the Jews need English imperialism. But its "support" is as harmful as is Arab resistance. English imperialism views with a favorable eye a weak Jewish immigration to constitute a counterweight to the Arab factor, but it is intensely hostile to the establishment of a big Jewish population in Palestine, to its industrial development, to the growth of its proletariat. It merely uses the Jews as a counterweight to the Arab threat but does everything to raise difficulties for Jewish immigration. Thus, to the increasing difficulties flowing from Arab resistance, there is added the perfidious game of British imperialism.

Finally, we must draw still one more conclusion from the fundamental premises which have been established. Because of its necessarily artificial character, because of the slim perspectives for a rapid and normal development of Palestinian economy in our period, the task of Zionist colonization requires considerable capital. Zionism demands incessantly increasing sacrifices from the Jewish communities of the world. But so long as the situation of the Jews is more or less bearable in the Diaspora, no Jewish class feels the necessity of making these sacrifices. To the extent that the Jewish masses feel the necessity of having a "country," to the extent also that persecutions mount in intensity, so much the less are the Jewish masses able to contribute to Zionist construction. "A strong Jewish people in the Diaspora is necessary for Palestinian reconstruction," states Ruppin. But so long as the Jewish people is strong in the Diaspora, it feels no need for Palestinian reconstruction. When it strongly feels this necessity, the possibility for realizing it no longer exists. It would be difficult today to ask European Jews, who have a pressing need to emigrate, to give aid for the rebuilding of Palestine. The day when they will be able to do it, it is a safe assumption that their enthusiasm for this task will have considerably cooled.

A relative success for Zionism, along the lines of creating a Jewish majority in Palestine and even of the formation of a "Jewish state," that is to say, a state placed under the complete domination of English or American imperialism, cannot, naturally, be excluded. This would in some ways be a return to the state of things which existed in Palestine before the destruction of Jerusalem and, from this point of view, there will be "reparation of a two-thousand-year-old injustice." But this tiny "independent" Jewish state in the midst of a world-wide Diaspora will be only an apparent return to the state of things before the year 70. It will not even be the beginning of the solution of the Jewish question. The Jewish Diaspora of the Roman era was in effect based on solid economic ground; the Jews played an important economic role in the world. The existence or absence of a Palestinian mother country had for the Jews of this period only a secondary importance. Today it is not a question of giving the Jews a political or spiritual center (as Achaad Haam would have it). It is a question of saving Judaism from the annihilation which threatens it in the Diaspora. But in what way will the existence of a small Jewish state in Palestine change anything in the situation of the Polish or German Jews? Admitting even that all the Jews in the world were today Palestinian citizens, would the policy of Hitler have been any different?

One must be stricken with an incurable juridical cretinism to believe that the creation of a small Jewish state in Palestine can change anything at all in the situation of the Jews throughout the world, especially in the present period. The situation after the eventual creation of a Jewish state in Palestine will resemble the state of things that existed in the Roman era only in the fact that *in both cases the existence of a small Jewish state in Palestine could in no way influence the situation of the Jews in the Diaspora.* In the Roman era, the economic and social position of Judaism in the Diaspora was very strong, so that the disappearance of this Jewish state did not in any way compromise it. Today the situation of the Jews in the world is very bad; so the re-establishment of a Jewish state in Palestine cannot in any way restore it. In both cases the situation of the Jews does not at all depend on the existence of a state in Palestine but is a function of the general economic, social and political situation. Even supposing that the Zionist dream is realized and the "secular injustice" is undone —and we are still very far from that— the situation of Judaism throughout the world will in no way be modified by that. The temple will perhaps be rebuilt but the faithful will continue to suffer.

The history of Zionism is the best illustration of the insurmountable difficulties that it encounters, difficulties resulting, in the last analysis, from the fundamental contradiction which tears it apart: The contradiction between the growing necessity of resolving the Jewish question and the growing impossiblity of resolving it under the conditions of decaying capitalism. Immediately following the first imperialist war, Jewish emigration to Palestine encountered no great osbtacles in its path. Despite that, there were relatively few immigrants; the economic conditions of capitalist countries after the war made the need to emigrate less pressing. It was, moreover, because of this light emigration that the British government did not feel obliged to set up bars to the entry of Jews into Palestine. In the years 1924, 1925, 1926, the Polish bourgeoisie opened an economic offensive against the Jewish masses. These years are also the period of a very important immigration into Palestine. But this massive immigration soon collided with insurmountable economic difficulties. The ebb was almost as great as was the floodtide. Up to 1933, the date of Hitler's arrival to power, immigration was of little importance. After this date, tens of thousands of Jews began to arrive in Palestine. But this "conjuncture" was soon arrested by a storm of anti-Jewish demonstrations and massacres. The Arabs seriously feared becoming a minority in the country. The Arab feudal elements feared being submerged by the capitalist wave. British imperialism profited from this tension by piling up obstacles to the entry of the Jews, by working to deepen the gulf existing between the Jews and the Arabs, by proposing the partition of Palestine. Up to the second imperialist war, Zionism thus found itself in the grip of mounting difficulties. The Palestinian population lived in a state of permanent terror. Precisely when the situation of the Jews became ever more desperate, Zionism showed itself absolutely incapable of providing a remedy. "Illegal"

Jewish immigrants were greeted with rifle fire by their British "protectors."

The Zionist illusion began to lose its attractiveness even in the eyes of the most uninformed. In Poland, the last elections revealed that the Jewish masses were turning completely away from Zionism. The Jewish masses began to understand that Zionism not only could not seriously improve their situation, but that it was furnishing weapons to the anti-Semites by its theories of the "objective necessity of Jewish emigration." The imperialist war and the triumph of Hitlerism in Europe are an unprecedented disaster for Judaism. Judaism is confronted with the threat of total extinction. What can Zionism do to counteract such a disaster? Is it not obvious that the Jewish question is very little dependent upon the future destiny of Tel Aviv but very greatly upon the regime which will be set up tomorrow in Europe and in the world? The Zionists have a great deal of faith in a victory of Anglo-American imperialism. But is there a single reason for believing that the attitude of the Anglo-American imperialists will differ after their eventual victory from their prewar attitude? It is obvious that there is none. Even admitting that Anglo-American imperialism will create some kind of abortive Jewish state, we have seen that the situation of world Judaism will hardly be affected. A great Jewish immigration into Palestine after this war will confront the same difficulties as previously. Under conditions of capitalist decay, it is impossible to transplant millions of Jews. Only a world-wide socialist planned economy would be capable of such a miracle. Naturally this presupposes the proletarian revolution.

But Zionism wishes precisely to resolve the Jewish question independently of the world revolution. By misconstruing the real sources of the Jewish question in our period, by lulling itself with puerile dreams and silly hopes, Zionism proves that it is an ideological excrescence and not a scientific doctrine.[16]

[16] In this chapter, Zionism has been treated only insofar as it is linked with the Jewish question. The role of Zionism in Palestine naturally constitutes another problem.

CHAPTER VIII

TOWARD A SOLUTION OF THE JEWISH QUESTION

It is incorrect to state that a solution for the Jewish problem has been needed for two thousand years. The very fact that in the course of this long period such a solution was not found best demonstrates that it was not necessary.

Judaism was an indispensable factor in precapitalist society. It was a fundamental organism within it. That is what explains the two-thousand year existence of Judaism in the Diaspora. The Jew was as characteristic a personage in feudal society as the lord and the serf. It was no accident that a foreign element played the role of "capital" in feudal society. Feudal society *as such* could not create a capitalist element; as soon as it was able to do so, precisely then it ceased being feudal. Nor was it accidental that the Jew remained a foreigner in the midst of feudal society. The "capital" of precapitalist society existed outside of its economic system. From the moment that capital begins to emerge from the womb of this social system and takes the place of the borrowed organ, the Jew is eliminated and feudal society ceases to be feudal.

It is modern capitalism that has posed the Jewish problem. Not because the Jews today number close to twenty million people (the proportion of Jews to non-Jews has declined greatly since the Roman era) but because capitalism destroyed the secular basis for the existence of Judaism. Capitalism destroyed feudal society, and with it, the function of the Jewish people-class. History doomed this people-class to disappearance; and thus the

Jewish problem arose. The Jewish problem is the problem of adapting Judaism to modern society, of liquidating the heritage bequeathed to humanity by feudalism.

For centuries Judaism was a social organism within which social and national elements were closely intermingled. The Jews are far from constituting a race; on the contrary, they are probably one of the most typical and conspicuous examples of racial mixture. This does not mean, however, that the Asiatic element is not very noticeable in the mixture — sufficiently outstanding, in any case, to set the Jew apart in the Western nations, where he is chiefly to be found. This real national "base" is supplemented by an imaginary, poetic base, formed out of the secular tradition which attaches the present Jew to his distant "ancestors" of biblical times. On this national base, the class foundation and the mercantile psychology were subsequently grafted. The national and social elements became mixed to the point of complete intermingling. It would be difficult to distinguish in a Polish Jew the part that his "type" has inherited from his ancestors and the part acquired from the social function that he fulfilled in that country for centuries. It must be agreed that the social base long ago acquired greater importance than the national base. At any rate, if the social element came to be added to the national element, the latter could persist only thanks to the former. It is thanks to his social and economic situation that the Jew was able to "preserve" himself.

Capitalism has posed the Jewish problem, that is to say, it has destroyed the social bases upon which Judaism maintained itself for centuries. But capitalism has not resolved the Jewish problem, for it has been unable to absorb the Jew liberated from his social shell. The decline of capitalism has suspended the Jews between heaven and earth. The Jewish "precapitalist" merchant has largely disappeared, but his son has found no place in modern production. The social basis of Judaism has crumbled; Judaism has become largely a declassed element. Capitalism has not only doomed the social function of the Jews; it has also doomed the Jews themselves.

Petty-bourgeois ideologists are always inclined to raise a historical phenomenon into an eternal category. For them the Jewish question is a function of the Diaspora; only the concentration of the Jews in Palestine can resolve it.

But it is pure childishness to reduce the Jewish question to a question of territory. The territorial solution has meaning only if it signifies the disappearance of traditional Judaism, the penetration of Jews into modern economy, the "productivization" of the Jews. By a detour, Zionism thus returns to the solution proposed by its worst enemies, the consistent "assimilationists." For the Zionists as well as for the assimilationists it is a question of doing away with the "cursed" heritage of the past, of making workers, agriculturalists, productive intellectuals, of the Jews. The illusion of Zionism does not consist in its desire to attain this result; that is a historical necessity which will cut its own path sooner or later. Its illusion consists in believing that the insurmountable difficulties which decaying capitalism puts in the way of these tasks will disappear as if by magic in Palestine. But if the Jews were unable to find a place in economic life in the Diaspora, the same causes will prevent them from doing so in Palestine. The world today is so much a unit that it is sheer folly to try to build within it a haven sheltered from its storms. That is why the failure of "assimilation" must of necessity be followed by the failure of Zionism. In this period when the Jewish problem takes on the aspect of a terrible tragedy, Palestine can be no more than a feeble palliative. Ten million Jews find themselves in a huge concentration camp. What remedy can the creation of a few Zionist colonies bring to this problem?

Well then —neither assimilation nor Zionism? No solution at all? No, there is no solution to the Jewish question under capitalism, just as there is no solution to the other problems posed before humanity— without profound social upheavals. The same causes which make the emancipation of the Jews an illusion also make the realization of Zionism impossible. Unless the profound causes for the Jewish question are eliminated, the effects cannot be eliminated.

The ghetto and the wheel [the badge that Jews sewed on their clothes in the Middle Ages] have reappeared— symbols, moreover, of the tragic destiny toward which humanity is being driven. But the very exacerbation of anti-Semitism prepares the road for its disappearance. The driving out of the Jews provides momentarily a kind of living-space for the petty bourgeoisie. "Aryanization" creates jobs for some tens of thousands of unemployed intellectuals and petty-bourgeois. But in attacking the apparent causes of their misfortunes, the petty bourgeoisie have merely strengthened the operation of the real causes. Fascism will accelerate the process of proletarianization of the middle classes. After the Jewish petty bourgeoisie, hundeds of thousands of shopkeepers and artisans were expropriated and proletarianized. Capitalist concentration made gigantic progress. "Improvement in the economic situation" took place only at the price of preparation for the second imperialist war, the cause of enormous destruction and slaughter.

Thus the tragic fate of Judaism mirrors with singular sharpness the situation of all humanity. The decline of capitalism means for the Jews the return to the ghetto—although the basis for the ghetto disappeared long ago, along with the foundations of feudal society. Similarly, for all humanity, capitalism bars the road of the past as well as the highway to the future. Only the destruction of capitalism will make it possible for humanity to benefit from the immense achievements of the industrial era.

Is it astonishing that the Jewish masses, who are the first to feel —and with special sharpness— the effects of the contradictions of capitalism, should have furnished rich forces for the socialist and revolutionary struggle? "On various occasions Lenin emphasized the importance of the Jews for the revolution, not only in Russia but in other countries as well... Lenin also expressed the thought that the flight of a part of the Jewish population... into the interior of Russia, as a result of the occupation of the industrial regions of the West, had been a very useful thing for the revolution —just as the appearance of a large number of Jewish intellectuals in the Russian cities during the war had also been useful. They helped to smash the wide-spread and extremely dangerous sabotage which confronted the Bolsheviks everywhere inmediately following the Revolution. Thus they helped the Revolution to survive a very critical stage."[1] The high percentage of Jews in the proletarian movement is only a reflection of the tragic situation of Judaism in our time. The intellectual faculties of the Jews, fruit of the historic past of Judaism, are thus an important support for the proletarian movement.

In this latter fact lies a final —and not the least important— reason for modern anti-Semitism. The ruling classes persecute with special sadism the Jewish intellectuals and workers, who have supplied a host of fighters to the revolutionary movement. To isolate the Jews completely from the sources of culture and science has become a vital necessity for the decaying system which persecutes them. The ridiculous legend of "Jewish-Marxism" is noth-

---

[1] S. Dimanstein, *Lenin on the Jewish Question in Russia* (Russian) Moscow, 1924. Quoted by Otto Heller, *Der Untergang des Judentums*, Vienna, [1931], p. 230.

ing but a caricature of the bonds that actually exist between socialism and the Jewish masses.

Never has the situation of the Jews been so tragic. In the worst periods of the Middle Ages entire countries opened their doors to receive them. Today capitalism, which rules the whole world, makes the earth uninhabitable for them. Never has the mirage of a Promised Land so haunted the Jewish masses. But never was a Promised Land less capable of resolving the Jewish question than in our time.

The very paroxysm, however, that the Jewish problem has reached today, also provides the key to its solution. The plight of the Jews has never been so tragic; but never has it been so close to ceasing to be that. In past centuries, hatred of the Jews had a real basis in the social antagonism which set them against other classes of the population. Today, the interest of the Jewish classes are closely bound up with the interests of the popular masses of the entire world. By persecuting the Jews as "capitalist," capitalism makes them complete pariahs. The ferocious persecutions against Judaism render stark-naked the stupid bestiality of anti-Semitism and destroy the remnants of prejudices that the working classes nurse against the Jews. The ghettos and the yellow badges do not prevent the workers from feeling a growing solidarity with those who suffer most from the afflictions all humanity is suffering.

And the greatest social explosion the world has ever seen is finally preparing the liberation of the most persecuted pariahs of our planet. When the people of the factories and the fields have finally thrown off the yoke of the capitalists, when a future of unlimited development opens up before liberated humanity, the Jewish masses will be able to make a far from unimportant contribution towards the building of a new world.

This does not mean that socialism, brought to maturity by a

wave of a magic wand, will remove all the difficulties that stand as obstacles to the solution of the Jewish question. The example of the USSR shows that even after the proletarian revolution, the special structure of Judaism —a heritage of history— will give rise to a number of difficulties, particularly during the transition periods. During the time of the NEP, for instance, the Jews of Russia, utilizing their traditional business experience, furnished numerous cadres for the new bourgeois class.

Moreover, the great mass of Jewish small tradesmen and petty artisans suffered greatly at the beginning of the proletarian dictatorship. It was only later, with the success of the Five Year Plan, that the Jews penetrated *en masse* into Soviet economic life. Despite certain difficulties, the experiment was decisive: hundreds of thousands of Jews became workers and peasants. The fact that white-collar workers and functionaries constitute a considerable percentage of wage-earning Jews must not be considered a matter for concern. Socialism is not at all interested that all Jews should take up manual occupations. On the contrary, the intellectual faculties of the Jews should be put to widest use.

It is thus clear that, even under the relatively difficult conditions of a backward country, the proletariat can solve the Jewish problem. The Jews have penetrated *en masse* into Russian economy. The "productivization" of the Jews has been accompanied by two parallel processes: assimilation and territorial concentration. Wherever the Jews penetrate into industry, they are rapidly assimilated. As early as 1926 there were hardly 40 percent of the Jewish miners in the Donetz Basin who spoke Yiddish. Nevertheless the Jews live under a regime of national autonomy; they have special schools, a Yiddish press, autonomous courts. But the Jewish nationalists are continually deploring the abandonment of these schools and this press, Only in those places where fairly dense masses of Jews have been colonized, especially in Birobidjan, do we witness a kind of "national renaissance."[2]

Thus life itself demonstrates that the problem which so bitterly divides Judaism —assimilation or territorial concentration— is a fundamental problem only to petty-bourgeois dreamers. The Jewish masses want simply an end to their martyrdom. That, socialism alone can give them. But socialism must give the Jews, as it will to all peoples, the possibility of assimilation as well as the possibility of having a special national life.

The end of Judaism? Certainly. Despite their apparently irreconcilable opposition, assimilationists and nationalists are agreed in combatting Judaism as history has known it — the mercantile Judaism of the Diaspora, the people-class. The Zionists never stop repeating that it is a matter of creating a new type of Jew in Palestine, altogether different from the Jew of the Diaspora. They even reject with horror the language and culture of the Judaism of the Diaspora. In Birobidjan, in the Ukraine and the Donetz Basin, even the old man discards his secular dress. The people-class, historical Judaism, has been definitively doomed by history. Despite all its traditional pretentions, Zionism will not culminate in a "national renaissance" but, at the most, in a "national birth." The "new Jew" resembles neither his brother of the Diaspora nor his ancestor of the era of the fall of Jerusalem. The young Palestinian, proud of speaking the language of Bar Kochba, would probably not be understood by his ancestor; in reality, the Jews in the Roman era spoke Aramaic and Greek fluently but had only a vague knowledge of Hebrew. Moreover, neo-Hebrew, in the nature of things, is going further and further away from the language of the Bible. Everything will add up to estrange the Palestinian Jew from the Judaism of the Diaspora. And tomorrow, when national barriers and prejudices begin to disappear

---

[2] We touch here on the Jewish problem in Russia only in passing.

in Palestine, who can doubt that a fruitful reconciliation will take place between the Arab and the Jewish workers, the result of which will be their partial or total fusion?

"Eternal" Judaism, which, moreover, has never been anything but a myth, will disappear. It is puerile to pose assimilation and the "national solution" as opposites. Even in those countries where Jewish national communities will eventually be created, we will be witnessing either the creation of a new Jewish nationality, completely different from the old, or the formation of new nations. Moreover, even in the first case, unless the people already established in the country are driven out or the rigorous prescriptions of Ezra and Nehemiah are revived, this new nationality cannot fail to come under the influence of the long-time inhabitants of the country.

In the sphere of nationality, only socialism can bring the widest democracy. It must provide the Jews with the opportunity of living a national existence in every country they inhabit; it must also give them the opportunity of concentrating in one or more territories, naturally without injuring the interests of the native inhabitants. Only the widest proletarian democracy will make possible the resolution of the Jewish problem with a minimum of suffering.

Clearly, the tempo of the solution of the Jewish problem depends upon the general tempo of socialist construction. The opposition between assimilation and the national solution is an entirely relative one, the latter often being nothing but the prelude to the former. Historically, all existing nations are the products of various fusions of races and peoples. It is not excluded that new nations, formed by the fusion or even the dispersion of nations now existing, will be created. However it may be, socialism must limit itself in this sphere to "letting nature take its course."

Thus in a certain sense socialism will return to the practice of precapitalist society. It was capitalism, by virtue of the fact that it provided an economic basis for the national problem, which also created insoluble national contradictions. Before the capitalist era, Slovaks, Czechs, Germans, French, lived in perfect understanding. Wars did not have a national character; they had interest only for the possessing classes. The policy of compulsory assimilation, of national persecution, was unknown to the Romans. Submission of barbarian peoples to Romanization or Hellenization was a peaceful process. Today, national-cultural and linguistic antagonisms are only manifestations of the economic antagonism created by capitalism. With the disappearance of capitalism, the national problem will lose all its acuteness. If it is premature to speak of a worldwide assimilation of peoples, it is nonetheless clear that a planned economy on a global scale will bring all the peoples of the world much closer to each other. But the hastening of this assimilation by artificial means would hardly seem to be indicated; nothing could do more harm. We still cannot foresee exactly what the "offspring" of present Judaism will be; socialism will take care that the "birth" will take place under the best possible conditions.

BIBLIOGRAPHY

Albertini, E. F. *L'Empire Romain.* Paris, 1929.
Ansiaux, Maurice. *Traité d'Economie Politique.* Paris, 1920-6.
Aristotle. *Politics.* Trans. by Benjamin Jowett. Oxford, 1885.
Autran, Charles. *Les Phéniciens.* Paris, 1920.
Avenel, Georges d'. *Histoire Economique de la Propriété,* etc. Paris, 1894.
Ballester y Castell, Rafael. *Histoire de l'Espagne.* Paris, 1928.
Bauer, Otto. *Die Nationalitätenfrage und die Sozialdemokratie.* Vienna, 1907.
Bédarride, I. *Les Juifs en France, en Italie et en Espagne.* París, 1867.
Beloch, K. J. *Griechische Geschichte.* Berlin, 1914-27.
Ben-Adir. "Anti-Semitism." In *General Encyclopedia* (Yiddish). Paris, 1936.
Böhm, Adolf *Die Zionistische Bewegung.* Berlin, [1935-7].
Brentano, Lujo. *Die Anfänge des Modernen Kapitalismus.* Munich, 1916.
Eine Geschichte der Wirtschaftlichen Entwicklung Englands. Jena, 1927-29.
Das Wirtschaftsleben der Antiken Welt. Jena, 1929.
Brutzkus, Dr. J. "History of the Jewish Mountaineers in Daghestan (Caucasia)." In *Yivo Studies in History* (Yiddish). Wilno, 1937, vol. II.
"Trade Relations of the West European Jews with Medieval Kiev." In *Writings on Economics and Statistics* (Yiddish). J. Lestschinsky, editor. Berlin, 1928.
Bühl, F. *Die Sozialen Verhältnisse der Israeliten.* Berlin, 1899.
Caro, Georg. *Sozial-und Wirtschaftsgeschichte der Juden im Mittellalter und der Neuzeit.* Frankfort, 1924.
Causse, Antonin. *Les Dispersés d' Israël.* Paris, 1929.
Clerc, Michel. *Les Métèques Atheniens.* Paris, 1893.
Cunow, Heinrich. *Allgemeine Wirtschaftsgeschichte.* Berlin, 1926-31.
Depping, G. B. *Histoire du Commerce entre le Levant et l'Europe.* Paris, 1830.
Les Juifs dans le Moyen Age. Paris, 1845.
Dubnow, S. M. *History of the Jews in Russia and Poland.* Philadelphia, 1916.
Die Neuste Geschichte des Jüdischen Volkes. Berlin, 1920-24.

Dubnow, W. "On the Economic History of the Jews in Russia." In *Writings on Economics and Statistics* (Yiddish), J. Lestschinsky, editor. Berlin, 1928.
Francotte, Henri. *L'Industrie dans la Grèce Ancienne.* Brussels, 1900-1901.
Frank, Tenney. *An Economic History of Rome to the End of the Republic.* Baltimore, 1920.
Friedländer, Ludwig. *Roman Life and Manners under the Early Empire.* London, 1910.
Furtenbach, Friedrich von. *Krieg gegen Russland und Russische Gefangenschaft.* Nuremberg, 1912.
Fustel de Coulanges, N. D. *The Ancient City.* Boston, 1874.
Histoire des Institutions Politiques de l'Ancienne France. Paris, 1888-92.
General Encyclopedia (Yiddish). Paris, 1936.
Gibbon, Edward. *The History of the Decline and Fall of the Roman Empire.* Heritage Press, New York, 1946.
Gide, Charles. *Principles of Political Economy.* Boston, 1905.
Graetz, Heinrich Hirsch. *Popular History of the Jews.* New York, 1919.
Gumplowicz, Ludwig. *The Outlines of Sociology.* Philadelphia, 1899.
Günther, Hans. *Rassenkunde des Jüdischen Volkes.* Munich, 1930.
Hasebroek, Johannes. *Staat und Handel im Alten Griechenland.* Tübingen, 1928.
Hatzfeld, Jean. *Les Trafiquants Italiens dans l'Orient Hellénistique.* Paris, 1919.
Heller, Otto. *Der Untergang des Judentums.* Vienna, [1931].
Herzfeld, Dr. L. *Handelsgeschichte der Juden des Alterthums.* Braunschweig, 1879.
Holleaux, Maurice. *Rome, la Grèce et les Monarchies Hellénistiques au IIIe Siècle avant J. C.* Paris, 1921.
Hölscher, Gustav. *Urgemeinde und Spätjudentum.* Oslo, 1928.
The Holy Bible. Thomas Nelson & Sons, New York, [1901].
Jannet, Claudio. *Les Grandes Epoques de l'Histoire Economique.* Paris, [1896].
Josephus, Flavius. *Works.* London, 1844.
Jüdisches Lexikon. Berlin, 1927-30.
Juster, Jean. *Les Juifs dans l'Empire Romain.* Paris, 1914.
Kautsky, Karl. *Are the Jews a Race?* New York, 1926.
Foundations of Christianity. New York, [1925].
Klatzkin, Jakob. *Probleme des Modernen Judentum.* Berlin, 1918.
Köhler, Dr. Max. *Beiträge zur Neueren Jüdischen Wirtschaftsgeschichte; die Juden in Halberstadt und Umgebung bis zur Emanzipation.* Berlin, 1927.
Krauss, Dr. Samuel. *Studien zur Byzantisch-Jüdischen Geschichte.* Leipzig, 1914.
Kriegk, Georg Ludwig. *Frankfurter Bürgerzwiste und Zustände im Mittelalter.* Frankfort, 1862.

Laurent, Henri. "Religion et Affaires." In *Cahiers du Libre Examen.*
Lavisse, Ernest. *Histoire Générale du IVe. Siècle à Nos Jours.* Paris. 1893-1904.
Legaret, Gustave. *Histoire du Développement du Commerce.* Paris, 1927.
Lenin, V. I. "The Development of Capitalism in Russia." *Selected Works.*
Lestschinsky, Jacob. *The Development of the Jewish People in the Last 100 Years.* (Yiddish). Berlin, 1928.
Der Wirtschaftliche Zusammenbruch der Juden in Deutschland u. Polen. Paris, 1936.
Lestschinsky, J., editor. *Writings on Economics and Statistics* (Yiddish). Berlin, 1923.
Lods, Adolphe. *Israel from Its Beginnings to the Middle of the Eighth Century.* London, 1932.
Lucas, Dr. Leopold. *Zur Geschichte der Juden im Vierten Jahrhundert.* Berlin, 1910.
Marx, Karl. *Capital.* Kerr Edition.
Selected Essays. New York, 1926.
Marx and Engels. *Selected Correspondence of Marx and Engels.* New York, 1942.
Menes, A. "Craft Industry among the Jews in Biblical and Talmudic Times." In *Writings on Economics and Statistics* (Yiddish), J. Lestschinsky, editor. Berlin, 1928.
Meyer, Eduard. *Blüte und Niedergang des Hellenismus in Asien.* Berlin, 1925.
Mommsen, Theodor. *The History of Rome.* London, [1911].
The Provinces of the Roman Empire. New York, 1887.
Montesquieu. *Spirit of the Law.* Cincinnati, 1873.
Philippson, Martin. *Neueste Geschichte des Jüdischen Volkes.* Leip-
Movers, F. C. *Die Phönizier.* Berlin, 1856.
zig, 1907.
Piganiol, André. *La Conquête Romaine.* Paris, 1927.
Pirenne, Henri. *Belgian Democracy, Its Early History.* London, 1915.
Histoire de Belgique. Brussels, 1902-32.
A History of Europe from the Invasions to the XVI Century. London, [1939].
Mohammed and Charlemagne. New York, [1939].
Les Villes au Moyen Age. Brussels, 1927.
Roscher, W., *Die Juden im Mittelalter.*
Roscher, W. "The Status of the Jews in the Middle Ages." In *Historia Judaica,* vol. VI.
Rostovtzev, M. *The Social and Economic History of the Roman Empire.* Oxford, 1926.
Roussel, Pierre. *La Grèce et l'Orient.* Paris, 1928.
Ruppin, Arthur. *The Jews in the Modern World.* London, 1934.
Salvian. *On the Government of God.* New York, 1930.

Salvioli, Giuseppe. *Der Kapitalismus im Altertum*, Stuttgart, 1922.
Sayous, André. "Les Juifs." In *Revue Economique Internationale*, March 1932.
Schipper, Ignaz *Anfänge des Kapitalismus bei den Abendländischen Juden in Früheren Mittelalter*. Vienna, 1907.
Jewish History (Yiddish). Warsaw, 1930.
Schubart, Wilhelm. *Aegypten von Alexander dem Grossen bis auf Mohammed*. Berlin, 1922.
Schulte, Aloys. *Geschichte des Mittelalterlichen Handels und Verkehrs zwischen Westdeutschland und Italien*. Leipzig, 1900.
Sée, H. E. *Economic and Social Conditions in France during the Eighteenth Century*. New York, 1927.
Esquisse d'une Histoire Economique et Sociale de la France. Paris, 1929.
Smith, Adam. *The Wealth of Nations*. Modern Library, New York, (1937).
Sombart, Werner. *L'Apogée du Capitalisme*. Paris, 1932.
The Jews and Modern Capitalism. London, 1913.
Strabo. *The Geography of Strabo*. London, 1854-7.
Thierry, Augustin. *History of the Conquest of England by the Normans*, London, 1856.
Toutain, J. F. *The Economic Life of the Ancient World*. New York, 1930.
Ullmann, Dr. Salomon. *Histoire des Juifs en Belgique jusqu'au 18e Siècle*. Antwerp, [192-?].
Vandervelde, Emile. *L'Exode Rural et le Retour aux Champs*. Paris, 1903.
Voitinski, Vladimir. *Tatsachen und Zahlen Europas*. Vienna, 1930.
Weber, Max. *General Economic History*. New York, 1927.
Weinryb, S. B. *Neueste Wirtschaftsgeschichte der Juden in Russland und Polen*. Breslau, 1934.
World Jewish Congress (Economic Bureau). *La Situation Economique des Juifs dans le Monde*. Paris, 1938.
Yiddishe Economic (Yiddish). Wilno.
Yivo Studies in History. Wilno, 1937.
Zeiller, Jacques. *L'Empire Romain et l'Eglise*. Paris, 1928.

FURTHER READING

THE REVOLUTION BETRAYED

WHAT IS THE SOVIET UNION
AND WHERE IS IT GOING?

Classic study of the degeneration of the Soviet workers' state under the domination of the privileged social caste whose spokesman was Stalin. Illuminates the roots of the crisis of the 1990s.
by Leon Trotsky, $19.95

QUESTIONS OF NATIONAL POLICY

Discusses the working-class view of "national culture," assimilation, the rights of national minorities, the fight against discrimination, and how to achieve unity of the toilers against capitalism.
by V.I. Lenin, $10.95

THE FOUNDING OF THE SOCIALIST WORKERS PARTY

MINUTES AND RESOLUTIONS, 1938-39

Documents from the founding convention of the SWP, on the eve of the Second World War, detail the building of a party of communist workers through the fight against imperialist war, fascism, and colonial and racial oppression. Includes 1939 "Theses on the Jewish Question."
by James P. Cannon et al., $20.95

FEBRUARY 1965: THE FINAL SPEECHES

Speeches form the last three weeks of Malcolm X's life presenting the still accelerating evolution of his political views.
by Malcolm X, $17.95

PALESTINE AND THE ARABS' FIGHT FOR LIBERATION

Palestinian resistance to the establishment by imperialism of the Zionist settler state of Israel, from the Balfour declaration of 1917 to the beginning of the intifada.
by Fred Feldman and Georges Sayad, $3.50

UNDERSTANDING HISTORY

How capitalism arose, why this exploitative system is historically outdated, and how revolutionary change in society and human development is fundamental to social and cultural progress.
by George Novack, $15.95

OTHER TITLES FROM PATHFINDER

THE STRUGGLE IS MY LIFE

"My political beliefs have been explained in my autobiography, *The Struggle Is My Life*"—Nelson Mandela.
by Nelson Mandela, **$15.95**

THE HISTORY OF THE RUSSIAN REVOLUTION

The social, economic, and political dynamics of the first victorious socialist revolution, as told by one of its central leaders. Unique in modern literature. Unabridged edition. 1,336 pages.
by Leon Trotsky, **$35.95**

TO SPEAK THE TRUTH
Why Washington's 'Cold War' against Cuba Doesn't End

Fidel Castro and Che Guevara explain why the U.S. government remains determined to destroy the example set by the Cuban revolution and why its effort will fail.
by Fidel Castro and Che Guevara, **$16.95**

COSMETICS, FASHIONS, AND THE EXPLOITATION OF WOMEN

How big business uses women's second-class status to generate profits for a few and perpetuate the oppression of the female sex and the exploitation of working people.
by Joseph Hansen, Evelyn Reed, and Mary-Alice Waters, **$12.95**

THE CHANGING FACE OF U.S. POLITICS
Working-Class Politics and the Trade Unions

Building a revolutionary workers' party in a world of capitalist economic crises, wars, trade conflicts, antiunion assaults, and attacks on workers' rights and individual liberties.
by Jack Barnes, **$19.95**

THOMAS SANKARA SPEAKS

Speeches and writings by the assassinated president of Burkina Faso tell the story of the 1983-87 revolution that unfolded in this West African country as peasants and workers began confronting hunger, illiteracy, the oppression of women, and other conditions perpetuated by capitalism. **$18.95**

HOW FAR WE SLAVES HAVE COME!

Speaking together in Matanzas, Cuba, in 1991, Mandela and Castro discuss the unique relationship and example of the struggles of the South African and Cuban peoples.
by Nelson Mandela and Fidel Castro, **$8.95**

THE STRUGGLE AGAINST FASCISM IN GERMANY

Writing in the heat of struggle against the rising fascist movement, the Russian revolutionary leader examines the origin and nature of fascism and advances a working-class strategy to combat it.
by Leon Trotsky, **$28.95**

FARMERS FACE THE CRISIS OF THE 1990s

Examines the deepening economic and social crisis in the capitalist world and explains how farmers and workers can unite internationally against the mounting assaults from the billionaire bankers, industrialists, and merchants.
by Doug Jenness, **$3.50**

THE COMMUNIST MANIFESTO

Founding document of the modern revolutionary workers' movement. Explains how capitalism arose as a specific stage in the economic development of class society, and how it will be superseded through the revolutionary action on a world scale of the working class.
by Karl Marx and Frederick Engels, **$2.50**

CHE GUEVARA AND THE FIGHT FOR SOCIALISM TODAY

Cuba Confronts the World Crisis of the '90s

Socialism can be built only by free men and women who consciously work together to lay the foundations for a new society, transforming themselves in the process. That course, which Ernesto Che Guevara championed in the early years of the Cuban revolution, remains central for Cuban working people today as they strive to find the way forward, confronting the biggest challenges yet in the history of the revolution. Also available in Spanish and French.
by Mary-Alice Waters, **$3.50**

THE EASTERN AIRLINES STRIKE

Accomplishments of the Rank-and-File Machinists

The story of the 686-day strike that demonstrated how a rank-and-file led resistance by IAM workers prevented Eastern's antiunion onslaught from becoming the road to a profitable nonunion airline.
by Ernie Mailhot and others, **$9.95**

TEAMSTER BUREAUCRACY

How the class-struggle leaders of the 1930s Midwest Teamsters union organized to oppose World War II, racism, and the bosses' attacks at home. Written by a central leader jailed for his opposition to the war.
by Farrell Dobbs, **$18.95**

New International

A MAGAZINE OF MARXIST POLITICS AND THEORY

IN ISSUE 7

Opening Guns of World War III:

WASHINGTON'S ASSAULT ON IRAQ

BY JACK BARNES

The U.S. government's murderous blockade, bombardment, and invasion of Iraq heralded a period of increasingly sharp conflicts among imperialist powers, more wars, and growing instability of international capitalism. 333 pp., $12.00

IN ISSUE 8

Che Guevara, Cuba, and the Road to Socialism

Exchanges from both the early 1960s and today on the lasting importance and historical weight of the political and economic perspectives defended by Ernesto Che Guevara. 204 pp., $10.00

IN ISSUE 5

The Coming Revolution in South Africa

BY JACK BARNES

The world importance of the struggle to overthrow the apartheid system and the vanguard role of the African National Congress, which is committed to lead the national, democratic revolution in South Africa to a successful conclusion. 198 pp., $9.00

IN ISSUE 6

The Second Assassination of Maurice Bishop

BY STEVE CLARK

The accomplishments and lessons of the Grenada revolution, 1979-83, and how it was overthrown from within by the Stalinist gang that murdered Maurice Bishop. 272 pp., $10.00

DISTRIBUTED BY PATHFINDER